YOUR CAR—
How to Buy It,
Take Care of It,
and Save Money

YOUR CAR—
How to Buy It,
Take Care of It,
and Save Money

BOOKS by U.S.NEWS & WORLD REPORT

Joseph Newman—Directing Editor

A division of U.S.News & World Report, Inc.

WASHINGTON, D.C.

Contents

    Illustrations / 7
    Acknowledgments / 11
   I What Every Motorist Needs to Know / 13
  II How to Buy a New Car / 25
 III How to Buy a Used Car / 51
 IV How to Finance Your Car / 65
  V Insurance: How Much Is Enough? / 75
 VI To Lease or Not to Lease / 97
 VII How to Buy Tires / 104
VIII Body Care—Outside and In / 125
 IX When to Trade In Your Car / 135
  X How to Sell Your Car / 149
 XI How Your Car Works / 159
 XII The Impact of Pollution Controls / 193
XIII The Mechanic: How to Deal With Him / 211
XIV An Ounce of Prevention . . . / 237
    Appendix / 269
    Index / 295

Illustrations

Tables and Charts
Cars and Population in the United States / 15
How Consumers Spend Their Dollars / 16
What Families Own / 19
Spending for Autos / 22
Work Hours Needed to Buy and Insure a New Car / 27
Buyers Favoring Smaller Cars / 29
Credit Sales of New Cars / 66
Holders of Installment Credit / 68
Types of Installment Credit Outstanding at Finance
    Companies / 69
Size of Auto Finance Contract Purchased by Finance
    Companies / 71
Purposes of Loans / 72
Types of Security Given for Loans / 72
Liability Insurance Required in the United States and
    Canada / 77

Deaths and Injuries Caused by Motor Vehicles / 78

Basic Coverages / 81

Motor Vehicles: The Worst Killer / 81

Accidents by Age of Drivers / 86

Economic Losses From Traffic Accidents Soar / 89

The Increase in Automobile Thefts / 90

Auto Thefts by State / 92

Costs of Leasing Cars / 102

Load-Carrying Capacity of Tires / 112

Degree of Friction for Good Tires on Various Road
    Surfaces / 112

Braking Distance in Feet From 20 MPH / 121

Tire Traction Ratings / 122

The Cost of Operating a Car / 142

Scrapped Autos Pile Up / 145

The High Cost of Cleaner Air / 203

The Decline in Auto Pollutants / 208

The Rising Cost of Auto Repairs / 215

Hydrometer Test and Hydrometer Corrections / 226

Oil Classifications / 242

Guide to SAE Viscosities of Motor Oil / 242

Protection Against Freezing / 249

Stopping Distances on Dry Pavement for Cars With Good
    Brakes / 266

State Motor Vehicle Registrations / 270

Taxes Paid by Highway Users / 272

Estimated Cost of Operating a Standard-Size 1972 Model
    Automobile / 274

Estimated Cost of Operating a Compact-Size 1972 Model
    Automobile / 278

Estimated Cost of Operating a Subcompact-Size 1972
    Model Automobile / 282

Tire Manufacturer Code Letters / 283

State "No-Fault" Laws / 284

Symptoms and Possible Causes of Car Trouble / 290

Photographs and Drawings

Bumper to bumper / 12
A new car / 24
Typical car sizes / 31
Convertible and hatchback / 33
Station wagon and camper / 34
Seat upholstery / 39
Air bags / 41
Used cars / 50
Flooded cars / 58
Page from *Official Used Car Guide* / 61
Auto accident / 82
Leasing showroom / 96
Tire construction / 106
Auto maker's sticker / 109
Old-time tire trouble / 114
Using a jack / 114-115
Removing and replacing wheel nuts / 115
Tire sidewall / 117
Tread-wear indicator bars / 119
Washing car / 126
Flushing dirt from trim / 126
Forcing water through car / 127
Cleaning headlights / 128
Repairing paint / 129
Polishing hardtop / 130
Repairing gaskets / 131
Cleaning windshield washer jet / 132
Seat belt / 134
Junked cars / 144
Used-car advertising / 148
Legalities in car sale / 154-155
Exploring the auto / 158
Basic auto parts / 160
Crankshaft / 161
Cylinder arrangements / 162

Valves / 163
Piston strokes / 164
Fueling the engine / 166
Carburetor / 168
Open and closed valves / 169
Supplying electricity to spark plug / 170
Spark plug / 171
Cooling system / 173
Lubrication system / 174
Piston rings / 175
Exhaust system / 176
How gears work / 178
Transmission and driveline / 179
Clutch / 180
Transmission gears / 182
Turning a corner / 183
Steering system / 185
Spring suspension / 186
Torsion bar suspension / 187
Rear suspensions / 188
Braking / 189
Drum brake / 190
Disc brake / 191
Air pollution / 192
Emission-control systems / 199
Catalytic converter / 201
Wankel engine / 204
Stratified-charge engine / 207
Auto mechanic / 210
Testing shock absorbers / 229
Certified mechanic patch / 234
Under the hood / 240
Tire inflations / 254
Rotating tires / 256
Tire wear causes / 258
Tire injuries / 260

Acknowledgments

The editors are indebted to Gerald S. Snyder for his work in researching and writing the manuscript for *Your Car— How to Buy It, Take Care of It, and Save Money*. Shirley Scalley edited the manuscript, and Roslyn Grant coordinated the editorial work.

Valuable assistance was also received from the American Automobile Association, American Motors Corporation, American Mutual Insurance Alliance, American Petroleum Institute, Automobile Club of Southern California, Automotive Information Council, Avis Rent a Car, Center for Automotive Safety, Covington and Burling, Executive Auto Leasing, Federal Trade Commission, Firestone Tire and Rubber Company, Florida Department of Agriculture and Consumer Services, Ford Motor Company, General Motors Corporation, General Services Administration, Goodyear Tire and Rubber Company, Pat Goss, an automotive expert, Hertz Corporation, Insurance Information Institute, Insurance Institute for Highway Safety, Monroe Auto Equipment Company, Motor Vehicle Manufacturers Association of the United States, National Automobile Dealers Association, National Bureau of Standards, National Business Council for Consumer Affairs, National Highway Traffic Safety Administration, National Institute for Automotive Service Excellence, National Tire Dealers and Retreaders Association, Office of Consumer Affairs of the Executive Office of the President, Riggs National Bank, State Farm Mutual Automobile Insurance Company, Taylor and Clark Insurance Services, Tire Industry Safety Council, United States Department of Commerce, and the United States Department of Transportation.

Despite the many problems motor vehicles create, their popularity is undiminished, and 126,800,000 of them are expected to be rolling on the nation's roads in 1980. In little more than half a century, the automobile has evolved from a novelty to a pervasive presence in American life.

CHAPTER 1

What Every Motorist Needs to Know

This book is for the nearly nine of every ten Americans who depend upon the automobile for transportation. To them—probably to you—the automobile is a necessity; in the eighth decade of the twentieth century, more people than ever feel that they cannot get by, that they cannot live well, without it.

In 1972, the nation's four major auto makers (Ford, General Motors, Chrysler, and American Motors) sold 9,321,502 cars—an increase of 7.4 percent over 1971. By 1975, predict the experts, some 125 million motor vehicles will be rolling over our country's highways and byways—an increase of 6 million over today's 119 million, 97 million of which are passenger cars.

So rapidly has the sale of cars been increasing that, second only to the home, the automobile is already solidly fixed as the most expensive purchase made by American consumers.

Consider the statistics: more than $100 billion worth of automobiles and auto parts sold each year by the automotive industry; about $33 billion spent annually on 10 million new motor vehicles; the same amount spent over the same period on about 22 million used cars (the average car remains in use for about ten years); and about $300 spent by the average motorist each year just to repair and maintain items that are critical for safety.

As each day passes, the commitment increases, with automobile buyers deeply entrenched as the biggest users of consumer credit. At the end of November, 1972, they owed $43.7 billion—$8 billion more than in the comparable period the previous year. Today the automobile installment debt is rising more rapidly than the borrowers' incomes— which means that the consumer is in danger of overextending himself.

Wages, it is true, have gone up, but in terms of purchasing power it takes more of a worker's earning capacity to buy a car now than it has in the past. Compared to four years ago, the average wage earner now has to work 30 hours longer to earn the price of a typical family car. That is the "real money" cost of buying America's favorite transportation machine.

Many motorists complain

Car owners are not really a happy lot for other reasons. As we have noted, the home, not the car, is the largest single personal expenditure for most people. Yet when it comes to evoking complaints, the automobile takes second place to nothing. Among the wailing chorus of complaints, we hear:

• My automobile insurance rates have gone up again.
• The state legislature has defeated no-fault.

Cars and Population in the United States

(1910-1980)

Year	Estimated Population (Millions)	Estimated Passenger Cars Registered (Millions)	Persons Per Car
1910	92.4	0.5	202
1920	106.5	8.1	13
1930	123.1	23.0	5.4
1940	132.5	27.5	4.8
1950	153.0	40.3	3.80
1951	155.3	42.7	3.64
1952	157.8	43.8	3.60
1953	160.5	46.4	3.46
1954	163.7	48.5	3.38
1955	166.7	52.1	3.10
1956	169.8	54.2	3.13
1957	172.8	55.9	3.09
1958	175.8	56.9	3.09
1959	178.7	59.5	3.00
1960	181.7	61.7	2.94
1961	184.6	63.4	2.91
1962	187.2	66.1	2.83
1963	189.9	69.1	2.75
1964	192.5	72.0	2.67
1965	194.6	75.3	2.58
1966	196.5	78.1	2.52
1967	198.5	80.4	2.47
1968	200.4	83.7	2.39
1969	202.6	86.9	2.33
1970	205.1	89.3	2.30
1971	207.3	92.1	2.25
1975	217.4	106.2	2.05
1980	233.8	126.8	1.84

Sources: Bureau of the Census, Federal Highway Administration, National Automobile Dealers Association Research Department

How Consumers Spend Their Dollars

Total Expenditures: $721 Billion

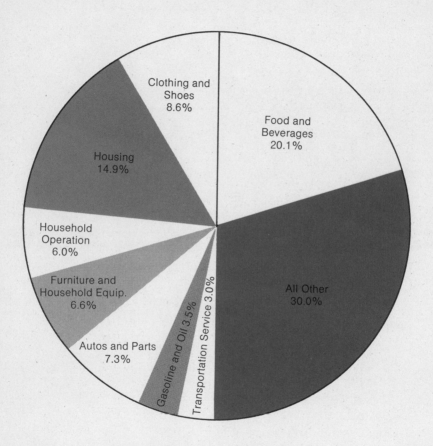

Source: Department of Commerce, 1972 figures

• My new tires went 3,000 miles and then I found out how little the warranty meant.

• My new car has been recalled.

• My tires have been recalled.

• My new car is in the shop for the fifteenth time.

• They overcharged me for repairs.

• They gave me repairs that I did not need and did not authorize.

• I wrote a letter and it took them a month to answer. And then all I got was the runaround.

Virginia H. Knauer, as special assistant to the President for consumer affairs, described the problems of the motorist as a "monotonous litany of complaints which deafens the ear with its intensity." For years, household appliances were the subject of most complaints. Now it is the automobile that holds this dubious distinction.

Auto manufacturers take action

While expending much time, energy, and money in hunting for a cleaner engine, one that will not pollute the air, auto makers also are taking positive action to answer as many complaints as they can. There are new warranty programs. Automobile designs are changing. One manufacturer even has a "We Listen" program to hear motorists' views. And change is coming in many other ways.

In the wake of skyrocketing auto insurance costs and the cries of motorists about rate increases, some states have changed their auto insurance laws in line with a plan that pays accident victims regardless of who is at fault—a system commonly called "no-fault." In one state alone, Massachusetts, the plan has cut premiums for bodily injury by more than 40 percent.

Yet no matter what is accomplished, it seems at times that nothing can be done to silence the deafening chant of consumer boos. The ire of car owners is directed everywhere—at dealers, manufacturers, even the United States government.

Effects of emission control

Under federal law, by 1976 cars must run 90 percent cleaner than automobiles manufactured in 1970, and a graduated schedule for reducing exhausts over the years in between has been formulated. This is making the air more fit to breathe. But the complex emission-control devices are adding to the woes of motorists because cars equipped with clean-air devices tend to run less smoothly and use more gas. In the words of one service station manager, "Everybody is for emission control until it affects them. Then they're not for it so much. People don't like the rough idling. We have to tell them it will never smooth out. They expect their cars to purr along like the old sixes and eights, and that just isn't going to happen."

As safety and pollution-control devices required by law are added, the family car might well become, as another observer expressed it, "as sophisticated as an airplane, as far as maintenance is concerned." Thus, it may become more complicated to analyze the engines and more difficult to repair them properly.

At the very heart of the problem is the complexity of the automobile itself, which can have as many as 15,000 parts. The staggering number and variety of makes and models compounds the problem. There are hundreds of different styles to choose from and so many options—such as radial tires, swivel seats, and vinyl tops—that repair work can become agonizingly complicated. About 81 percent of all cars contain power steering; 63 percent have factory-built air conditioning; and 3.6 percent contain stereo-tape players.

Motorists need to know more

It is not enough for you to drive well, to obey traffic laws and road signs, to reduce your speed when the weather is

What Families Own

(Percent of Total Households in 1971)

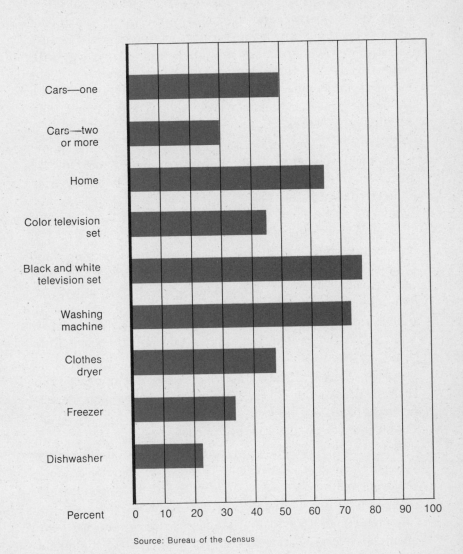

Source: Bureau of the Census

bad, and to drive defensively to avoid accidents. Because a car that is properly cared for is safer, reduces pollution, costs less to operate, and has more resale value, you should know something about mechanical maintenance. Because something, indeed almost anything, can go wrong with your car at any time, you should know something about how the automobile works. And because you can fall prey to the dishonest repairman, you should know something about how *he* works.

There are many other reasons why you need to know more about your automobile. Before you buy a new car, for instance, you should be thoroughly aware of how the price is arrived at by the dealer, what models and options are available, and what you can do to ensure that the car is delivered to you in the best working condition.

When it comes to used cars, the problem is further compounded. If you ever have tried to trade in a car, you have perhaps felt some conspiracy to cheat you as the car salesman pulled out a little book, thumbed through it quickly, and quoted a "book value" that was far below what you had expected. Who published the little book? How did it arrive at the figure?

As this book will show, there is no need for mystery; the little dealers' guides, from one of which we have reproduced a page, are important and widely used tools in the big business of buying and selling used cars.

You should, yourself, refer to one of these guides before you purchase a used car, but there is much, much more that you will need to know. You will, for instance, have to know something of the techniques employed by used-car salesmen. A sociologist who made a study of the used-car business concluded, not entirely in jest, that if diplomats want to learn how to make peace, they should study the techniques of used-car salesmen. Far from the cliché of the salesman as someone who is automatically out to take unfair advantage of you, the sociologist found the used-car salesman confident, motivated, and reasonable.

A concession is made in the study, however, that there can be much cynicism and bitterness in the bargaining process that goes on in every used-car sale. So you should know as much as you can about how to deal with the situation. Contrary to popular opinion, the buying of a used car can be a wise financial move on your part—if you avoid the pitfalls before signing on the dotted line. This means that you must thoroughly check the used car—and this book will tell how. And from whom should you buy a used car? From a private owner? The used-car department of a new-car dealer? A dealer who sells used cars only?

Many questions answered

This book will answer these and many other questions that you are likely to have about the business of keeping wheels under you and your family.

It is possible for anyone, with the help of this book, to learn enough about the basic functioning of the automobile to be able to discuss intelligently its inner workings. And when a person knows how a car works, he will not be an easy mark for unscrupulous salesmen and mechanics.

More people than ever are heeding this counsel. And they are not only males. In the "Women on Wheels" program of one manufacturer, for instance, some 18,000 women quickly signed up for courses on how a car operates, what to do if there is a problem, and how to recognize when serious trouble is developing. Women, indeed motorists in general, are tired of that helpless feeling. The high cost of automobiles and auto repairs has shocked them into realizing that if they knew more about the inner workings and maintenance needs of cars it would be possible to bring their operating costs down.

Very possibly, they also might help to save lives. In 1972 a record 57,000 persons died in automobile accidents in the

Spending for Autos

(Billions of Dollars)

Year	Total Personal Outlays (P.O.)	Total Auto & Auto-Related Outlays*		Outlays For Autos	
		Amount	% of P.O.	Amount	% of P.O.
1962	363.7	44.5	12.2	18.8	5.2
1963	384.7	47.8	12.4	20.6	5.3
1964	411.9	50.1	12.2	21.7	5.3
1965	444.8	56.9	12.8	25.8	5.8
1966	479.3	59.1	12.3	25.3	5.3
1967	506.0	60.6	12.0	24.9	4.9
1968	551.2	69.3	12.6	30.4	5.5
1969	596.3	74.3	12.5	31.7	5.3
1970	633.7	74.1	11.7	28.0	4.4
1971	680.7	84.9	12.5	35.3	5.2

Year	Auto-Related Outlays							
	Total Amount	% of P.O.	Gas and Oil	Repairs Greasing, Washing, Parking, Etc.	Tires, Tubes, Accessories and Parts	Insurance	Interest on Auto Debt	Tolls
1962	25.7	7.0	12.9	5.2	2.6	2.0	2.7	0.3
1963	27.2	7.1	13.5	5.6	2.7	2.1	3.0	0.3
1964	28.4	6.9	14.0	5.6	2.9	2.1	3.4	0.4
1965	31.1	7.0	15.3	6.1	3.2	2.2	3.9	0.4
1966	33.8	7.0	16.6	6.4	3.5	2.7	4.2	0.4
1967	35.7	7.1	17.6	6.6	3.8	2.9	4.3	0.5
1968	38.9	7.1	19.0	7.3	4.5	3.0	4.6	0.5
1969	42.6	7.2	21.1	7.9	5.1	3.0	5.0	0.5
1970	46.1	7.3	22.9	8.7	5.6	3.2	5.2	0.5
1971	49.6	7.3	24.4	9.6	6.1	3.3	5.6	0.6

*Excludes trailers

Source: Department of Commerce

United States. Each day, some 150 Americans are killed in traffic accidents and 5,400 others injured. Since 1933, about 52 million people have been injured by automobiles and the death toll has risen to the staggering figure of about one and a half million. Many of those lives might have been saved if the brakes had not failed at a crucial moment or if a badly worn tire had not suddenly blown out.

The total financial loss from automobiles is estimated at $179.4 billion since 1933. But much of the current economic loss can be prevented. Each year, for example, tens of thousands of motorists are bilked of billions of dollars in unnecessary repairs. Senator Philip A. Hart of Michigan, as chairman of the Senate Antitrust and Monopoly Subcommittee of the Judiciary Committee, estimated the annual cost of unnecessary or wrongful repair work as between $8 and $10 billion—almost a third of the amount spent each year on automobile repairs.

Some think that even the $10 billion figure is conservative. As one consumer advocate put it, "When you begin adding all the time lost from work, car rentals, and repairs to repair work, you are not talking about $10 billion, although God knows that is horrifying enough, you are talking in the neighborhood of $100 billion."

More than ever before, then, today's motorist needs help to cope with the cost and complexity of running a car. This book aims to provide it.

Practical thoughts and emotional reactions often are at war in the prospective buyer when the new car models make their appearance each year. Those who wish to save money on their purchase are advised to let practicality win.

CHAPTER 2

How to
Buy
a New
Car

Observe the light in the eyes of the prospective buyer browsing in the glitter of the new-car showroom. It is obviously a romance, and a serious one. In 1972 alone, 10.9 million new automobiles were bought in the United States. This is about half a million more than were bought in the previous year, and 1973 sales are estimated at 11.2 million.

Of course, not everyone buys a car as a symbol of beauty, adventure, and power. The increase in small-car sales in the last few years has proved that many people are more interested in acquiring economical transportation than status.

Assuming that your desire to buy stems more from practical than emotional considerations—that is, you have not "fallen in love" with any one car—you should carefully plan and research your purchase before approaching a dealer. Knowing exactly what you want and what you can afford—and sticking to your decisions in the face of sales pressures—could result in a saving of hundreds of dollars.

Remember, there is no fixed price for any automobile. The price can and should be negotiated between you and the dealer. If you do your homework before you approach a dealer, you will be in a much better bargaining position.

Planning your budget

Your first step should be to determine how much money you can afford to spend—not only on the purchase price of the car, but also on such things as insurance, taxes, gasoline, and repairs. Keep in mind that buying the car is just the beginning of your automotive expenditures.

There are no hard and fast rules to guide you in determining how much you can afford to pay for a car. You will, of course, have to estimate your annual income and then subtract your taxes, payments on outstanding loans, and expenses for food, clothing, medical care, housing, and entertainment. This will give you an idea of how much you have left for buying and operating the car. If, after you have worked out your budget, you are still uncertain how much you should spend, talk to your local banker. He has had considerable experience in these matters and should be able to give you some solid advice.

Some believe the best way to buy a car is to pay cash—unless your money is earning more interest than you would have to pay on an automobile loan. If you are like most people, however, you will need to finance your car. Even so, you will have to make some kind of down payment—either cash or an equity in your present car, or a combination of both—and your budget should provide for this. You will probably have to put down 20 to 30 percent of the price of the car. Of course, the more you can put down, the less you will have to finance and thus the less you will have to pay in interest. To get an idea of how much your present car is

Work Hours Needed to Buy
and Insure a New Car

The number of hours the average wage earner must work to purchase a new moderate-priced automobile increased 9.3 percent from 1968 to 1972, while the hours necessary to purchase auto insurance increased 3.1 percent over the same period. In 1968, it required 750.9 hours at the nation's median wage of $4.31 an hour to acquire the $3,241 purchase price of a popular automobile, while in 1972 it took 820.8 hours at $5.14 an hour to earn $4,223 for the latest model of the same car. For auto insurance (10/20/5 liability coverage, $100 deductible collision, and full comprehensive), it took 36.4 hours to earn the 1968 premium of $157.19 and 37.5 hours to earn the 1972 premium of $193.13.

Hours Worked to Buy Car	Hours Worked to Buy Insurance
1968 750 hours 55 minutes	1968 36 hours 25 minutes
1972 820 hours 48 minutes (+9.3%)	1972 37 hours 30 minutes (+3.1%)

Sources: U.S. Census Bureau, Insurance Services Office

worth, consult one of the recognized used-car price guidebooks (see page 61). You may not be offered the price
listed, but it will give you some idea of what the dealer
will offer.

Determining how much it costs to operate a car is somewhat complicated. A great deal depends on the type of car
you drive and how you drive it. A subcompact is obviously
going to cost less to operate than a large, luxury car. And
constant stop-and-start city driving is harder on a car, in
terms of wear and tear, than steady freeway driving. However, the Department of Transportation study on the costs
of operating a car (see Appendix III) should be helpful to
you in projecting your expenses.

Until you decide to buy a specific car, you will not be
able to do anything more than estimate your insurance and
finance charges. After you read the chapters on insurance
and financing, you can talk to your insurance agent and
banker or loan official to get a general idea of what your
costs are going to be.

Shopping at home

Determining how much money you have available is only
the first part of your homework. Next you should decide on
the size and type of car and the options you want and can
afford. It cannot be emphasized too strongly that these are
decisions you should make at home. You will be faced with
many temptations in the new-car showroom, and a good
salesman could influence your choice unless you are absolutely sure of what you want to buy.

These are the sizes of cars available:

Subcompact. These cars have a low initial cost and, because they usually have small, four-cylinder engines, they
give excellent gasoline mileage. In general, operating expenses are low. Their small size makes them easy to handle,
but space for passengers and luggage is limited. They are
good cars for use by one or two people.

Buyers Favoring Smaller Cars

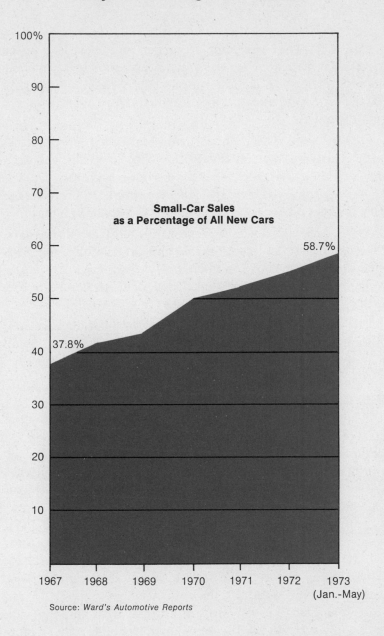

Small-Car Sales
as a Percentage of All New Cars

37.8%

58.7%

1967   1968   1969   1970   1971   1972   1973
(Jan.-May)

Source: *Ward's Automotive Reports*

Compact. They are slightly larger and more expensive than subcompacts. Operating costs are still low, and gas mileage is good. Like the subcompacts, they are easy to handle in traffic and to park. Compacts are good cars for small families.

Intermediate. These cars provide more room and comfort with relatively low-cost operation. They are excellent family cars and are good for long-distance highway driving. However, they must be specially equipped with a V-8 engine if extra power is needed for hill or country driving.

Full size or luxury. The largest and most expensive cars, they are roomy and comfortable and are the best for long-distance driving and for towing. However, they are costly to buy and to operate, and may be difficult to handle in city traffic.

The chart opposite gives typical dimensions for these cars. Although these dimensions are not strictly adhered to by all manufacturers, they do provide guidelines for you to use.

Why size matters

When deciding on the size car to buy, remember that smaller cars are less costly to operate than larger ones. On the other hand, if safety is high on your list of priorities, you may want to consider that in the battle of small cars versus big cars, the big fellows usually win—as a matter of physics. According to five independent studies, made by the University of North Carolina, the New York State Department of Motor Vehicles, the New Jersey Highway Authority, the University of Michigan, and the Insurance Institute for Highway Safety, small-car accidents cause up to three times as many fatal injuries as accidents involving big cars. When small cars were test-crashed with standard-size automobiles made by the same manufacturer, the results were always the same—the large cars were consistently safer. If a small car and a larger one traveling at the same

Typical Car Sizes

SUBCOMPACT
Wheelbases about 94" to 101"

COMPACT
Wheelbases about 102" to 111"

INTERMEDIATE
Wheelbases about 112" to 118"

FULL SIZE
Wheelbases from 119" up

high speed collide, the smaller car will sustain greater damage.

An engineer explained: "While engineering improvements *are* being made in smaller cars to make them as safe as possible, the safest of small cars almost always will come out second best in a head-on collision with a larger vehicle. The same disadvantage would apply to the larger car if it were to collide head-on with a heavy-duty truck."

After you have decided on the size car you want, you will have to decide what type of vehicle you want (or need). Here are some pointers to help you decide:

Two-door sedan. If you have small children and definitely want no doors in the rear, this may be the car for you. The two-door sedan has a strong body design, but passengers in the rear may find it awkward getting in and out, and the wider doors may make it difficult for anyone to leave or enter the car in tight parking spaces.

Four-door sedan. This is a good car for a family of four or more. The extra doors make it easier to get in and out, which will be especially welcome to older people who need to enter and exit easily. The posts between the side windows (a feature also found on two-door sedans and station wagons) offer sturdy construction and protection in the event the car should roll over. Be advised, however, that more squeaks can develop as the result of more doors, and children in the rear can easily get to the door locks and handles.

Two- and four-door hardtops. Because they are judged to be smarter in appearance than sedans, hardtops cost more and have had a better resale value. But they are not as rigid as sedans. Most have no body pillars at all. Some do have thin pillars—giving them the name "pillared hardtops."

Station wagon. These versatile, rugged, and adaptable vehicles come in all four sizes and, depending on the size, can seat from four to eight adults. Because the main function of these vehicles is to haul cargo, all of the seats behind the front one can usually be folded down to form a floor. Although station wagons are higher priced than sedans, they have a good resale value. They also are more subject to squeaks and rattles than sedans, and the larger ones take longer to heat or to cool.

Convertibles—long the glamour cars on American roads—may soon become extinct, doomed by the increasing concern for safe motoring. The 1974 Cadillac Fleetwood Eldorado (above) could be among the last of the happy-go-lucky breed made in the United States. Making up in convenience what it lacks in glamour, the hatchback, such as the Chevrolet Vega (below), is moving toward the top of the popularity ratings.

The urge to get away from crowded urban areas and the rising cost of vacationing at resorts have combined to boost the popularity of recreational vehicles, such as the one at right, which enable families to camp at moderate cost. Also popular with families is the station wagon, above, because of the space it provides for cargo and children.

Hatchback. These vehicles, available in subcompacts and compacts, are becoming increasingly popular because they combine some of the roominess of a station wagon with the styling of a sedan. The trunk area is not totally enclosed; the trunk lid and rear window are made in one piece which opens upward to permit access to a much longer trunk area. And this area can usually be further enlarged by putting the rear seat down.

Convertible. This type, which is fast becoming extinct, is the least rigid of all cars. It has a heavier, lower-center-of-gravity construction to make up for its lack of roof strength, but has poor rollover protection. Other disadvantages are: limited rear visibility when the top is up; the fabric roof and raise-lower mechanism need upkeep; a greater tendency than other cars to develop squeaks and rattles; and a thief or vandal could easily get into it by slashing the roof.

Specialty. These are sporty-looking cars that have powerful, high-performance engines. Their initial cost can vary considerably, but they tend to be relatively expensive to operate, maintain, and insure.

Van and recreational vehicle. These are becoming increasingly popular among motorists who have large families, or who carry large or heavy loads, or who like to go camping.

Considering the options

After you make your decisions about the size and type of car you want, you should think about options—and here you will have a great deal to think about. This is where, if you are not careful, the price of your car can easily jump hundreds of dollars. Also remember that the more gadgets you buy, the more potential repair trouble you are inviting.

There are many options available. Some, like air conditioning, are for comfort; some, like automatic speed control, are for convenience; some, like day-night rearview mirrors, are for safety; some, like stereo-tape players, are for pleasure; some, like spare-tire locks, provide security against theft; and some, like vinyl roofs, are for appearance. Some options, then, are almost necessities; others are luxuries.

You should be careful and logical when choosing options, buying those you need and can afford and foregoing those you would like to have but cannot afford. Be sure to consider optional equipment as a factor in the resale value of the car. Sometimes it is worth spending a few extra dollars now if it will mean a few more dollars in your pocket when the time comes to sell the car. A car equipped with options such as power steering and power brakes will be much more attractive to the next buyer than a car not so equipped. And finally, when you are comparing different cars, remember that certain equipment will be standard on some while being sold as options on others.

Choosing the engine

When considering options, the first thing you need to think about is the size of engine you will need or want. Will the standard engine be adequate for your needs? Or will you want a more powerful engine for pulling heavy loads? Will you need four, six, or eight cylinders? And there are various kinds. Will you want a big six-cylinder, a small V-8, or a larger eight?

Ask yourself, "Do I need an extra powerful engine?"— one that will produce more than 70 horsepower per 1,000 pounds of car weight? When you talk to the dealer, ask him the weight of the car and the horsepower of the engine that comes with it so that you can determine how much power the engine provides.

Here is a rule for deciding which engine you should select. If you generally drive only short distances in level country, carry no heavy loads, do not tow a trailer, and will not have any power-draining extra equipment on your car, the standard-equipment engine should be adequate for your needs. But you may want the greater power of a larger engine if your car has air conditioning or if you live in hilly country, do a great deal of long-distance turnpike driving, or know that you will carry passengers and cargo and perhaps tow a trailer.

Types of transmission

As for the transmission that will go with the engine, there are two basic types: manual and automatic. The essential difference between these two types is that a manual transmission requires the driver to operate a clutch pedal in order to shift gears. In an automatic transmission, the functions of the clutch are handled mechanically inside the transmission. Clearly, then, the driver will have more work to do if the car has a manual transmission. On the other hand, some people feel that a manual transmission gives the driver more control over the car.

There is only one type of manual transmission, but it may have three or four forward speeds. It is generally available on small, intermediate, and sports cars, and because the mechanism is simpler than an automatic transmission, it is less costly.

There are several variations on the automatic transmission, and again, the less work the driver has to do and the more work the transmission has to do, the more costly the transmission will be. The so-called semiautomatic transmission, which is the least expensive, is available only in some foreign cars. It is designed to give the driver the feel of a manual transmission and the ease of an automatic transmission. There is usually a gearshift lever mounted on the floor to the right of the driver, and he must shift the lever for each gear.

With the so-called fully automatic, the gearshift lever is either on the floor or mounted on the steering column, but there is almost always a pointer that visually tells the driver which gear he is in. A fully automatic will have either two or three forward speeds. If it has two speeds, all of the work of shifting will be done in the transmission. If it has three speeds, the driver has two choices: he can either put the car in the drive gear and the shifting will be done automatically, or he can use the shift lever to select whichever gear he wants. Three-speed automatics give the driver more control in difficult situations, such as when driving up a steep hill or in snow. And because there are more gears, there is not as much wear and tear on the engine.

Fully automatic transmissions are available on most cars except subcompacts. While they are expensive to buy, they generally have a good resale value.

Options add to comfort

Just as there is a greater market for cars having an automatic transmission, there is a greater one for cars equipped with power brakes, power steering, air conditioning, and a radio. All of these items contribute to the ease and comfort of driving and thus will be attractive to the next buyer.

When considering what equipment to get with the car, do not take the suspension system for granted. This includes the shock absorbers and springs at all four wheels and sometimes a stabilizer bar at the front and possibly the rear wheels. While for average driving, the original equipment will be adequate, those who drive on poor roads or frequently carry heavy loads or pull trailers will be wise to consider ordering a heavy-duty suspension.

Most police cars and taxicabs, which are subjected to hard use, have heavy-duty brakes, cooling systems, and batteries as well as heavy-duty suspensions. Depending on the type of driving you do, you may want to ask about getting similar equipment. You should be aware, however, that the

Usual Types of
Seat Upholstery

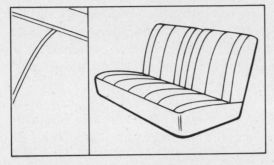

Smooth, grained, or pleated vinyl: durable, easily washable.

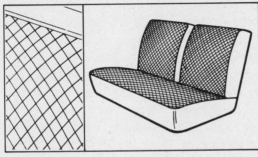

Knitted or woven vinyl: durable, washable, not too hot or cold.

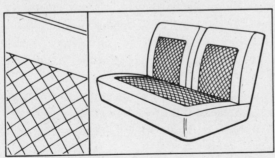

Cloth and vinyl combined: vinyl protects hard-wear areas.

Leather and vinyl combined: attractive, comfortable; needs upkeep.

ride in a car equipped with a heavy-duty suspension will be harder than that in a car with regular suspension, and you will probably feel the bumps more. Also, if you do order a heavy-duty suspension, you may need wider wheels and tires.

Although tires are an important part of any car, most people do not give them a thought until the time comes to buy replacement tires. This can be a mistake. Depending on their driving habits, where they live, and the kinds of roads they will be driving on, some motorists should consider buying as optional equipment a different kind of tire than that which comes with the car. Our chapter on tires will help you determine what your tire needs are.

Some options are controversial. Take power windows, for example. If you have children, you might like the idea of being able to open and close the windows from your seat so the youngsters cannot manipulate them. However, power windows are a potential hazard since a child could be injured if an inadvertently activated power window closed on his arm or neck. Another controversial option is fancy hubcaps which add little or no value to the car, and, in the opinion of some safety experts, may cause wheel balancing problems and undue tire wear.

And some options can be considered more necessities than luxuries, such as a rear-window defroster, day-night rearview mirror, rubber bumper guard, under-the-hood light, and trunk light.

Weighing the safety features

Finally, don't forget to consider safety features. One thing often overlooked is the color of the car. This can be an important safety factor, especially in night driving. According to the New York Port Authority, light-colored cars —preferably cream, yellow, and white—have significantly fewer collisions than dark-colored cars. Black is difficult to see at night or in inclement weather, while all shades of

Offered as an option in some cars beginning in 1974, air bags may eventually replace seat belts as safety devices. The type developed by General Motors consists of two cushions (being inflated above), one in the hub of the steering wheel and the other behind the instrument panel. When the bags fully inflate (below) within a fraction of a second after an accident, the occupants are protected by a pillow of air as the crash impact throws them forward.

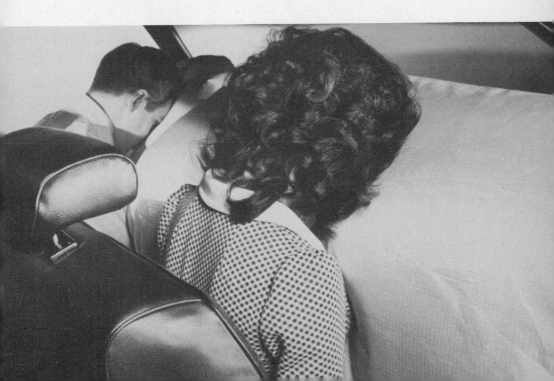

yellow are highly visible, as testified to by the great number of taxicabs, school buses, and police cars painted that color.

Do not concentrate on the appearance of bumpers, but on their ability to offer crash protection. Although all cars manufactured since 1973 must meet federal standards that permit no damage to safety-related equipment in front-end crashes at 5 mph and rear-end crashes at 2.5 mph, newer cars have bumpers that will withstand rear-end as well as front-end crashes at 5 mph.

There are other important safety factors that can be checked only when you get to the showroom:

• Have a small child stand close to the car and then slowly move around it. When in the driver's seat, you should be able to see the child at all times.

• Be sure that the vision through all windows is clear and undistorted. The only acceptable kind of tinting is that which runs across the top edge of the windshield. Fully tinted windshields dangerously reduce dusk and night vision.

• Check to see that the headrests do not block any part of your line of vision through the rearview mirror. This mirror should be located high enough that it does not obstruct your forward vision, and you should be able to see the outside rearview mirror without turning your head too far to the side.

• Look at the tail lights. High tail lights are more visible to the driver behind you and might prevent a rear-end collision.

Lastly, the dealer must, by law, supply you with certain safety facts about his cars. This is useful information to have when comparing safety features.

The National Highway Traffic Safety Administration's consumer information regulations require that, if requested, your dealer must tell you:

1. *Stopping distance*—how many feet the car will move

at various speeds before coming to a full stop.

2. *Acceleration and passing ability*—how much time and distance are needed to pass another car at certain speeds.

3. *Tire reserve loads*—how much extra weight can be added to the car's load without the risk of a blowout or damage to the tires.

Dealing with the dealer

Now that you have decided on the car and options you want, you should make up your mind whether you are going to hold out for this combination or whether you are going to compromise with the dealer. The dealer will have on his lot many cars with different kinds of extra equipment and, because he has paid for or is financing these cars, he is going to be more interested in selling you one of them than in ordering a car to your specifications. If you settle for a car he has immediately available, you may get options you do not need or want, and you may not get options you do need and want. This can be expensive as well as disappointing. It is best to know exactly what car you want and be willing to wait for its delivery from the factory. If the dealer will not order the car, you might want to take your business elsewhere.

You should, when you are planning your car-buying campaign, collect as many different brochures as you can from the various automobile manufacturers. Each manufacturer makes a model that will suit your needs. Make a list of each of the cars you would be interested in and the options you want, and take this list with you when you go to compare prices. When you do compare prices, keep in mind the fact that some options come as standard equipment on some cars and as extras on other cars. You will have to take this into consideration so that the prices you compare will actually be comparable.

Before you begin checking on prices, however, you should decide which dealers to do business with. Your first consideration is the dealer's location. You might, for example, be able to save $100 by trading with a dealer located fifty miles from your home. Should you decide to accept his offer, you may later find yourself in trouble trying to get warranty work done. Before you make a firm commitment to any dealer, examine the wording in the warranty carefully. You will find that most warranties are between you and *the selling dealer*. This means that unless you move to another city or your car breaks down away from home, only the selling dealer is required to do your warranty work. If, then, you buy a car for $100 less but fifty miles away, you may find that you have to drive fifty miles to get warranty work done. This kind of inconvenience may not be worth $100.

The reason the manufacturers include this provision is that dealers make little profit on warranty work and should not have to sustain a loss that rightfully belongs to the dealer who made the profit on the sale of the car. It is logical, too, that the selling dealer will be more interested than some other dealer in taking good care of your car and thus retaining your good will.

Most warranties will cover for one year or 12,000 miles any part of the car made or supplied by the auto manufacturer that is found to be defective in material or workmanship. Any defective part will be replaced or repaired without charge. Tires and batteries are usually warranted separately by their manufacturers.

Check dealer's reputation

What you should do, then, is to find a dealer reasonably close to your home or office who has a good reputation—particularly when it comes to servicing cars. To check on a particular dealer, one thing you can do is to call the Better Business Bureau and ask if any complaints have been lodged against him. But be fair—even honest businessmen are bound to be the subject of some complaints. If you get a negative report, ask for the nature of the complaint and how it was settled so that you can try to determine who was at fault.

One observer provides what is probably the best advice for finding a good dealer: "Good dealers enjoy a favorable word-of-mouth reputation in their communities. When people are pleased with everything—sales, service, and price —they are inclined to talk about it. Customers are equally inclined to spread the word when they are dissatisfied. Ask around."

Now, at last, it is time to visit the showroom. If you are like most people, the first thing you will do is look at the "window" or "sticker" price on a car. This represents the recommended retail price that the manufacturer is required by federal law to put on the car. But it is only a *suggested* retail price; it is not the price you will have to pay. Read the sticker carefully and you will see that it lists the base price of the car, the shipping charge, and the price of optional equipment.

Prepare to bargain

Because dealers often sell at well below the sticker price, especially in high-competition urban areas, this price really represents a "bargaining bench mark" from which the actual price will be determined. To prepare yourself for the bargaining that will go on inside the showroom, you should know the cost to the dealer of the new car and each of the possible options. You can usually obtain this information from any one of several publications sold at newsstands. If you cannot find the specific figures there, you should know that the sticker price ranges from 17 to 25 percent higher than the factory price to the dealer, depending on the size of the car. For a subcompact or compact, deduct 17 percent from the sticker price; for an intermediate-size car, deduct 20 percent; for a full-size car, deduct 22 percent; and for a luxury model, deduct 25 percent.

The dealer, of course, must add to the factory price his profit margin and expenses, including overhead, advertising, and salesmen's commissions. The minimum profit most dealers will settle for is $125—usually they try to get a price 5 to 10 percent above the list price.

If you know, then, the cost of the car to the dealer and how much profit he needs to make on the car, you will know just how much you can bargain and still have a possibility of success.

Unfortunately, there is no definite rule as to which type of dealer will give you the better price—the large, high-volume dealer or the small, low-volume dealer. However, the smaller dealer often has lower overhead expenses and can better afford to cut his profit on a car.

Timing your purchase

If it is particularly important to you to get the lowest possible price on a car, consider the timing of your purchase. For example, salesmen have monthly quotas. As they try to reach their quotas or better their sales of the previous month, they will be inclined to give you a better deal at the end of the month.

The end of the model year is also a time when you might get a better-than-usual deal. During the three months from August through October, dealers are usually offered special rebates by the manufacturers, and many dealers will turn this saving over to their customers. The rebate saving is generally 5 percent. On the other hand, you might not get a good deal in June or July because the dealer's stock may be low and he may have to make more profit on each car to cover his overhead.

You should also be aware that the depreciation loss could outweigh the rebate saving. In other words, the minute a car you buy in September is taken off the lot, it will have depreciated as much as the same car purchased eight months earlier. The model year, not the month of purchase, always determines the resale price. Because first-year depreciation can be as much as one-fourth to one-third of a car's price, the loss you would sustain by buying late in the model year may be greater than the rebate saving passed on by the dealer. This might not be an important factor, however, if you plan to keep the car for at least five years.

In addition to a lower price, another potential plus in buying late in the year is that by then any defects in the particular car you want may have been discovered and corrected. In any case, you can benefit from the experience others have had with the car—either through firsthand reports from friends or through newspaper and magazine reports.

Tips on bargaining

Regardless of when you buy, you may be able to save several hundred dollars on the cost of the car and options you want—perhaps as much as $500—by shopping around. You might have to talk to five or more dealers to get the lowest price. Use the telephone if you prefer, and do not be reluctant to tell one dealer the price another has quoted. If there is one dealer you would rather buy from but his price was not the lowest, do not hesitate to call him back and tell him about the lowest price asked. He may decide to match it.

When you begin your bargaining, some experts recommend that you do not tell the salesman you have a car to trade. If the salesman immediately knows that you have a car to trade, he might make you an extremely attractive offer on your old car—and then not give you as great a discount on the new car. Suppose the wholesale value of your old car is $200. The salesman could offer you $300 for the car, and then not give you the $100 discount he might have given you on the new car. This is just a matter of juggling figures, because in actual practice the salesman will never give you more than the wholesale value of your old car.

The main advantage in not telling him that you have a car to trade until after you have agreed on a price for the new car is that you will have a clearer idea of exactly how much the new car is going to cost you and exactly how much your old car is worth.

The time to talk about a trade-in, then, is *after* you have agreed on a price for the new car. And if you plan to pay cash or finance the car with a bank loan, the time to tell the salesman about that also is after you have agreed on the price for the new car. This is because a dealer could make a 2 or 3 percent profit on any car loan he arranges with a finance company. If the dealer knows that you are going to pay cash or will finance the car through a bank loan, he might not discount the 2 or 3 percent figure from the new car price he quotes you. If you agree on a price and then tell the dealer that you will handle the financial arrangements yourself, the dealer will not be able to recoup his 2 or 3 percent loss by raising the price of the car.

Get prices in writing

Whatever prices you agree on for the new car and for your old car, make sure that you get them in writing and that the estimate carries the signature of the sales manager, not just the salesman. This is to ensure that the dealer will honor the prices he originally quotes. Be sure to ask, too, how long the price on your old car will remain in effect. If you fail to do this, you could find that by the time you are ready to sign the contract, your car will have suffered a sizable depreciation.

In order to be certain that you are getting a reasonable price for your old car, check one of the used-car price guidebooks. Be sure to look for the average wholesale, not retail, value of your old car and either add to or subtract from the price according to the instructions in the guidebooks that refer to optional equipment and general car condition.

Before signing the purchase order for your new car, make sure it states that you have the right to give the car a complete check and road test *before* you take delivery. And, as you did on the estimate, be sure that the contract carries the signature of the sales manager, not just the salesman.

Check everything before you buy

These are the things you should do before you take possession of the car:

• Check the operation of *everything* in the car: heater, air conditioner, radio, *all* of the lights, turn signals, windshield wipers, door latches, door locks, seat belts, cigarette lighter, clock, clutch, brakes, steering wheel—anything and everything that performs some mechanical function.

• Make sure all the options you ordered are there and are operative—and that there are no options you did not order.

• Check the exterior of the car for any signs of damage that has or has not been repaired. Many cars sustain damage to the body and the tires en route from the factory to the showroom.

• Take the car for a short road test.

If, after you have thoroughly inspected and road tested the car, you find anything that is not to your complete satisfaction, do not accept the car until the problem has been corrected. It might not be easy to get the work done *after* you have driven the car off the lot.

Properly done, the process of buying a new car is time consuming and complicated. But the satisfaction you will get from owning a car that operates properly, that is just what you want, and that fits comfortably into your budget will be reward enough for your trouble.

A used car in good condition is the practical answer for those who need a second car or who must economize. Finding a good one requires considerable attention to detail, but the time and effort are repaid by the acquisition of reliable, relatively inexpensive transportation.

CHAPTER 3

How to Buy a Used Car

How many times have you heard it said, "Buy a used car and you buy someone else's problems"?

Contrary to popular belief, however, a used car can be a practical buy for those who cannot afford high payments for a new car or who need a second car.

Most American cars have an average useful life of 100,000 to 150,000 miles—and most are traded in long before they are ready for the junkyard. Furthermore, a used car can provide more economical transportation than a new car, because a used car—even if it is only one year old —will have already depreciated by a major amount, which means that the new buyer will not suffer this loss and that his operating costs per mile will be lower than they would be for a new car. And the used-car buyer many times has the advantage of being able to purchase a fairly new automobile that has already had any of its defects corrected.

This is not to say that buying a used car is a simple matter. It isn't. And it can be risky. But if you shop carefully and cautiously, you could find a real bargain.

What kind of car to buy

As with a new car, you should first consider how much you can afford to spend and gear your choice to this. You might want to consider the long-term economics of your choice, too, such as how much gas the car uses and what kind of replacement tires it will need.

Most experts agree that the best used-car buys are the newer and originally lower-priced autos. So look for recent models of subcompact, compact, intermediate, or lower-priced full-sized cars.

But what if you find a large, luxurious, late-model car that you would love to own but cannot afford to buy new? It would not make sense economically to buy such a car if you could buy a smaller new car for the same price.

In the end, then, choosing the kind of car you want is a matter of preference tempered by judgment. And you can do an important part of this kind of shopping at home. Read the newspaper advertisements, and get a current issue of one of the guides to used-car prices (see page 60). Then check to see what the going prices are for cars you think you might be interested in buying. This not only will give you an idea of what kinds of cars you can afford and thus the kinds of cars you should look for, but will also provide a scale against which to measure the prices being asked by the sellers you will be contacting.

There are also, incidentally, numerous publications available on the newsstands that tell what kinds of problems various cars have had, such as whether or not a certain model has had more, or less, than normal trouble with its electrical system, piston rings, or valves. This actually offers you a great advantage over the new-car buyer, who cannot profit from the experiences—good and bad—of other car owners. Friends are also a good source of this kind of information.

Where to buy your car

The two main sources of used cars are private parties—friends, neighbors, coworkers, newspaper advertisers—and dealers. There are advantages and disadvantages in buying from each source.

One of the really important things to know about a used car is who owned it previously. If you know this, you can usually find out what kind of care the car has had and what problems the owner has had with it. This kind of information is more accessible if you buy from the original owner. And if you buy from a friend or neighbor, you have the added benefit of dealing with a known and trusted individual.

If you buy from a private party, you can expect to pay less than the average retail price, and sometimes considerably less. This is because a private seller may not know the true value of his car, or may just accept the best offer in order to get on with the business of buying a replacement car. But, on the other hand, the seller will not have made any repairs to the car to prepare it for sale and will not offer any kind of guarantee or warranty. Taking care of mechanical defects after you buy the car will be strictly your problem.

In contrast, a dealer will probably recondition the car—although this may be nothing more than cover-up work so that the car will pass your inspection. He will also offer you some kind of minimal guarantee. But you will have to pay for these possible advantages in a higher price for the car. The dealer, after all, is in business to make a profit after he has recovered these expenses as well as the price he paid for the car.

If you want to buy from a dealer, you need to decide

whether to buy from a used-car or new-car dealer. Most consumer-advisory groups tend to recommend the franchised new-car dealer over the dealer who handles used cars exclusively. The reason is that your chances of getting a one-owner car are better.

Used cars come from many sources, and it is improbable that all the cars on any used-car dealer's lot come from private owners. Many may have given their best miles to police departments, government agencies, taxicab companies, and rental firms. Each week, used-car dealers buy and sell between 25,000 and 30,000 cars at auctions open only to these dealers. It is small wonder that the dealers have little or no information about the previous history of these cars.

Whatever dealer you decide to buy from, be sure to check his reputation with friends and acquaintances. Call, too, the Better Business Bureau or perhaps the dealers' association, and do not hestitate to go to three or more dealers to compare cars and prices.

Is it a "lemon" or mechanically sound?

By now you should be ready to get down to the actual business of answering ads and making the rounds of dealers to inspect particular cars. And this is where you should be prepared to exercise extreme caution.

Resolve not to become emotional. The minute you do, you will become vulnerable to making an unwise choice. Before you even consider buying any car, you should carefully inspect its condition. You should, in fact, have those you are seriously considering checked out by a mechanic of *your* choice. But you should first weed out as many "lemons" as you can and take only those worthy of his attention to your mechanic. This can save you a considerable amount of money since the mechanic's fee can run as high as $25. As a matter of fact, just telling the seller your intentions can save you time and effort. If he has nothing to hide, he will be willing to let the car go for inspection. If, however, he knows the car is defective, he will be reluctant to have a mechanic look it over. In this and everything else, do not be put off by a refusal. Take your business elsewhere if the seller is uncooperative.

How, then, do you go about inspecting a car? It is really not very difficult. First of all, always examine cars on a bright, sunny day. Never inspect them at night or when it is raining. Darkness can hide many defects, as can rain. "Rain," a former used-car salesman says, "can hide the worst paint job and the worst bumped-out fender job. Some engines even run better in the rain. And you are less likely to crawl under the car and spend the time necessary to give it a good going-over if it's raining."

First check the exterior

The first thing to check, then, is the exterior of the car. This will give you many clues about the treatment the car has had or whether it has been in an accident. Look down the side of the car to see if there are any ripples in the metal. Examine the paint job closely to see whether all the paint matches. Be especially alert about cars that are several years old but entirely free of nicks and scratches. Such a car was entirely repainted for some reason—possibly extensive accident damage. Frequently, you can determine the original color of the car, and thus whether or not it was repainted, by looking at the fire wall that separates the engine from the driver. It is almost impossible to repaint this area. If you suspect that the car was damaged in an accident but are still interested in it, have a mechanic check it to make sure the frame was not bent.

While checking the body, be sure to look at the tires—including the spare. If the car is more than two years old, you probably will have to observe only the amount of tread left because the tires most likely have been replaced. But if the car is almost new or supposedly has low mileage, the tires can be a good indicator of the car's condition. The original tires should still be on the car. If they have been replaced, if the rear ones are different than those in front, or if there are signs of uneven wear, you should ask why. The front end may be out of alignment or the car's mileage may be higher than that indicated on the odometer.

Look underneath the car

By now you probably are tempted to get inside the car to start the engine. Don't. At least not yet. Instead, get down on your knees and look underneath the car, checking for rust spots and holes. "Crawl over the car, under it, and through it," one expert in used cars advises. "Don't be shy. If they see that you are insistent about seeing everything, they won't try to sell you a lemon." Also check for rust spots behind the bumpers and in and around the doors. A car that is beginning to rust badly should usually be eliminated from further consideration.

While searching underneath, look for excessive amounts of mud or some other signs that would indicate the car has had hard use by a contractor or someone who has frequently used the car off the road. It is difficult to remove all caked mud that may have built up over the years without doing a steam-cleaning or sand-blasting job.

Also look under the car for signs of oil and water leakage. Look *on the car*, not on the ground—there is no way of telling how many cars have been in that exact spot, so oil or water patches on the ground could be meaningless. If some spots on the car are wet with oil or water, your mechanic could determine the source. The leak could come from a broken $2 hose, but it also could be a sign of a cracked engine block.

Next, check the suspension system for signs of wear. Test the shock absorbers by pushing down on each corner of the car and then letting go. The car should move up and then stop in its normal position. If it continues to bounce, the shock absorber probably should be replaced. Another test for shock absorbers is to brake the car several times when traveling about 5 mph. The front end should not bounce up and down. If you suspect worn shock absorbers, check with your mechanic.

Check the interior

Now it is time to inspect the interior of the car. Do not be satisfied with an interior that merely looks good on first glance. Check the operation of the windows, door locks, seat adjustments, and air conditioner. Inspect the upholstery beneath the seat covers. Lift up the rubber floor mats and examine the carpeting. Feel the carpeting to see if it is bumpy, and look at it closely to determine if its appearance is new, which may mean it has been replaced.

To avoid getting a former taxi, look for holes drilled under the dashboard where a two-way radio or taxi meter may once have been installed. Look also for a new ceiling liner that may cover the patchwork resulting from the removal of roof lights.

Remember, too, that the interior includes the trunk. This can be one of the most revealing places to help you diagnose a used car's condition. If the mats and carpeting have been taken out and the interior sprayed with paint, the car may have been utilized commercially—by a construction worker, for instance, who used the paint to cover scrapes made by his tools.

While still examining the interior, step down on the brake and hold the pressure steady for a minute. If the pedal continues to sink, the car may need serious brake repairs. Also look for depressions in the driver's seat or a badly worn steering wheel rim, which would indicate hard use. Stains on the upholstery might indicate rain leaks.

Look for flood damage

Finally, check for signs of flood damage. Many flood-damaged cars turn up on used-car lots, especially under "spe-

One of the hazards in selecting a used car is the possibility of buying one that has been damaged in a flood. Many such cars are offered at bargain prices on used-car lots but are a waste of the buyer's money.

cial purchase" or "hundreds under cost" labels. Such cars are risky buys and sooner or later will cause their owners grief from leaking brake cylinders, defective wheel bearings, knocking engines, and rusting bodies. Some signs of flood-damaged cars are:

• Rust under the carpets, on the turn signal and transmission control levers, and around chrome screws.

• Musty, stale odor.

• A waterline or warpage on the back cushion of the rear seat.

• A film of moisture on the inside of the glass covering the instruments on the dashboard.

If a car has passed your inspection so far, it is time to start looking at the engine. First lift the hood of the car and check the consistency of the engine oil. If the rings or bearings are worn, the dealer may put in heavy oil to keep the engine quiet. Next check the color of the engine oil. Any oil that has been run through an engine for more than twenty minutes will have become dark. If the oil is remarkably light in color and clean, it has just been changed—and you should find out why. And if the oil is gritty, there could be sand in the engine.

Then check the transmission oil; the engine must be running when you do this. Again, be sure that it is not a heavy oil. If it looks or smells burned, this could mean serious trouble.

When you start the engine make sure that all the warning lights go out, and then listen for loud or unusual noises. Pay attention to how the engine idles. If it is noticeably or objectionably rough, have your mechanic check for internal engine problems, such as valve damage.

Next operate all the gadgets to make sure they work—the horn, windshield wipers, lights, turn signals, radio, and so on.

Price Guidelines for Used Cars

We often hear the term "book value" used in regard to cars, yet few know exactly what this means. In fact, it can mean a great many things. This is what it is all about.

Reproduced here is a page from the *Official Used Car Guide,* published monthly in nine regional editions by the National Automobile Dealers Association (NADA). This is the most popular, in terms of the number of subscribers, of several publications that list either the current wholesale values or the current wholesale and retail values of cars. The wholesale value is the price the dealer will probably give you if you trade in your car; the retail value is what you will probably pay for a used car—or get for your car if you sell it yourself.

Other monthly publications of this type include *The Red Book,* published in Chicago, primarily for the midwestern region; *The Black Book,* published in Gainesville, Georgia, mainly for the southern region; and the *Kelley Blue Book Auto Market Report,* published in Los Angeles for the western part of the country. *AMR* (Automotive Market Reports), published in Pittsburgh, Pennsylvania, and *Galvs Auto Price List,* published in The Bronx, New York, are two more guides to auto values.

One or more of these publications are available to you either through your dealer, your bank, or your local library, and they can be invaluable aids when buying a used car or trading in or selling your old car.

In preparing its guide, NADA takes reports of actual transactions by dealers and wholesalers, tabulates them by date and state, and puts them into a computer, which averages the prices. These prices, whether wholesale or retail, should be regarded only as "guides," however. At different times and places, the price of a particular make, model, and year of car may vary by hundreds of dollars for a number of reasons, such as the mileage on the car, its general condition, and the kind of extra equipment it may have.

For example, the averages assume that a car is clean, and the NADA guide states: "Appropriate deductions should be made for reconditioning costs incurred to put the car in salable condition. An exceptional clean car or one which has been dealer reconditioned and bears a warranty or guarantee should bring a premium price."

Also note that the guides usually have instructions for adjusting the listed price for such variables as special equipment that may be on the car.

Be sure, then, whenever someone starts talking to you about the "book value," to ask which book value—wholesale or retail.

Wholesale Price

Retail Price

Adjustments to make to the listed price

Av'g. Trade-In	Ins. Sym.	BODY TYPE	Model	Fact. A.D.P.	Ship. Wgt.	Av'g. Loan	Av'g. Retail
1972 CHEVELLE—AT—PS—continued							
STATION WAGONS—V8		Veh. Ident.: 1(X X X)2( )100001 Up.					
2125	4	Nomad 4D 2S	1B36	$3016	3732	1925	2600
2325	4	Greenbrier 4D 3S	1C46	3247	3870	2100	2800
2200	4	Greenbrier 4D 2S	1C36	3140	3814	2000	2675
2425	4	Concours 4D 3S	1D46	3351	3909	2200	2900
2300	4	Concours 4D 2S	1D36	3244	3857	2075	2775
2575	5	Concours Estate 4D 3S	1H46	3538	3943	2325	3075
2450	5	Concours Estate 4D 2S	1H36	3431	3887	2225	2925
75		Add Vinyl Top		$ 92		75	100
250		Add Factory Air Conditioning		397		225	325
100		Add SS Pkg.		350		100	125
75		Add AM/FM Stereo		233		75	100
125		Add AM/FM Stereo W/Tape		363		125	150
200		Deduct 3 Spd. Trans.				200	200
150		Deduct 4 Spd. Trans.				150	150
125		Deduct Conventional Steering				125	125
1972 CAMARO—AT—PS						**Start Sept. 1971**	
CAMARO—6 Cyl.		Veh. Ident.: 1Q87D2( )100001 Up.					
2300	4	Hardtop Sport Coupe 2D	1Q87	$2730	3121	2075	2775
CAMARO—V8		Veh. Ident.: 1Q87( )2( )100001 Up.					
2425	4	Hardtop Sport Coupe 2D	1Q87	$2820	3248	2200	2900
75		Add Vinyl Top		$ 87		75	100
250		Add Factory Air Conditioning		397		225	325
100		Add SS Pkg.		306		100	125
25		Add Rally Spt. Pkg.		118		25	50
200		Deduct 3 Spd. Trans.				200	200
150		Deduct 4 Spd. Trans.				150	150
125		Deduct Conventional Steering				125	125
1972 MONTE CARLO—AT—PS						**Start Sept. 1971**	
MONTE CARLO—V8		Veh. Ident.: 1H57( )2( )100001 Up.					
2600	4	Hardtop Coupe 2D	1H57	$3362	3506	2350	3100
75		Add Vinyl Top		$ 123		75	100
250		Add Factory Air Conditioning		397		225	325
75		Add AM/FM Stereo		233		75	100
125		Add AM/FM Stereo W/Tape		363		125	150
200		Deduct Manual Trans.				200	200
1972 CHEVROLET—AT—PS						**Start Sept. 1971**	
BISCAYNE—6		Veh. Ident.: 1K69D2( )100001 Up.					
1650	4	Sedan 4D	1K69	$3074	3857	1500	2075
BEL AIR—6		Veh. Ident.: 1L69D2( )100001 Up.					
1775	4	Sedan 4D	1L69	$3204	3854	1600	2200
IMPALA—6		Veh. Ident.: 1M(X)D2( )100001 Up.					
1900	4	Sedan 4D	1M69	$3369	3928	1725	2350
2025	4	Hardtop Sport Coupe 2D	1M57	3385	3864	1825	2500
BISCAYNE—V8		Veh. Ident.: 1K69( )2( )100001 Up.					
1775	4	Sedan 4D	1K69	$3408	4045	1600	2200
BEL AIR—V8		Veh. Ident.: 1L69( )2( )100001 Up.					
1900	4	Sedan 4D	1L69	$3538	4042	1725	2350

DEDUCT FOR HIGH MILEAGE
EASTERN EDITION

Page from the Eastern Edition of the NADA Official Used Car Guide

Road test the car

If everything has checked out to your satisfaction so far, you should take the car for a road test. See if you like the way it handles. Check the steering wheel—there should be no more than a total of two inches of free play. More than this means serious problems in the steering linkage. The car is, in fact, unsafe to drive in this condition.

If you are able to take one with you, have a friend watch as you drive down the road. He or she should observe whether the car rides level and in a straight line, that the tires do not wobble or bounce about, and that there is no excessive exhaust smoke when you accelerate or decelerate. Make this test recommended by the Automobile Club of Southern California: "Either descend a long grade with your foot off the accelerator or, in a flat area, decelerate from 50 mph to about 15 mph without using the brake. Then step hard on the accelerator. If there is heavy blue exhaust smoke, the car may need new piston rings, or the engine may need overhauling."

You should be aware, however, that an engine can burn a lot of oil and yet emit little smoke out of the exhaust. Such an engine could be plugged up with sludge. This is why it is vital that your mechanic remove one of the valve covers and look inside the engine.

Be sure, also, to drive the car on a stretch of rough road. This will reveal rattles, poor steering control, or weak shock absorbers.

Make sure that the transmission shifts relatively evenly, but do not be alarmed if it is not as smooth as you think it should be. Many people think that they should not feel an automatic transmission shift. Actually, sometimes the more durable the transmission, the more noticeable the shift. If you think the shift is too noticeable, bring this to the attention of your mechanic.

While you are road testing the car, make sure that the engine does not race between shifts. Also listen for any humming or whining sounds from the rear that could indicate something wrong with the gears in the differential.

If, while you are driving, the engine overheats, this could be caused by a loose fan belt—but it could also be caused by a plugged, damaged, or defective radiator, internal engine problems, or a cracked engine block. Check with your mechanic.

Have a mechanic check the car

If a car gets through this kind of an inspection, you are justified in taking it to your mechanic. Have him check out any specific problems you have noticed, and then let him do his own thorough check. He should examine the brakes, the exhaust system, the suspension system, the electrical system, and the transmission. He should remove one of the valve covers to check for sludge, and he should perform a cylinder compression test and leakage test. He should do any other tests and checks he thinks necessary, and, of course, he should road test the car. If a car passes all of these tests, with perhaps only a few minor repairs needed, you have probably found a good buy.

If you are buying from a dealer and find that some repairs are needed, get the dealer to make them before you buy the car. Ask him to note on the deposit receipt that the sale is contingent on your approval of the car after the complaints have been remedied and after an inspection by your own mechanic. No reputable used-car dealer should refuse to do this.

Do not expect too much in the way of a guarantee and warranty on a used car. Guarantees usually cover the car for only thirty days and stipulate that the seller and the buyer will share the cost of any repair work. If you find a used car still covered by the manufacturer's warranty, it should be worth more to you than a car not so covered. But check with an authorized dealer to be certain that the warranty is valid and can be transferred to you.

Points to keep in mind

Here are some other tips on buying used cars:

• Do not pay too much attention to the mileage on a car. Most experts agree that the important thing is the age of the car and how it has been cared for—not the number of miles it has been driven.

• Do not think that by taking over the payments on a repossessed car, you are getting a bargain. If an individual is unable to keep up with his car payments, often he is also unable to take proper care of the car.

• If your state requires that all cars be inspected, insist that the car be passed before you sign a contract.

• Many cars are recalled each year because they have defects. If you buy from a private seller, your chances are good of finding out whether the car you want to buy was recalled and whether the repairs were made. If, however, you buy from a dealer, he may not be able to give you this information. What you might do in this case is to get a list of all the cars that have been recalled and the reasons for the recalls. To get this information, write to the U.S. Government Printing Office, Washington, D.C. 20402. Ask for all the quarterly or yearly reports on "Motor Vehicle Safety Defect Recall Campaigns" that have been issued since the car you want to buy was manufactured. Even with this information, you still will not know for sure whether your car was involved in a recall or whether the defect was corrected, but you will know if your car might have been involved. If this is the case, have your mechanic check the part and advise you whether repairs are necessary.

It is no easy task, but if all the rules for used-car buying are followed, its purchase can be a most practical answer to the transportation question.

CHAPTER 4

How to Finance Your Car

Many people go to a great deal of trouble to shop around for the lowest possible price on a car and are extremely pleased when they are able to save one or two hundred dollars. Then they carelessly lose this money on the financing of the car.

The best way to buy a car, of course, is to pay cash. But if you cannot do this, or if you do not want to because your money is earning more interest than you would have to pay on a loan, try to borrow at the lowest possible rate of interest. The price you must pay for credit can add hundreds of dollars to the cost of the automobile, so shop around and investigate several sources. Talk to at least three different lenders, compare their deals, and then select the best one.

Shopping for a loan has been greatly simplified since the passage, in 1969, of the truth-in-lending legislation. Under

Credit Sales of New Cars

(As Percentage of Total Sold)

Month	1962	1963	1964	1965	1966	1967	1968	1969	1970	1971
Jan.	53%	58%	59%	53%	57%	61%	59%	63%	61%	51%
Feb.	56	57	58	57	60	65	64	61	58	58
Mar.	55	56	62	61	65	65	61	69	66	64
Apr.	59	61	61	64	67	63	69	69	67	68
May	60	61	63	64	75	65	67	66	66	63
June	65	64	73	68	76	69	67	69	66	67
July	76	74	77	77	81	75	78	77	79	73
Aug.	77	78	77	82	85	84	81	81	79	83
Sept.	73	77	69	86	76	70	73	65	81	62
Oct.	57	60	74	58	62	65	61	64	65	56
Nov.	57	58	56	62	62	64	59	58	67	62
Dec.	57	60	57	65	61	60	63	65	66	68
Annual Percentage	61%	63%	65%	66%	68%	67%	67%	67%	68%	65%

Source: Board of Governors of the Federal Reserve System

this law, all lending institutions must express interest in terms of the annual percentage interest rate and the dollar amount of interest. This has eliminated much of the confusion that previously existed, because now the interest on any loan is always calculated the same way. This means that a 9 percent loan from one organization is exactly the same as a 9 percent loan from another one. The only thing you need to be concerned about, then, is finding the agency that will offer you the lowest annual percentage interest rate.

The sources of credit available to you are commercial full-service banks, savings banks, credit unions, the car dealer himself, and finance companies. In addition, some insurance companies handle auto financing for their policyholders at favorable interest rates. There is no rule to guide you to the lending institution that will give you the best interest rate. Rates fluctuate not only with the state of the economy, but also with the financial condition and goals of the particular lending agency.

Although it is often true that banks and credit unions offer the lowest rates, and finance companies offer the highest rates, this is not always the case. The rates offered by dealers usually lie somewhere in the middle.

You are not obliged to let the dealer handle the financing of your car, but you might want to explore this possibility. Be cautious, however. While the dealer will offer you the convenience of one-stop shopping, you may pay a premium for this convenience in terms of high interest rates.

Remember that the dealer usually makes a profit on loans he places with his finance company or bank. What happens here is that the dealer arranges with the lender to finance his cars at a specified interest rate. The dealer then charges the customer a higher rate—and he keeps the difference between what the customer pays and what the lender gets. This is called the dealer's reserve. A result of this method of financing is that some automobile dealers actually charge

Holders of Installment Credit

(Millions of Dollars)

	Outstanding Year-end 1971	Extensions 1972	Repayments 1972	Outstanding Year-end 1972
Total installment credit	111,295	142,951	126,914	127,332
Commercial banks	51,240	59,339	50,796	59,783
Finance companies	28,883	38,464	35,259	32,088
Credit unions	14,770 }	20,607	18,117	{ 16,913
Miscellaneous lenders*	2,251 }			2,598
Automobile dealers	226 }	24,541	22,742	{ 261
Other retail outlets	13,925 }			15,689
Automobile Paper	38,664	40,194	34,729	44,129
Commercial banks	23,114	24,879	20,897	27,096
Purchased	(13,837)	—	—	(16,320)
Direct	(9,277)	—	—	(10,776)
Finance companies	9,577	8,879	8,282	10,174
Other financial lenders*	5,747	6,111	5,260	6,598
Automobile dealers	226	325	290	261
Other consumer goods paper	34,353	55,599	49,872	40,080
Commercial banks	13,343	18,399	15,546	16,196
Mobile homes	(4,423)	(3,231)	(1,868)	(5,786)
Credit card plans	(4,419)	(10,145)	(9,276)	(5,288)
Other	(4,501)	(5,023)	(4,402)	(5,122)
Finance companies	5,613	11,611	10,719	6,505
Mobile homes	(2,561)	(1,430)	(1,075)	(2,916)
Other	(3,052)	(10,181)	(9,644)	(3,589)
Other financial lenders*	1,472	1,373	1,155	1,690
Retail outlets	13,925	24,216	22,452	15,689
Personal loans	32,865	43,152	39,095	36,922
Commercial banks	11,547	13,871	12,471	12,947
Check credit plans	(1,497)	(2,517)	(2,225)	(1,789)
Other	(10,050)	(11,354)	(10,246)	(11,158)
Finance companies	13,446	17,539	16,073	14,912
Other financial lenders*	7,872	11,742	10,551	9,063
Home repair and modernization loans	5,413	4,006	3,218	6,201
Commercial banks	3,236	2,190	1,882	3,544
Finance companies	247	435	185	497
Other financial lenders*	1,930	1,381	1,151	2,160

Note: Parts may not add to totals due to rounding.

* Miscellaneous lenders include savings and loan associations, and mutual savings banks. Credit unions and miscellaneous lenders are combined as "other financial lenders" in the Federal Reserve reports on extensions and repayments.

Source: Federal Reserve Board

Types of Installment Credit Outstanding at Finance Companies

End of 1972 Total: $32.1 Billion

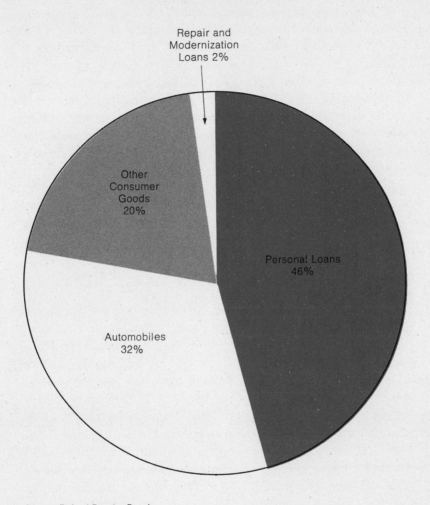

Repair and
Modernization
Loans 2%

Other
Consumer
Goods
20%

Personal Loans
46%

Automobiles
32%

Source: Federal Reserve Board

their customers the highest interest rate permissible by law.

This is why experts recommend that you not only shop around for your loan, but also postpone any discussion with the dealer about financing until after you have agreed on a price for the car. If he knows before you start talking about price that you are going to pay cash or finance the car elsewhere, he will be less apt to discount from the price of the car the profit he might make on the financing. After you have agreed on a price, you can then ask him what his finance charges will be and compare his charges with those of other lending companies.

Be wary, too, if the dealer makes you a no-down-payment offer. This means that he will finance the car twice—through a small finance company and through the bank with whom he usually does business—and the interest charges will be extremely high.

Other loan possibilities

Banks offer several types of loans that are not available elsewhere. If you have a large enough amount in your savings account, you can sometimes secure a passbook loan. What you do here, in effect, is to borrow against the money in your account. Some banks will also accept good-quality common stocks as security for the loan. Either way, the interest rates are usually lower than those on a straight automobile loan because there is less risk to the bank.

When shopping for a loan, you should also understand that the longer the loan period, the greater the amount of interest you will have to pay. This is because interest is calculated each month on the unpaid balance of the loan. You will not, however, actually pay a different dollar amount of interest each month. When you first secure the loan, the total interest charge for the period of the loan will be calculated, and you will repay the principal and the interest in equal monthly installments. Because you must pay interest only for those months when you are using the

Size of Auto Finance Contract Purchased by Finance Companies

(Averages for Selected Years)

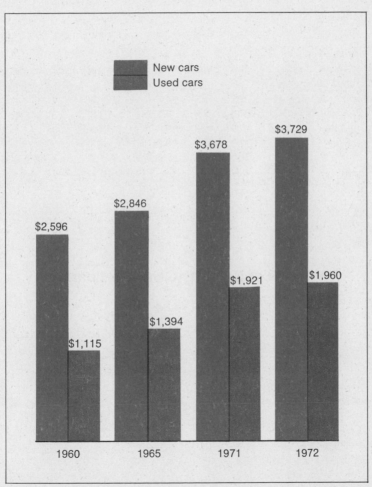

New cars
Used cars

	1960	1965	1971	1972
New cars	$2,596	$2,846	$3,678	$3,729
Used cars	$1,115	$1,394	$1,921	$1,960

Source: Federal Reserve Board

Purposes of Loans

(Estimated in Percent)

Purpose	1950	1954	1958	1960	1964	1966	1971
To consolidate existing bills	30.2	33.7	39.5	40	46	44	46
Travel, vacation, education expenses	7.4	8.4	9.3	10	8	8	7
Automobile purchase or repair	4.5	4.7	5.5	7	11	12	10
Home furnishings and appliances	5.1	5.2	4.7	8	3	3	3
Household repairs	7.3	6.8	5.1	4	3	3	4
All other purposes	45.5	41.2	35.9	31	29	30	30
Total	100.0	100.0	100.0	100	100	100	100

Source: National Consumer Finance Association

Types of Security Given for Loans

(Estimated in Percent)

	1950	1954	1958	1962	1966	1969	1971
Automobiles, household goods, and other chattels	63.3	62.2	61.1	61.2	51.4	58.7	63.2
Unsecured notes	25.4	27.3	27.4	28.9	35.2	31.1	24.0
Endorsed and/or co-maker loans	4.2	3.6	2.7	2.2	2.4	2.5	2.0
Wage assignments	6.2	6.1	7.7	5.7	8.6	4.3	5.3
Real estate	0.4	0.3	0.3	0.4	0.5	0.3	1.0
Other	0.5	0.5	0.8	1.6	1.9	3.1	4.5
Total	100.0	100.0	100.0	100.0	100.0	100.0	100.0

Source: National Consumer Finance Association

lender's money, you will get a refund of interest if you repay the loan faster than required in the contract. You should always, then, borrow money for the shortest possible period of time—and if you can repay it faster than scheduled, that will be to your further advantage.

Credit life insurance

When you borrow money, the question of credit life insurance is apt to be raised. This insurance, which will pay for the car if you should die before you have paid off the loan, could be a good idea because it will protect your estate from any claims made by the lending institution. However, the lender always has some security for his loan—the car itself, your savings passbook, or something else of monetary value—so many experts question the importance of this coverage. The American Automobile Association says: "If you are young and in good health, or if you have substantial life insurance already, consider whether you really need credit life insurance on your car loan at all." You should know, too, that the truth-in-lending laws prohibit lending institutions from making this insurance a condition of the loan. Your decision, then, should be based on the deal that your lender will offer you. If the cost of this insurance lies in the area of ½ of 1 percent, you might be wise to buy it; if the cost approaches 1 percent or more, you should seriously consider doing without this coverage.

Before you sign the contract for your loan:

• Read and understand the contract. Do not rush. If you do not understand it, have some qualified person explain it to you.

• Never sign a contract with spaces left blank. Even if you are told that the typist has left for the day and will not be back until Monday, do not sign it until the blanks are filled in.

• Be sure the contract tells *exactly* what you will have to pay: the purchase price of the car and each piece of extra equipment; the total price including sales and license taxes; the trade-in allowance; the cost, if any, of insurance; the down payment made and the total amount due; the finance charges in dollars and annual percentage rate; and the amount and number of payments and the dates due.

• Make certain that all the figures in the contract are accurate and that there are no extra charges you do not understand.

• Know to whom you make all payments.

• Get a copy of the contract for your records.

• Be aware that there may be a penalty for late payment. In some instances, this could be 5 percent or more of the payment. If you make all the payments on time, this clause will not cost you. But if you fall behind on your payments, it can add an extra financial burden.

• Understand the conditions under which the car can be repossessed.

• Find out what refund of interest you will get if you are able to repay the loan faster than scheduled. Under the 1969 law, the method of computation of refund for prepayment must be shown on the contract.

• Beware of a contract calling for a large, final "balloon" payment. In order to keep the monthly payments low, some lenders make the last payment very large. If this payment is not made, the borrower could lose the car or have to refinance it at a higher rate. This practice is now against the law.

• Do not sign away any of your legal rights.

• Read everything on the contract, including the fine print.

CHAPTER 5

Insurance: How Much Is Enough?

Step into any automobile and you step into the expensive world of auto insurance. Consider, for instance, liability insurance, which is the most important coverage you can have. According to a United States Department of Transportation study, this kind of insurance has the "dubious distinction of having probably the highest cost/benefit ratio of any major compensation system currently in operation in this country."

There are, however, ways to cut your insurance costs. Whether you are buying for the first time or are planning to change your present coverage, it will be to your advantage to examine carefully the cost and types of protection available. You could have too little, too much, the wrong kind of coverage, or you could be paying too much for the coverage you have.

Types of insurance

With an eye, then, to saving money on auto insurance, let us examine the five basic types of coverage:

Liability. Don't drive without this most vital kind of auto insurance. If you do not have this coverage and are sued as the result of an accident, you could lose many of your personal assets, including your savings and some of your future salary.

If you, or anyone else driving your car with your permission, are found to be at fault, your liability coverage will pay claims for injury or damages made against you by passengers in your car, passengers in the other car, and any pedestrians involved in the accident. This insurance will pay their claims for medical bills, lost wages as a result of injury, burial expenses, and damages for "pain and suffering." It will cover the cost of repairs to other cars involved or other property damaged, such as a neighbor's fence. It will not cover injury to you or damage to your property.

In a majority of states, motorists who buy liability coverage are required to have a minimum of "10/20/5," which means that for any single accident, the insurer will pay up to $10,000 for an individual's injuries, up to $20,000 if there is more than one person hurt, and up to $5,000 for automobile or other property damage. The table opposite shows the liability coverage required by the different states. Some states have compulsory liability insurance laws, requiring you to have the minimum insurance before you can register your car and get license plates.

The amounts in the table represent minimum coverage limits. But this is not the place to scrimp, so you should explore the wisdom of increasing your coverage. Remember that your insurer will pay up to the dollar limit of your policy. If a court should award an amount over that limit, you—not your insurer—will have to pay the difference.

You should buy enough of this insurance to cover the maximum amount of claim against you that you can rea-

Liability Insurance Required in the United States and Canada

UNITED STATES State	Liability* Limits	State	Liability* Limits
Alabama	10/20/5	North Dakota	10/20/5
Alaska	15/30/5	Ohio	12.5/25/7.5
Arizona	15/30/10	Oklahoma	5/10/5
Arkansas	10/20/5	Oregon	10/20/5
California	15/30/5	Pennsylvania	10/20/5
Colorado	15/30/5	Rhode Island	10/20/5
Connecticut	20/40/5	South Carolina	10/20/5
Delaware	10/20/5	South Dakota	15/30/10
District of		Tennessee	10/20/5
Columbia	10/20/5	Texas	10/20/5
Florida	25/25/5	Utah	10/20/5
Georgia	10/20/5	Vermont	10/20/5
Hawaii	10/20/5	Virginia	20/40/5
Idaho	10/20/5	Washington	15/30/5
Illinois	10/20/5	West Virginia	10/20/5
Indiana	15/30/10	Wisconsin	15/30/5
Iowa	10/20/5	Wyoming	10/20/5
Kansas	15/30/5		
Kentucky	10/20/5		
Louisiana	5/10/1	**CANADA**	*inclusive** *
Maine	20/40/10		
Maryland	15/30/5	Alberta	$35,000
Massachusetts	5/10/5	British Columbia	$50,000
Michigan	20/40/10	Manitoba	$50,000
Minnesota	10/20/5	New Brunswick	$35,000
Mississippi	10/20/5	Newfoundland	$35,000
Missouri	10/20/2	Nova Scotia	$35,000
Montana	10/20/5	Ontario	$50,000
Nebraska	10/20/5	Prince Edward	
Nevada	15/30/5	Island	$35,000
New Hampshire	20/40/5	Quebec	$35,000
New Jersey	15/30/5	Saskatchewan	$35,000
New Mexico	10/20/5	Northwest	
New York	10/20/5	Territories	$35,000
North Carolina	10/20/5	Yukon	$50,000

* The first two figures refer to bodily injury liability limits and the third figure to property damage liability. For example, 10/20/5 means coverage up to $20,000 for all persons injured in an accident, subject to a limit of $10,000 for one individual, and $5,000 coverage for property damage.

** The "inclusive" limit means there is $35,000 of liability insurance available to settle either bodily injury or property damage claims—or both—up to that amount.

Source: American Insurance Association

Deaths and Injuries Caused by Motor Vehicles

Deaths and injuries caused by motor vehicle accidents in the United States from 1947 to 1971 are tabulated, along with the annual number of accidents since 1966, the first year such national statistics were compiled.

Year	Accidents	Deaths	Injuries
1947		32,697	1,365,000
1948		32,259	1,471,000
1949		31,701	1,564,000
1950		34,763	1,799,000
1951		36,996	1,962,000
1952		37,794	2,090,000
1953		37,955	2,140,000
1954		35,586	1,960,000
1955		38,426	2,158,000
1956		39,628	2,368,000
1957		38,702	2,525,000
1958		36,981	2,825,000
1959		37,910	2,870,000
1960		38,137	3,078,000
1961		38,091	3,057,000
1962		40,804	3,345,000
1963		43,564	3,460,000
1964		47,700	3,840,000
1965		49,163	3,982,000
1966	15,896,000	53,041	4,192,000
1967	16,978,000	52,924	4,353,000
1968	18,631,000	54,862	4,356,000
1969	22,025,000	56,000	5,010,000
1970	22,116,000	54,800	4,983,000
1971	22,650,000	54,700	4,994,000

Sources: Insurance Information Institute, National Safety Council, Travelers Insurance Companies

sonably foresee. When deciding on the amount to buy, you should consider the average size of the court awards made in your state, the amount of your existing personal assets and your future income potential, and the recommendation of your insurance agent or company.

Additional protection is not as expensive as you might imagine. One large company, for instance, charges an annual premium of $40.95 for liability coverage with a $20,000 limit for bodily injury to one individual and a $40,000 limit if two or more persons are injured. For an annual premium of $48.35—less than $8 more a year—this same company offers a policy with limits of $100,000 and $300,000. Another company offers 10/20 insurance for $100. This coverage can be increased to 25/50 for less than $15 and to 100/300 for less than $35. With some companies, you could increase your property damage protection from $5,000 to five times that amount—$25,000—for an additional premium of only $3. The basic coverage is the major expense; it usually can be increased many times over for only a modest increase in cost.

Someone of substantial financial standing might well consider an "umbrella" policy. This increases liability coverage to $1 million for an added yearly premium of about $60, and provides coverage for everything from a car wreck to a boating accident. However, this kind of insurance can be obtained only by those who already have 100/300 automobile liability protection as well as a homeowner's liability policy of $50,000.

Many motorists who have just bought a new car mistakenly believe that liability insurance is included in their car payments. While lending institutions do require collision and comprehensive insurance to protect their investment, they usually do *not* require liability coverage.

Medical benefits. This coverage pays medical and hospital expenses for anyone traveling in your car. It also covers you if you are injured by a car even when you are not a

passenger. Medical benefits coverage may duplicate the
health insurance you already carry, but you would be wise
to have it as supplemental insurance. It also covers passengers in your car, which your health insurance does not do.

This is one of the cheapest kinds of insurance you can
buy. The cost runs about $7 a year for coverage of $500
per person, $8 for $750, $9 for $1,000, $11 for $2,000, and
$19 for $10,000. When deciding on how much insurance to
buy, consider the kind of driving you do. If you regularly
carry passengers, such as neighborhood children, you
should get higher coverage.

Collision. This insurance pays for repairs to your car regardless of who is at fault. If the other driver is to blame,
your company will pay you and then attempt to collect
from his insurance company. As with other types of insurance, costs for collision coverage vary widely. But because
collision insurance policies are of the deductible type, this
is one place where you can save money. Most policies offer
$50, $100, or $250 deductible. As a general rule, the larger
the deductible amount, the smaller the premium. If there is,
for example, $100 deductible, the policyholder pays the first
$100 of repair costs, and the insurer pays the rest. You
should, therefore, buy a policy with as large a deductible as
you are prepared to pay in repair costs.

It may surprise some drivers to know that collision insurance is one kind they may be able to dispense with alto-
gether. If you have a car five to ten years old, the coverage
may cost you more than the car is worth. Assume, for example, that your car is worth $500. You would have to de-
cide whether it would be wise to pay $50 for $100 deductible collision insurance which would pay you a maximum of
$400. One basis on which you could make this decision
would be your driving record. Because you generally receive collision benefits when an accident is your fault, you
could probably do without this coverage if you have a consistently good driving record. If your record is poor, it

Basic Coverages

Bodily Injury Coverages:	Policy-holder	Other Persons
Bodily Injury Liability	No	Yes
Medical Payments	Yes	Yes
Protection Against Uninsured Motorists	Yes	Yes

Property Damage Coverages:	Policy-holder's Automobile	Property of Others
Property Damage Liability	No	Yes
Comprehensive Physical Damage	Yes	No
Collision	Yes	No

Source: Insurance Information Institute

Motor Vehicles: The Worst Killer

	1971	1972	% Change
All Accidents	115,000	117,000	+2
Motor Vehicle	54,700	56,600	+3
Home	27,500	27,000	−2
Work	14,200	14,100	−1
Public (Not Motor Vehicle)	22,500	23,500	+4

Note: Death figures shown for the four separate classifications total more than the "all accidents" figure because some deaths are included in more than one classification.

Source: National Safety Council

A familiar scene on the nation's roads, auto accidents result in an enormous and ever-increasing economic loss from deaths, injuries, property damage, and insurance costs. Motor vehicles are now America's No. 1 killer.

might be more costly in the long run to drop this insurance, regardless of how much your car is worth.

You should not, then, be arbitrary about picking a cutoff date for your collision insurance. You should consider your driving record and the current value of the car, which can be affected by the type of car you own, by its age, and by how much wear and tear you have subjected it to.

If, for example, you have a three-year-old Mercedes-Benz, you certainly should keep the collision insurance in effect, as you also should for a three-year-old Volkswagen, which is more apt than most cars to retain much of its original value. On the other hand, many cars are not worth much more than $500 after three years of hard use, and after five years almost all cars, regardless of their make, have depreciated enough to raise the question of the value of retaining collision insurance.

Comprehensive. This type of insurance provides financial protection against theft, vandalism, or damage caused by hail, flood, fire, and windstorm. Like collision insurance, comprehensive can sometimes be bought on a deductible basis. If your company offers it, always compare the cost of full comprehensive against that of $50 and $100 deductible. Your premiums will be less if you buy the deductible type of comprehensive coverage.

If you live in a high-theft area, your premiums for comprehensive may run quite high. But this protection could be invaluable if your car is stolen and not recovered. As with collision insurance, however, you may want to consider dropping comprehensive if your car is not worth enough to justify the cost.

Uninsured motorists. Whether or not you have to carry this protection depends upon your state's financial responsibility laws. Regardless of this, however, it is worthwhile to carry an uninsured-motorists clause in your policy. This will cover medical treatment for injuries inflicted on you and your passengers by a hit-and-run driver who is never caught or by a driver who either does not have liability insurance or is insured by an insolvent company. This insurance also covers lost wages and pain and suffering incurred as a result of such an accident. In some states, uninsured-motorists protection will provide benefits if your property is damaged by an uninsured or hit-and-run driver.

Miscellaneous. In addition to these basic coverages, there are many insurance "frills" available. For example, you may want to consider emergency road service, which will cost from $1 to $3 a year and pay up to $25 each time towing is necessary. Be aware, though, that if you belong to an auto club, you probably already have this kind of coverage.

Buying your insurance

You can buy auto insurance from four main sources:

• Independent insurance agents, who often represent several companies and sell many kinds of insurance on a commission basis;

• Agents who sell the insurance of only one company or group of associated companies on a commission basis;

• Associations, which include auto clubs and other organizations and which sell insurance to their members at special group rates; and

• Direct writers, which are companies that do not employ agents and sell insurance directly through the mail.

There are two considerations when choosing an insurance company. The cost, of course, is important, but it is also vital to consider the company's performance record.

To determine how well or poorly a company performs, the first thing you should do is to look in *Best's Insurance Reports* to find the company's General Policyholders Rating. Note, however, that although *Best's* will tell you about a company's financial stability, it will not tell you anything about the quality of its service. To get this information, talk to friends and relatives who may have submitted claims to their insurance companies. Were they satisfied with the service? Did the company pay the claim promptly and fairly? Did it answer questions and respond to complaints? Did it stick with the policyholder after he or she had been involved in an accident or had received a traffic ticket? What reasons—if any—were given for cancellation or nonrenewal?

And find out from the various companies themselves whether or not they offer "around-the-clock" nationwide claim service. Ask what their policies on cancellation or nonrenewal are, and note whether they are patient in explaining their policies and answering questions.

Your next step is to shop around for the best prices. Check with at least four companies, and compare their rates. The rates asked by various companies for identical coverage of the same car and driver(s) will differ significantly.

Special discounts offered

Some companies offer special discounts. Be sure to ask whether a company offers discounts to:
- Owners of two or more automobiles.
- Owners of small cars.
- Young drivers who have completed a formal driver-education course.
- Young drivers who receive good marks in school.
- Drivers who have good driving records.
- Nonsmokers and nondrinkers of alcoholic beverages.
- Owners of cars with the new, improved bumpers.

Obviously, whenever an insurance company feels it is running the risk of having to pay out a great deal of money in claims, it is going to charge proportionately more for coverage. Newer and more expensive cars cost more to repair—and so cost more to insure. The more miles a car is driven, the greater the risk of accident—and so insurance rates are often geared to your average mileage. Cars used for business and cars driven only in congested cities also

Accidents by Age of Drivers

Compilations based on reports from state traffic authorities show that drivers under age 30 are involved in a disproportionately high number of traffic accidents. In 1971, drivers in that age group comprised 31.8 percent of the motoring population of the United States, but were involved as drivers in 47 percent of all accidents and 45.9 percent of fatal accidents. The highest rate of involvement in fatal accidents is among drivers 20 through 24 years of age.

Age Group	Number of Drivers	% of Total	Drivers in All Accidents	% of Total	Drivers in Fatal Accidents	% of Total
0-19	11,700,000	10.3	4,700,000	16.6	10,100	14.9
20-24	12,900,000	11.3	5,200,000	18.4	12,800	18.9
25-29	11,600,000	10.2	3,400,000	12.0	8,200	12.1
30-34	10,900,000	9.6	2,700,000	9.6	7,100	10.4
35-39	10,900,000	9.6	2,400,000	8.5	5,150	7.6
40-44	11,300,000	9.9	2,100,000	7.4	5,150	7.6
45-49	11,200,000	9.8	2,100,000	7.4	4,800	7.1
50-54	9,900,000	8.7	1,650,000	5.8	3,700	5.4
55-59	7,800,000	6.8	1,450,000	5.1	3,100	4.6
60-64	6,000,000	5.3	1,000,000	3.5	2,700	4.0
65-69	4,500,000	3.9	850,000	3.0	1,900	2.8
70-74	3,100,000	2.7	350,000	1.3	1,350	2.0
75 and over	2,200,000	1.9	400,000	1.4	1,750	2.6
Total	114,000,000	100%	28,300,000	100%	67,800	100%

Source: National Safety Council

run greater risks. If the car is located in a high-theft area, the cost of comprehensive insurance will be high. Younger people are involved in more accidents than older people—so their premiums are usually higher. And a driver's accident record is very important in determining rates. In fact, people involved in many accidents have difficulty getting insured at all. Often such a driver is "assigned" to a particular insurance company by the state. In this way, each company carries its proportionate share of these drivers. Even so, the coverage is usually minimal, and the premium extremely high.

In general, then, the amount of the premiums you will have to pay will be determined by:

• The make, model, and year of your car.

• Where you live in the country, and whether you live in a rural area or in a city.

• The age, sex, and marital status of the drivers of the car.

• The driving records of the drivers.

• Whether the car is used primarily for business, for commuting to work, or merely for pleasure.

How often you pay your premiums is another factor that can influence the cost of insurance. A special handling charge of $1 may be imposed by some companies if you pay on a quarterly or semiannual basis instead of annually. If you pay on a monthly basis, the handling charge may be higher. You can save money if you pay annually, making less bookkeeping work for the company.

High cost of insurance

Why does insurance cost so much? The main reason is the high cost of fixing vehicles. To get an idea of how high this is, consider that if a $3,500 car were destroyed, it would cost about $15,000 in parts and labor for a repair garage to restore the vehicle to proper working order. Of course, no one would spend $15,000 to repair a totally destroyed car. But the point is that if a $3,500 car suffered damages of only 10 percent in a crash, the cost to repair it would not be 10 percent of $3,500, or $350, but more likely $1,500, or 10 percent of the $15,000 it would cost the repair garage to fix the entire car.

Claims for damaged cars outnumber those for bodily injury by more than seven to one, and that is why two-thirds of most auto insurance premiums go for vehicle damage coverage.

The situation shows some sign of improving, however, with a noticeable decline in damage to late-model autos in low-speed crashes. Recent data show that the average repair costs for rear-end damage sustained in test crashes at 2.5 mph dropped from $56 for 1972 models to $22 for 1973s, and for crashes at 5 mph, they have fallen from $229 to $117. For front crashes at 5 mph, repair costs dropped from $244 to $15. At 10 mph, they dropped from $712 to $389.

In 56 percent of all accidents reported under collision insurance and 34 percent reported under property damage liability, it is the front fender which needs repair or replacement. According to a study conducted by four large auto insurers in conjunction with the research department of the American Mutual Insurance Alliance, the front bumper assembly is involved in 48 percent of collision and 25 percent of all liability claims. In 39 percent of collision claims and 47 percent of liability claims, the rear quarter panel needs repair, and in 24 percent of collision and 36 percent of liability claims, the rear bumper assembly needs repairs.

Of all crashes reported in the study, the right front corner of the car was the principal point of impact, being involved in a crash 16 percent of the time and costing an average $382 to repair.

The American Mutual Insurance Alliance report was based on inspections of 89,060 collision-damaged cars. Ex-

Economic Losses From Traffic Accidents Soar

Economic losses in the United States have been propelled upwards by increases in accidents, deaths, and injuries, and by the rising costs of automobile repairs and medical care. The economic loss figure includes the cost of
paying for property damage; legal, medical, surgical, and hospital bills; loss of
income due to absence from work; and the administrative costs of insurance.

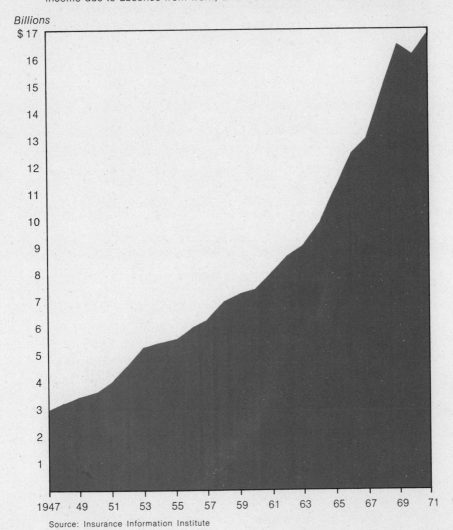

Billions

Source: Insurance Information Institute

The Increase in Automobile Thefts

Police estimate that 80 to 85 percent of all cars stolen are taken by nonprofessional thieves, mainly juveniles, for transportation or personal profit from the sale of the cars or parts. Although 84 percent of all stolen vehicles are recovered, an estimated 30 percent of the recovered cars have been damaged or stripped of parts—many to the extent that they represent total losses.

Year	Passenger Car Registrations	Thefts	Ratio of Cars Stolen/ Registered
1952	43,823,097	215,310	1 in 204
1953	46,429,270	226,530	1 in 205
1954	48,468,418	215,940	1 in 225
1955	52,144,739	227,150	1 in 230
1956	54,210,901	263,720	1 in 206
1957	55,917,897	265,178	1 in 211
1958	56,890,558	282,787	1 in 201
1959	59,453,984	293,779	1 in 202
1960	61,682,304	325,900	1 in 189
1961	63,417,358	333,700	1 in 190
1962	66,108,282	364,300	1 in 181
1963	69,055,428	405,400	1 in 170
1964	71,982,740	469,500	1 in 153
1965	75,260,847	493,400	1 in 153
1966	78,315,000	557,300	1 in 141
1967	81,051,000	655,200	1 in 124
1968	83,698,100	778,200	1 in 108
1969	87,153,381	872,400	1 in 100
1970	89,861,000	921,900	1 in 97
1971	92,082,000	941,600	1 in 98

Sources: Federal Bureau of Investigation, Bureau of Public Roads

perienced automotive damage appraisers did the inspecting. The study revealed:

• As cars become larger and more expensive to buy, they cost more to repair. For example, subcompacts average $303 to repair, compacts $312, semisport models $317, intermediate and standard-size cars $320, specialty cars $402, compact station wagons $312, full-size wagons $331, and luxury cars $409.

• Some 70 percent of all auto crashes involve impacts at either the front or rear ends at speeds under 10 mph.

• More than half of all auto crashes and more than one-fourth of the repair dollars involve damages costing less than $250 to repair.

• Damage to front ends is more frequent and more costly than damage to rear ends but "front and rear ends are involved about equally in low-speed crashes, indicating economic justification for added protection at the rear as well as at the front."

In addition to expensive repairs, an important factor influencing insurance rates is that most of the money is used to cover an insurer's overhead costs. A Department of Transportation study has determined that only 44 cents of the liability premium dollar is ever returned to the policyholder in terms of benefits. Fewer than half the 500,000 people who are killed or seriously injured in automobile accidents each year are involved in cases of reimbursement by liability insurance, according to the DOT study. For those who lose $25,000 or more as the result of accidents, the average recovered is only one-third of the loss. However, small claims—amounting to not more than $500—are likely to be settled quickly and, in fact, the claimants frequently are overpaid.

Protect your car against theft
One way that drivers can help to bring premiums down, say the insurers, is to protect their cars against theft. Dur-

Auto Thefts by State

State	1970	1971	% Change
Alabama	7,696	7,696	—
Alaska	1,666	1,636	—1.8
Arizona	8,883	8,336	—6.2
Arkansas	2,096	2,186	4.3
California	137,514	144,375	5.0
Colorado	12,988	12,895	—.7
Connecticut	14,682	16,611	13.1
Delaware	3,064	3,263	6.5
Florida	26,930	27,652	2.7
Georgia	14,164	14,078	—.6
Hawaii	4,474	4,476	—
Idaho	1,028	1,219	18.6
Illinois	57,551	53,267	—7.4
Indiana	22,275	20,229	—9.2
Iowa	4,945	4,372	—11.6
Kansas	5,772	5,504	—4.6
Kentucky	11,150	10,905	—2.2
Louisiana	14,016	14,786	5.5
Maine	1,452	1,419	—2.3
Maryland	21,478	21,072	—1.9
Massachusetts	49,955	56,709	13.5
Michigan	41,184	44,793	8.8
Minnesota	13,153	13,314	1.2
Mississippi	1,737	2,213	27.4
Missouri	25,156	23,848	—5.2
Montana	1,540	1,572	2.1

State	1970	1971	% Change
Nebraska	4,331	3,850	—11.1
Nevada	3,229	3,074	—4.8
New Hampshire	1,269	1,402	10.5
New Jersey	39,957	42,346	6.0
New Mexico	3,983	4,599	15.5
New York	124,092	126,051	1.6
North Carolina	7,653	7,669	.2
North Dakota	562	542	—3.6
Ohio	52,488	53,501	1.9
Oklahoma	7,049	7,264	3.1
Oregon	6,961	7,790	11.9
Pennsylvania	40,107	43,086	7.4
Rhode Island	8,158	9,402	15.2
South Carolina	6,385	5,529	—13.4
South Dakota	624	558	—10.6
Tennessee	11,353	12,111	6.7
Texas	44,153	42,289	—4.2
Utah	3,350	3,608	7.7
Vermont	551	637	15.6
Virginia	13,824	13,867	.3
Washington	12,335	11,874	—3.7
West Virginia	1,612	1,942	20.5
Wisconsin	9,614	10,771	12.0
Wyoming	547	618	13.0
District of Columbia	11,158	8,770	—21.4

Source: Federal Bureau of Investigation estimates

ing the past decade, while the number of cars has risen about 25 percent, automobile theft has more than doubled, and insurance companies estimate their bill for stolen cars at more than $825 million a year.

Statistics indicate that every forty seconds a car is stolen somewhere in the United States. If you live in New York City or Saint Louis, for example, the odds are one in five that your car will be stolen. If you live in Chicago, the odds are one in nine, and they are one in fifteen in Los Angeles.

To protect your car from theft:

• Keep its doors locked and windows tightly closed at all times.

• Never leave the car unattended while the engine is running.

• Remove the keys from the ignition even when leaving the car for an errand.

• Do not "hide" an extra key under the floormat, seat, hood, or elsewhere in the car.

• Do not expose valuable items in the car.

• Park in areas that are well lighted.

By taking these precautions you will be doing your part to hold down auto insurance premiums.

Is no-fault the answer?

Accidents are always costly—in terms of both time and money. But the cost is often excessive when lawsuits are instigated to obtain compensation for such intangibles as "pain and suffering."

Some types of coverage—such as comprehensive and collision—are already no-fault. That is, your insurance company pays you regardless of who was at fault. What some legislators are now seeking is an extension of this kind of coverage to liability insurance. Lawsuits to recover damages are costly not only in terms of money paid out by the insurance companies, but also in terms of lawyers' fees, court costs, and the amount of time it takes to conclude such a suit. And, of course, they are costly in terms of the premiums the motorist has to pay. It is contemplated that no-fault insurance would eliminate many of these costs. The insurance company would pay its policyholder his out-of-pocket expenses—without delay and regardless of who was at fault.

Many lawyers, not surprisingly, are opposed to this concept. They argue that such a plan would deprive an individual of his common-law right to compensation for his "human losses." Nevertheless, states that have adopted such an insurance plan (see Appendix V) have reported encouraging results. In Massachusetts, where no-fault was first used, bodily injury premiums were cut 15 percent during the first year of the plan's operation. Because of the lower costs of settling claims under the new plan, further reductions in premiums were made in subsequent years. Not only was the settlement of claims quicker during the first year of operation, the number of claims was 37 percent lower than in the previous year. Florida, the second state to adopt a no-fault plan, experienced similar results —premiums for bodily-injury and property-damage liability were reduced by 15 percent the first year with further reductions in subsequent years, claims were settled faster, and fewer cases crowded the courts.

Under most no-fault plans, lawsuits for damages can be instituted under special circumstances. In Massachusetts, a lawsuit for negligence can be filed if the individual incurs at least $500 in medical expenses or if the injury results in death, dismemberment, or disability. Under the Florida law, lawsuits are permitted when medical expenses mount to $1,000.

If no-fault insurance becomes the standard for the country, we can all look forward to more stabilized insurance costs. Until then, we can help to cut our costs by buying insurance wisely and driving carefully.

The advantages of leasing a car rather than buying one are attracting a growing number of drivers, expected to number about two million by 1975.

CHAPTER 6

To Lease
or
Not
to Lease

There is a relatively recent way of putting yourself behind the wheel of a brand-new automobile, and close to one million Americans think it is a good way. That is the number who are leasing their cars instead of buying them. This figure stems from an increase of 15 to 20 percent each year in the number of cars leased during the past decade. By 1975, according to industry experts, some two million motorists will be leasing instead of buying autos.

Is leasing for you? It may be, but before you sign a contract, consider carefully the pros and the cons. First, the *pros*:

• For many people, leasing is simply a less troublesome way of getting a new car. It eliminates the need to shop for a new car and haggle over prices and trade-ins every year or two.

• If you now own a car and are thinking of leasing, the leasing company (called the "lessor") will probably offer you the wholesale value of your car minus any costs of getting it into suitable resale condition. The lessor also may pay you in cash at the time the lease is signed—provided, of course, that there are no finance charges outstanding on the car.

• Under most leases, you do not need a down payment, so you can direct toward some other purpose the cash you might have used this way. When a down payment is required, it is usually lower than the down payment required to buy a car. As one major auto leasing company puts it: "The prime motivation for leasing is 'cash conservation.' It makes more sense to lease than to buy because when leasing you pay only for the use of the car; you do not buy the entire car only to have to sell it two or three years later. Nor do you have to borrow money or tie up capital or become involved in a credit squeeze."

• You (the "lessee") will have the opportunity of driving a new, well-equipped car of the make and model you want. Leasing companies generally handle only cars that have an automatic transmission, power steering, power brakes, air conditioning, a radio, and whitewall tires. Their cars usually are top-of-the-line models because the leasing company is anticipating the time when it will have to sell the car, and lower-priced, poorly equipped models do not have a high resale value.

• Under some contracts, you will not have the trouble or expense of arranging for license plates and insurance. These are included in the leasing fee.

• Some lessors make available insurance coverage at group rates that are often lower than any you would be likely to obtain by yourself.

• Under certain kinds of contracts, you do not have to worry about maintenance expenses. Because you know in advance what your expenses will be, with no "hidden" or unexpected costs, you will be better able to plan your budget.

• Because the leasing company has a vested interest in the car—it is the owner—you are more likely to get quick, dependable service if trouble occurs.

• Professional people, such as doctors, lawyers, and ministers, find that the monthly billing statements enable them to keep simplified expense records for tax purposes. It is a relatively easy process, for example, to prorate expenses for tax returns if you keep your canceled checks and a record of mileage each year. Also you may be able to reduce the net cost of the lease by submitting the part attributable to business expense on your tax return.

• When the lease expires and the time comes to pick up a new car, the leasing company will handle the resale of the old car and save you the trouble of selling it yourself.

Consider the disadvantages

Given this impressive list of the advantages in leasing, you may feel the urge to sign quickly on the dotted line. Before you do, however, you should consider these *cons* of leasing:

• First of all, you must be a first-class credit and insurance risk. Leasing companies carefully investigate their customers, and if you cannot afford to buy a new car, you should forget about leasing one. To qualify for a lease, you will need: (1) a good credit rating; (2) a stable employment record; (3) a good driving record; and (4) an income commensurate with the size of your leasing obligation.

• You can rent a car by the day, week, or month, but you can lease only for a long term. The minimum contract is for six months; most contracts run for twenty-four to twenty-six months.

• If you want to lease, but know that you will have only short-term use of the car, you will still have to sign a contract for at least six months. Under these conditions, whether you use the car or not, the bills will keep coming.

• If you change your mind during the leasing period and decide that you should buy a car instead, you cannot simply return the leased car. A leasing company executive explained: "Lease rates are predicated on set depreciation schedules, and should you cancel your contract prior to accrual of the established depreciation reserve, you would be responsible for the balance." In other words, you, not the lessor, would have to assume the remaining depreciation loss on the car when the company tries to sell it as a used car.

• Leasing is not cheap. Even though leasing companies have special arrangements with auto dealers, they still have to make a profit above what they pay for the cars. So leasing could be at least as expensive for you as buying a car.

• Under most contracts, after you have paid off the lease and returned the car, you have no equity in it. If you had bought the same car and made loan payments for two or three years, you would ultimately own a car still worth hundreds, and possibly thousands, of dollars. Some leases give you the option to purchase the car you leased at the wholesale market value after the leasing period expires. However, if you do this, you may find that you would have come out ahead financially if you had bought the car in the first place.

• Under many agreements, the lessor reserves the right to recall the car after 18 months or to leave it in service for a few months after the lease has expired. This allows the lessor to dispose of the car at a time when used-car prices are higher than usual.

Three types of leases

If, after considering the pros and cons, you think it might be to your advantage to lease, you should examine the three basic types of leasing arrangements. They are:

Open-end. As a general rule, this is the least expensive

type of lease arrangement. It is also the most popular. Under it, you assume all operating costs of the car in addition to the leasing cost. You are responsible for keeping the car in good condition and for servicing it according to the manufacturer's recommendations.

The unique thing about an open-end lease is that you must guarantee that the lessor receives the depreciated value of the car on the used-car market when the lease expires. If the car sells for less than the depreciated value, you pay the difference. If it sells for more, you get the profit.

This type of lease, then, is risky. If the market value of the car declines sharply or if the vehicle is not in good condition, you may have to make a substantial cash outlay at the end of the leasing period.

Closed-end. This kind of agreement is substantially the same as an open-end agreement except that you do not guarantee to the lessor the depreciated value of the car when the lease expires. When you turn the car in, with normal wear and tear, the lessor, not you, will have to worry about the price it may bring on the used-car market. The monthly payments, however, are higher under a closed-end lease, and are comparable to what you would pay if you were buying a car.

Full-maintenance. This arrangement, which is usually closed-end, is the most expensive type of lease because, for a fixed fee, the lessor offers complete maintenance, including tire repairs, tune-ups, oil changes, lubrication, and emergency service. You pay for only gas and oil. The full-maintenance lease will even provide a replacement vehicle if the leased car breaks down. This type of lease is primarily used by large companies that maintain fleets of cars for their executives and do not want to be involved in servicing the cars.

When selecting the kind of car to lease, you should use the same criteria that you would when choosing a new car.

Costs of Leasing Cars

This is a typical open-end fee schedule
based on a thirty-six-month lease:

1973 Model		Monthly Charges
Plymouth Cricket Chevrolet Vega Ford Pinto	Standard factory equipment plus 4-cylinder engine, automatic transmission, radio, whitewall tires.	Under $59
Plymouth Satellite Sebring Chevrolet Malibu Ford Torino Pontiac Le Mans	Standard factory equipment plus V-8 engine, automatic transmission, power steering, radio, whitewall tires, wheel covers.	$79
Plymouth Gran Coupe Chevrolet Impala Ford Galaxie Pontiac Catalina	Standard factory equipment plus V-8 engine, automatic transmission, power steering, power brakes, radio, whitewall tires, wheel covers.	$91.50
Chrysler Newport Buick Custom LeSabre Ford Country Squire Pontiac Grand Ville	Standard factory equipment plus V-8 engine, automatic transmission, power steering, power brakes, radio, whitewall tires, wheel covers, air conditioning, tinted glass.	$119.75

Chrysler Imperial
Cadillac Coupe
  de Ville
Buick Electra
  Custom 225
	Standard factory equipment plus V-8 engine, automatic transmission, power steering, power brakes, power windows, power seats, air conditioning, whitewall tires, AM/FM radio, wheel covers, tinted glass, vinyl roof.	$174.50

But remember that your leasing costs will vary with the type of car and the kind of equipment you want as well as with the terms of the lease.

For a specific dollars-and-cents answer to the question of what it costs to lease, you should discuss your requirements with a reputable leasing company representative. In general, monthly charges range anywhere from $60 for a small foreign compact to $300 or more for a large luxury car.

Always be sure to examine closely the terms of any leasing contract. In some leases, you may find an extra mileage clause stating that if you drive more than the maximum allowed mileage—probably 20,000 miles a year—you will have to pay one to three cents a mile for every extra mile driven. You should also ensure that the contract provides for adequate insurance (to judge this, see Chapter 5).

Above all, comparison shop among leasing companies— just as you would for a new car. Find out about special deals and terms, and remember to weigh all the pros and cons.

CHAPTER 7

How
to
Buy
Tires

At one time or another, the guessing game about what kind of tires to buy is played by nearly all motorists. It is a guessing game because most car owners know little about tires. Tires may all look alike on the outside, but there are important differences on the inside. Understanding these differences will enable you to buy just as much tire—and only as much tire—as you need for comfort, safety, and long wear.

There are three major types of tires widely available today: bias ply, belted bias, and radial. And each of these types is constructed differently to do a different kind of job.

Bias ply. This was the standard automobile tire until the mid-1960s, when new tire construction techniques were introduced. The body of the tire is made up of two or four plies, or layers, of fabric cord that cross at roughly a thirty-five-degree angle to the centerline of the tire.

The cord in these tires is made of either rayon, nylon, or polyester. Rayon gives a smooth ride, but is not as durable as the other materials. It is largely being replaced by polyester, which is stronger and is not affected by moisture and oils. Nylon tires tend to develop flat spots after they have been standing for a time. This causes them to give a bumpy ride when they are cold, but when they warm up, they give a smooth ride. Of these three materials, polyester is the strongest.

Belted bias. The cords in the body of these tires are arranged in a crisscross pattern similar to that in bias ply tires. But in addition to the cords, which are made of rayon, nylon, polyester, or fiberglass, these tires have two or more belts under the tread. These belts are made of strands of rayon, fiberglass, or steel coated with brass. Of these belting materials, steel is the strongest and most expensive. Fiberglass is not as puncture resistant as steel, so if your tires would be vulnerable to this kind of damage, steel would be a better choice.

The belts in these tires give greater firmness to the tread, reducing tread motion during contact with the road and thus increasing tread life and traction. These tires run cooler than bias ply tires and are more suitable for sustained high-speed driving. Because the firmer tread reduces rolling resistance, belted tires will not only wear longer than bias ply tires, they may even increase gasoline mileage.

Radial. These are the tires of the future. Most foreign cars come equipped with radials, and they are now standard or optional equipment on most American cars.

In these tires, the body cords do not crisscross, but extend in a radial, or circular, fashion at an angle of about ninety degrees to the centerline of the tire. They, too, have belts under the tread. The body cords are made of rayon or

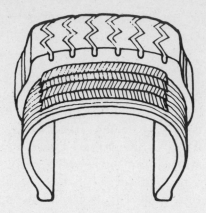

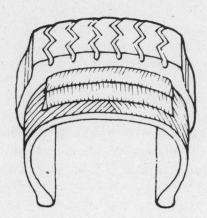

The three most widely used types of tire construction are, from the top, radial, belted bias, and bias ply. Radials provide the most rigidity and tread life, and the performance of the belted bias is also superior to the bias ply.

polyester; the belts are made of rayon or steel. Rayon belts are not as durable as steel, but they will give the same superior handling.

Radial tires combine all the advantages of belted bias tires with even better handling and longer wear. According to the National Bureau of Standards, the radial tire "offers superior cornering and greater safety at sustained turnpike speeds." Unlike other tires, no part of the tread of a radial tire ever leaves the road, even when negotiating corners.

This is not to say, however, that radial tires are the best for everyone. They do have some disadvantages. Because of their firmer construction, they give a rather harsh ride at low speeds, the sidewalls are much more susceptible to bruising, and, not only are they individually expensive, they should be used in sets of four on the road.

Quiz to help you decide

To determine which type of tire you should buy, you might want to take this short quiz and mark down your points.

(1) How often do you drive over 60 mph?
Seldom	1 point
Frequently	2 points
Mostly	3 points

(2) How often do you drive on rough roads?
Seldom	1 point
Frequently	2 points
Mostly	3 points

(3) How often do you drive on expressways?
Seldom	1 point
Frequently	2 points
Mostly	3 points

(4) How often do you drive with a heavy load (two or more adult passengers, heavy cargo, or both)?

Seldom	1 point
Frequently	2 points
Mostly	3 points

(5) How many miles will you drive this car? (Multiply the miles per year by the number of years you will keep the car.)

10,000 or less	1 point
25,000 or less	2 points
40,000 or more	3 points

(6) How do you rate yourself as a driver?

Easy	1 point
Average	2 points
Hard	3 points

The tire manufacturer who made up this quiz as a guide to consumers recommends that if your points total fewer than 9, you should probably use a bias ply tire; if they total from 10 to 13, you should use a belted bias tire; and if they total over 14, a radial tire might be best.

As your answers to the quiz should have indicated, a bias ply tire should wear very well if your driving consists mainly of short trips between home and work or between home and shopping. These tires are particularly suitable for smaller cars—subcompacts and compacts.

If your driving patterns are similar to the above, but perhaps you do more high-speed driving and your car is somewhat larger—an intermediate size, for example—you might want to buy the sturdier belted bias tire.

If you drive predominantly at high speed and expect to put well over 50,000 miles on your car, you might consider using tires that are one grade better than those that came as original equipment on the car. You should even consider doing this when you purchase a new car. You can usually buy, as optional equipment, different types of tires than those the manufacturer supplies with the car.

Follow auto maker's advice

There is much more you should know before you buy tires. Here are some pointers:

You should buy only the types of tires that the automobile manufacturer recommends for your car. You will find this information on the sticker somewhere in your car—in the glove compartment, on the dashboard, or on a door

GM RECOMMENDED TIRE PRESSURES		
(PSI COLD)		
VEHICLE LOAD	FRONT	REAR
UP TO VEHICLE CAPACITY	24	28
UP TO 5 OCCUPANTS 250 LBS MAXIMUM	24	24

RECOMMENDED TIRE SIZE(S)
(USE ONLY IN SETS)   LOAD RANGE **B**
E78-14/E70-14
BECAUSE OF POSSIBLE ADVERSE EFFECTS ON VEHICLE HANDLING, DO NOT MIX RADIAL TIRES WITH OTHER TYPE TIRES ON THE SAME VEHICLE.

VEHICLE CAPACITY

BENCH SEAT	BUCKET SEAT
6 OCCUPANTS 3 FRONT 3 REAR 200 LBS TRUNK LOAD	5 OCCUPANTS 2 FRONT 3 REAR 200 LBS TRUNK LOAD
TOTAL 1100 LBS	TOTAL 950 LBS

SEE OWNERS MANUAL FOR ADDITIONAL INFORMATION

ZN   334408   PRINTED IN USA

Sticker gives auto maker's recommendations concerning tires.

post. This is particularly important with regard to radial tires—*never* put them on your car unless the manufacturer has approved. If you do not follow these instructions, you will probably experience either excessive tire wear or dangerous handling problems.

When it is time to replace one or two tires, many motorists are tempted to change from one type of tire to another. Although mixing different types of tires is discouraged by some experts, others say that you may do it if you follow these general rules:

Never mix tires of different sizes or different constructions on the same axle. You may mix bias ply and belted bias tires if you have two of each and put two of the same type of tire on the same axle. Also, you will have better handling if you put the belted bias tires on the rear axle. You may mix two radial tires with two of either 83-, 78-, or 70-series bias ply or belted bias tires, provided you put the two radials on the *rear* axle. If you put the radials on the front, you will have serious handling problems.

Before you mix radials, however, check the instructions in your owner's manual or on the tire sticker in your car. Many automobile manufacturers strongly advise against mixing radials with other tires, and specify that radials always be used in sets of four on the road. The possible exception to this would be if you have a late-model car equipped with four radials and a spare tire of the deflated "space maker" type. Because these new spare tires are never radials, you should know that in an emergency, you can use them with your radials on any axle as long as you drive only at a moderate speed for a short distance. Be sure, then, to have the radial repaired and remounted on the car promptly.

Because of their extreme width and low profile, 60- and 50-series tires should *never* be mixed with any other type of tire.

The National Highway Traffic Safety Administration,

which recommends that for the best handling and safest operation of your car you never mix tires, says:

> In general, the hazard of mixing tire types relates to the erratic or dangerous vehicle performance which may result. Under various driving conditions requiring dependable vehicle control, especially in cornering, "mixed-tire" performance has been compared to the effect of wearing a rubber-soled shoe on one foot, a new leather sole on the other—or a pair of ice skates, of which only one is newly sharpened.
>
> The radial tire has an increased ability to keep its entire "footprint" on the road surface, even under cornering stresses which might cause other types to lift or skid laterally. If the radial tire has increased handling stability in some situations, a "mix" of radials on the front wheels with some other tire type on the rear wheels could produce a breakaway with little or no control as the rear of the auto loses traction at a different spin-radius than the vehicle's front portion. Obviously, random "mixing" front and rear or on the same axle can produce unpredictable, sometimes dangerous handling difficulties.

When buying tires, you also have to consider the size. Here again, follow the instructions on the sticker in your car. It is best to buy the same size tire that came as original equipment on the car, unless you are planning to carry extra heavy loads or pull a trailer.

Tire code explained

Tire manufacturers use numbers and letters to indicate the size of a tire. A tire size might read: F78-14 (Replaces 7.75-14). Here is how you would interpret this:

The letter "F" is a code for the load-carrying capacity of the tire. When inflated to 24 pounds per square inch (psi), an "F" coded tire can carry 1,280 pounds regardless of

Load-Carrying Capacity of Tires

As a tire's inflation is increased, so is its carrying capacity. These are the weights that can be carried by a tire with the given code letter when the tire is inflated to 24 pounds per square inch.

lbs.	lbs.	lbs.	lbs.
V —650	A— 900	E—1,190	J —1,580
W—710	B— 980	F—1,280	K—1,620
Y —770	C—1,050	G—1,380	L —1,680
Z —830	D—1,120	H—1,510	M—1,780
			N—1,880

Degree of Friction for Good Tires on Various Road Surfaces

Type of Pavement	Dry	Wet
Concrete	.90	.60
Asphalt	.85	.65
Brick	.85	.65
Oiled gravel	.90	.65
Gravel, cinders	.65	.65
Packed snow	.45	.45
Ice or sleet	.20	.20
Mud on pavement	.20	.30

other size factors. The load capacity increases as the inflation pressure increases. The table opposite will give you the carrying capacity indicated by the different code letters.

The "78" means that the height of the tire from inner rim to tread surface is 78 percent of the tire's width. This is the "aspect ratio." Tires come in 50, 60, 70, 78, and 83 series. A 50-series tire is the lowest and widest. Belted bias and radial tires are sized this way, but bias ply tires are still sometimes sized in the old numerical way represented by the figures in parentheses—7.75-14. The "7.75" represents the section width of the tire (the distance across the widest point).

Radial tires were formerly sized according to the metric system, and a similar tire would be marked 195R14. The "195" refers to the approximate cross section width in millimeters. Most radial tires today are sized under the new system. Such a tire would be designated FR 78-14—the "R" standing for radial.

The "14" in our example refers to the rim size. You should never choose a tire with a rim size different than that of the wheel. The wheel rim size will determine the maximum width of tire permissible for your car.

Changing tire size

The main consideration for changing the size of tire on your car is the weight of the load you plan to carry. The maximum weight capacity of your car is posted in the car and cannot be increased by the use of oversize tires. If you plan to carry loads that call for inflation pressures exceeding the maximum for your tires, buy the next larger size tire, but only if permitted by the manufacturer. To obtain tire size, load, and inflation tables, write to Tire Safety, Box 726, New York, New York 10010, and ask for the free Consumer Tire Guide.

If you plan to pull a trailer, you should read and follow

Women drivers have come millions of miles since her day, but changing a tire is still an operation many women feel inadequate to perform.

How to Change a Tire

In spite of the new tubeless tires and the fact that help is usually as close as the nearest telephone, there are times when tires go flat and assistance is not at hand. It is useful, then, to know how to change a tire.

1. You will, of course, irreparably damage a tire if you drive any distance when it is flat. Drive the car only as far as necessary to get it well off the road and onto level ground. Do not park on a hill or near a ditch, because the car might fall off the jack. Shut off the engine, but if you are close to traffic, leave the ignition key in the "accessory" position and turn on the hazard warning lights or the left turn signal lights. Set the parking brake and put the gear selector in the "park" position if the car has an automatic transmission or in first or reverse gear if it has a manual transmission. Then block the wheel diagonally opposite the wheel to be changed with a piece of 2 x 4 (which you might want to carry in the trunk at all times) or anything available, such as a large rock or brick.

Example of Jacking Car at Bumper

(front)

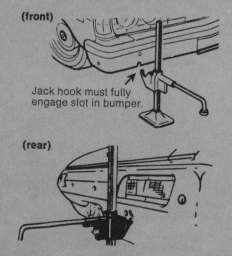

Jack hook must fully engage slot in bumper.

(rear)

2. Remove the jack and the spare tire from the trunk. You will have to consult your owner's manual for the proper operation of the jack.

3. Operate the jack only until it is set—do not yet lift the car so that the tire is off the road. With the flat end of your wrench, pry off the hubcap or wheel cover at a point 180 degrees from the valve stem. Then loosen—but do not remove—the wheel nuts by turning them counterclockwise. (Turn them clockwise if there is an "L" on the end of each lug bolt.) Do not remove or replace the nuts in a random order, because this might damage the brakes. In general, alternate every other nut, as shown in the diagrams below.

Example of
Jacking Car at Side

(front)

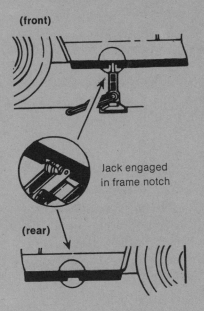

Jack engaged
in frame notch

(rear)

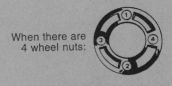

4. Jack the tire up off the road and remove the wheel nuts, putting them in the upturned wheel cover so that they cannot get lost. Then pull the wheel off the car.

5. Mount the spare tire and replace the nuts with the beveled end facing in toward the wheel. Lightly tighten the nuts in the same order shown below. Lower the car so that the tire is again on the road. Tighten the nuts, replace the wheel cover, and then remove the jack from under the car and the block from under the opposite wheel.

6. Finally, put the damaged tire, the jack, and any other tools and equipment into the trunk—and you are ready to go again.

Remove and replace lug nuts in this sequence.

When there are
4 wheel nuts:

When there are
5 wheel nuts:

---

the special instructions in your owner's manual or discuss the matter with your dealer.

The diagram opposite of the sidewall of a tire shows you the kind of information you will find on the tire. In addition to the size designation, it will give you the load range or ply rating of the tire. The load range is indicated by a letter—usually B, C, or D for passenger car tires. This is a new system that has been developed to replace the old ply rating system. Even so, the ply rating is sometimes given in parentheses after the load range—for example, load range B (4-ply rating). If it is not, you should know that load range B has a 4-ply rating, load range C has a 6-ply rating, and load range D has an 8-ply rating. To say that a tire has a 4-ply rating means that it is as strong as a tire with 4 plies, even though the tire may actually have only 2 plies. A 2-ply tire with a 4-ply rating is not only as strong as a 4-ply tire, it may even be better. A 2-ply tire may run cooler because of less flexing and may give a softer ride.

Underneath the load range or ply rating, you will find the maximum load limit and the maximum inflation pressure. The line in our example reads: "Max. load 1500 lbs. @ 32 psi. max. press." You should never exceed the load limit specified on the tire. For normal operation, you should not inflate the tire to the maximum pressure, but only to the pressures recommended by the car manufacturer. *Never* exceed the maximum load and pressure recommended for your tire.

The other markings on the tire give the number of plies and their composition, tell whether the tire meets Department of Transportation tire safety standards, and indicate whether the tire is of the tube type or is tubeless. The word "radial" will also appear on that type of tire.

When to buy replacement tires

It is important that the tread of your tires be deep

enough to provide the traction you need to control your car. When the tread depth is less than 1/16th of an inch, the tire must be replaced. In fact, many states require this by law.

Tread depth can be determined in three ways. The simplest way is to look for the tread wear indicator bars that are built into the grooves of all tires manufactured since

By reading a tire's sidewall, the motorist can gain valuable information needed to maintain his car's tires. Data includes size, load range, maximum inflation pressure, number of plies, and type of cord material.

1968. When the tread has worn down so that these bars are exposed—producing a smooth line across at least two adjacent grooves, the tread is worn to less than 1/16th of an inch.

There are also special tread depth gauges that you can buy, or you can use a Lincoln penny. If you insert the top edge of the penny in a groove and Lincoln's head is entirely exposed, the tread depth is less than 1/16th of an inch. Also, if the depth of two or more adjacent grooves in an area without an indicator bar measures less than 1/16th of an inch, it is time to replace the tire.

Tires should also be replaced when the cord or fabric is exposed, when there is a break in the fabric, when the tread or sidewall is cracked, cut, or snagged deeply enough to expose the body cords, or when there are bumps, bulges, knots, or separations.

Using snow tires

Snow tires should always be the same size and type as those on the front of the car. Tread selection should be based on the type of driving you expect to do. Your tire dealer can tell you which type of snow tire would be best in your locality.

Keep in mind when using snow tires that the deep, open design of the treads will cause them to wear rapidly on dry roads. And, because the rubber in these tires is specially compounded for cold conditions, there is a heat buildup problem if they are used during warm weather. For these reasons, you will shorten the life of your winter tires considerably if you use them in the summer.

As for the controversial studded snow tires, their use is illegal in some states and restricted to the winter months in others. It is important, therefore, to check the laws of your state before using them. If you are planning to drive with these tires in Canada, be sure to check their laws, too.

The reason for these laws is that studded tires may dam-

When tread-wear indicator bars appear on two or more adjacent grooves, as is shown circled with chalk here, the tire is unsafe and should be replaced.

age the road surface. This not only is costly, but also can be dangerous. Repeated stops and starts at intersections by cars with studded tires may cause shallow ruts in the road. In freezing weather, ice can form in these ruts, creating a hazardous condition.

In order to decide whether or not to use these tires, you should know that they are most effective on icy roads when the temperature is between 0° and 32° F. Furthermore, although in these weather conditions pullaway traction is vastly improved with studded tires on the drive wheels only, stopping and cornering traction is significantly improved only when studded tires are mounted on all four wheels. In snow and slush, traction may be slightly improved. And on a clear road surface, particularly concrete, the stopping ability of studded tires can actually be less than that of regular tires. In addition, prolonged driving at high speeds or on a dry surface causes rapid wear and harmful tread heat buildup.

Cautions about snow tires

If you do decide to get these tires:

• Never insert the studs yourself. Have a qualified dealer or serviceman insert studs matched to the wear rate of your tires and your driving habits.

• Never permit the dealer to insert more than 150 studs in a tire. Traction decreases as the number of studs over 150 increases. This is especially true on a concrete surface.

• Never ask your dealer to insert studs in a tire that has been used or to restud an old tire. Dirt in the holes of a used tire will cause the studs to seat improperly and to loosen.

• Always remount a studded tire so that it rolls in the same direction. When you remove them, mark the direction of roll on each tire and mark them "left" or "right."

When storing snow tires—or tires of any kind—place

Braking Distance in Feet From 20 MPH

(Reaction time averages ¾ of a second and adds 22 feet to figures shown.)

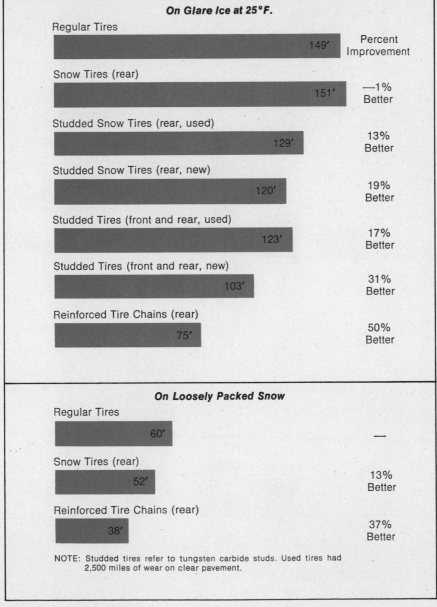

On Glare Ice at 25°F.

Tire Type	Distance	Percent Improvement
Regular Tires	149'	
Snow Tires (rear)	151'	—1% Better
Studded Snow Tires (rear, used)	129'	13% Better
Studded Snow Tires (rear, new)	120'	19% Better
Studded Tires (front and rear, used)	123'	17% Better
Studded Tires (front and rear, new)	103'	31% Better
Reinforced Tire Chains (rear)	75'	50% Better

On Loosely Packed Snow

Tire Type	Distance	Percent Improvement
Regular Tires	60'	—
Snow Tires (rear)	52'	13% Better
Reinforced Tire Chains (rear)	38'	37% Better

NOTE: Studded tires refer to tungsten carbide studs. Used tires had 2,500 miles of wear on clear pavement.

Source: National Safety Council

Tire Traction Ratings

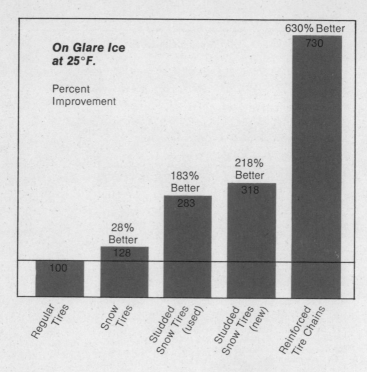

**On Glare Ice
at 25°F.**

Percent
Improvement

630% Better
730

218%
Better
318

183%
Better
283

28%
Better
128

100

Regular
Tires

Snow
Tires

Studded
Snow Tires
(used)

Studded
Snow Tires
(new)

Reinforced
Tire Chains

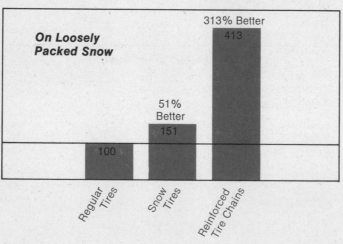

**On Loosely
Packed Snow**

313% Better
413

51%
Better
151

100

Regular
Tires

Snow
Tires

Reinforced
Tire Chains

NOTE: Studded tires refer to tungsten carbide studs. Used tires had
2,500 miles of wear on clear pavement.

Source: National Safety Council

them flat in a cool, dry area, away from electrical motors and sunlight. Place white sidewall against white sidewall to keep them clean. It is also a good idea to reduce the air pressure to about ten pounds if the tires are mounted on extra wheels.

Here are some final words of advice about new tires:

• Always observe a break-in period. Hold your speed to 60 mph for the first 50 miles of driving in order to give the tires a chance to set.

• Inspect and replace, if necessary, the valve stems when you buy new tires. Sudden valve stem failure produces the same result as a blowout.

• Be sure to have the tires balanced. Either spin or bubble balancing is satisfactory.

Quality standards for tires

There are no industry-wide standards of quality at the present time. The Department of Transportation is establishing its own standards, and these should be in effect in late 1974. Under this system, tires will be graded against model tires for tread wear, traction, and high-speed performance.

While these new standards may be helpful, they will not solve all your tire-buying problems. Tire wear is related not only to driving habits, but to road and weather conditions. Thus, the same quality tire may not wear as well for one driver as for another and may wear out faster in one part of the country than in another. One major tire manufacturer, for example, became perplexed when they received numerous complaints about rapid tire wear in an area of the country where this sort of complaint was unusual. Later they found that the dropoff in complaints coincided with the smoothing down of a newly built turnpike in the area.

In general, your best bet in buying tires is to follow the advice in this chapter and then buy from a reputable local dealer. You should not try to find bargains in tires, but you do not need to buy the most expensive ones either. For the maximum in safety and long wear, buy tires that conform to your car, the loads you plan to carry, the type of roads you will be driving on, and your driving habits.

CHAPTER 8

Body Care— Outside and In

At a small cost in time and energy, that "new-car look" can be preserved on the oldest of cars. Regular exterior and interior maintenance requires little special equipment, and not only will add to the life of your car, but could pay off in hundreds of extra dollars at trade-in time.

Here is what you can do:

Wash your car. Frequent washings—once or twice a month—are a must. If your car is exposed to salt air, ash from furnaces or industrial plants, or chemicals used to melt ice and snow, wash the car even more frequently. All of these substances are highly corrosive.

Do not wipe off dirt with a dry cloth—dirt particles are abrasive and may scratch the finish. Thoroughly wet the car with warm or cold water, and then wash it with a mild laundry detergent or a special car wash compound that can

Wash your car at least once a month, using a detergent or special compound.

be bought at most auto supply stores or gas stations. After soaping the car well, remove all the dirt and salts in joints and crevices and behind metal trim by directing a high-pressure jet of water to these areas. Use your garden hose or, better yet, one of the high-pressure sprayers at a do-it-yourself car wash.

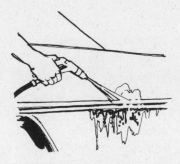

Flush dirt from behind metal trim with a hose or high-pressure sprayer.

It is most important to get mud and salt out of all the nooks and crannies in your car. Rust starts where water gets trapped, and mud is often the cause; it can get packed into small spaces and trap water there. Salt, on the other hand, mixes with water to produce hydrochloric acid, which will eat sheet metal. In this respect, you should know that salt will not damage the car if the temperature is below 25 degrees, but it will do its worst damage when the temperature is between 25 and 40 degrees. If you live in an area where the winters are hard and salt is used to remove snow and ice from the streets, get to work on your car as soon as the outside temperatures permit. And if you live in an area where there is a considerable amount of salt in the air, wash your car frequently.

After you have sprayed all the nooks and crannies in the upper body of the car, get all those places underneath the car, especially under the wheels.

Then use your hose or sprayer to flush out the rocker panel drains. Direct the water through the hood-level air intakes and keep it running through until you see the water drain out near the rear wheels.

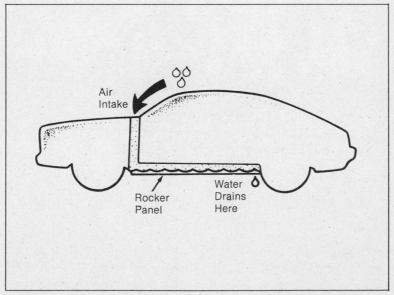

Force water down the air intake until it drains out near the rear wheels.

Finally, use a large quantity of fresh water to flush away any remaining soap on the body of the car, and use a sponge or towel to wipe off the excess water.

Immediately after washing, remove any road tar, bug stains, tree sap, or other spots. Resist the temptation to use kitchen cleansers on stubborn spots; all are abrasive and some contain bleach that can discolor the car's finish. Use tar remover to get the tar off; use a prewax cleaner on the other stains. Then rewash these areas to remove any traces of these cleaners.

You can use steel wool soap pads to polish chrome trim, but use a cleaner-polish on aluminum. If the chrome is pitted, you can use a rubbing compound to smooth and polish the area before you wax it.

Wash headlights more often than the car. Dirt reduces the light output.

When washing their cars, many people often forget about the headlights. These should be washed frequently, because dirt there can act like the filter on a camera lens, cutting down the light output.

How to do touch-up painting

Repair the paint. A good time to fix up nicks and scratches in the paint is just after you have washed the car. For superficial scratches, dab or spray on some touch-up paint. Be sure to first remove with steel wool any rust that may have formed in these spots, because paint will not stick to rust.

A more serious problem is caused by drivers who bump your car door when they open theirs. To repair these deep, rust-breeding chips, first apply a paste body solder with a putty knife. After the solder has dried, use fine (200-grit) sandpaper to make the area flush with the rest of the paint. Then, in a piece of cardboard, cut a hole a little

Touch up chips by spraying paint through a hole in a piece of cardboard.

larger than the area you wish to touch up. Hold the hole alternately close to and far from the area, and spray touch-up paint through in short bursts. Allow a couple of minutes for the paint to dry, spray again, and repeat this process four or five times until the paint builds up to the desired thickness. Then remove the cardboard and spray paint again so that the touched-up area will blend with the larger area. After this has dried, polish with a rubbing compound. Finally, if you are not planning to wax the whole car, wax and buff the affected area.

Wax your car. It is advisable to give your car a hard-wax finish at least once a year. Liquid wax is good for a temporary shine, but for the longest lasting protection, use a hard wax. Try to wax your car on a cool day—or during a time of the day when the paint is not hot. To avoid scratching the finish, apply the wax only after the car has been thoroughly washed. You should wash the car even if the label on the wax can says that the product contains a cleaner. With a folded pad of dampened cheesecloth, spread the wax over each two-foot-square area of the car in turn, and then buff each area with a clean pad as soon as the wax has dried. Be sure to clean the buffing pad at frequent intervals.

Use vinyl wax, shoe polish, or baby oil to make a vinyl hardtop shine.

You may not have to wax a new car for at least a year, unless there is a heavy fallout of industrial pollutants in your area. Consult your owner's manual for the specifics about your car.

If you wash your car in a commercial car wash, remember that the harsh detergents used in many of these places may partially remove or thin out any protective coating you have put on your car. This is true even if the car is waxed during the washing process. If you have your car washed this way often, you should probably give it a hard wax finish at least twice a year.

Excessive exposure to the sun can also affect the finish of a car. In hot weather, drops of dew and rain settling on the car act as tiny lenses to intensify the heat. So protect the finish by applying a barrier of hard paste wax more often —at least every six months.

Shine and waterproof vinyl hardtops. After washing, use spot remover if the vinyl is badly soiled. Then apply several coats of either vinyl wax, which can be purchased at an auto supply store, shoe polish of the same color as the top, or baby oil. Whatever you use, apply it with a sponge and rub it well into the grain. Then buff with a shoe brush.

Clean whitewall tires. Use a white tire cleaner, taking care to follow the instructions on the container. Remove tar from the wheels with tar remover, and clean the black part of the tire with rubber renewer.

Reset loose rubber gaskets with a suitable cement after cleaning them.

Repair loose rubber gaskets on windows, doors, and the trunk lid. Lift and clean the gaskets until they are free of dust and old adhesive. Then reset them with contact cement, rubber cement, or special rubber-to-metal cement as directed by the manufacturer.

How to clean glass

Protect windshield and windows. Never wipe them with
a dry cloth or paper towel when they are dry and covered
with dust or grit. This could scratch the glass. Only a wet
or damp cloth or paper towel should be used on thoroughly
wet glass. Use commercial glass-cleaning liquids for all car
glass—inside and out—or try a mixture of one part vinegar to twenty parts water.

Clean clogged windshield washer jets by carefully inserting a fine wire.

Never chip at the glass with anything hard. If the windows are covered with ice, start the car and turn on the
heater and the rear window defroster. While the car is
warming up, spray the windows with deicer spray. The
combination of the heat from the car and the deicer spray
should loosen the ice fairly quickly, and it can then be removed with a plastic—not metal—scraper.

If you do not have an automatic windshield washer, keep

a supply of antifreeze windshield washer solvent (which will not freeze in the winter as glass cleaner may) in a spray bottle that you can store in the car. While the car is parked, spray the glass and then operate the windshield wipers. Never operate the wipers when the glass is dry.

If you do have an automatic windshield washer and the jets become clogged, you can clear them by inserting a fine wire into the holes. Take special care, however, not to enlarge the holes.

Polish interior surfaces. All you need usually do is wipe the instrument panel, instrument covers, and door panels with a rag dampened with the vinegar and water solution mentioned above. Do not use steel wool or strong solvents, which may fog up the covers over the instruments. You can repair any nicks or scratches in the paint with touch-up paint and wax the interior painted surfaces just as you would the exterior. A pipe cleaner is excellent for cleaning dust out of hard-to-reach spots, like the spaces between the push buttons on the radio.

Clean fabric upholstery. Use a vacuum cleaner or whisk broom to remove light dust and dirt. Then wash with a foam fabric shampoo of the kind used for household upholstery or some other upholstery fabric cleaner. Next, use a waterproofing spray so that subsequent spills and stains can easily be wiped from the fabric.

Clean vinyl upholstery. First wipe with a damp cloth or sponge to remove light dust or dirt. Then use a special vinyl upholstery cleaner or a mild detergent and water. Never use strong soaps or detergents.

Clean leather upholstery. Wipe the leather with mild soapsuds and then buff with a dry cloth. Never use gasoline or any other volatile fluid, such as naphtha, turpentine, or carbon tetrachloride to clean the interior of your car. Some of these fluids could ignite if you rub too hard on them.

You can cover up small nicks and scratches by rubbing in a little shoe wax of the same or a similar color.

Clean seat belt webbing. Use soap and water or, if very dirty, a mild detergent. Do not use bleach or dye on the webbing because this might weaken the belts, and avoid getting the buckles wet because moisture might corrode them.

Clean seat belt webbing with soap and water. Do not use bleach or dye.

Keep carpeting clean. First vacuum the carpeting, being sure to include any carpeting in the trunk. Then use any home carpet cleaner or shampoo. After the shampoo is applied, rub it in with a brush and allow it to dry before stepping on it.

Clean rubber floor mats. Scrub with soap and water—nothing more. Then rinse and wipe dry.

CHAPTER 9

When to Trade In Your Car

In the life of every car there comes a time, sooner or later, when its owner begins to wonder whether he should continue to spend money on repairs or whether he should buy a new car and look forward to a few years of hopefully troublefree driving. Is it more feasible economically to have the valves repaired now and risk the necessity of further major surgery soon or to buy a new car and look forward to twenty-four or thirty-six months of car payments?

There is no single answer for everyone. When you should trade in your car will depend on many factors, including where you live, the number of miles the car has been driven, the way it has been maintained, and your driving habits—all of which will affect your annual repair and maintenance costs.

For some people, particularly those who take good care

of their cars, long-term ownership pays off. For others, it does not. To determine when to trade in your car, you should, therefore, first try to develop a personal philosophy about car ownership. Ask yourself how often you can afford to trade cars. Study how well the car runs. Keep car expense records and determine the frequency and cost of repairs. Compare expenditures with those for previous cars you may have owned and kept for various lengths of time. While you do so, take into account the three major cost factors: purchase price, depreciation, and maintenance expenses.

But bear in mind that for some motorists none of these factors may be of primary concern. To many owners, the major factor may be that a new car is simply more reliable than an old one. Other owners may feel a real need for a new car to "keep up with the Joneses" or because they are not comfortable in the old car. Still others may like the fact that well-maintained new cars emit less pollution than well-maintained older models. And yet other motorists may favor the idea of trading because the new cars contain many important safety features, including energy-absorbing steering columns, improved windshield safety glass, and retractable bumpers.

Life history of a car

Whatever your reason for wanting to trade, statistics compiled by the Department of Transportation can be useful in helping you to decide when it would be most advantageous for you to do so. In its study, DOT estimated the costs of owning and operating a standard-size, four-door 1972 automobile costing $4,379 and equipped with automatic transmission, power steering and power brakes, air conditioning, a V-8 engine, tinted glass, radio, clock, whitewall tires, and body protective molding. The study assumed that the car would be operated for ten years, or 100,000 miles, which it cited as the life expectancy of the average automobile in its long journey from assembly line to junk-yard.

In order to approximate the typical history of a stand-ard-size car which is used first as primary transportation and later as a second or even third car and which may have as many as three owners, the study assumed that the car would be driven fewer miles each year, beginning with 14,500 miles in the first year, and in succeeding years drop-ping off to 13,000 miles, 11,500, 10,000, 9,900 (for the fifth and sixth years), 9,500, 8,500, 7,500, and 5,700. All the costs —fuel, repairs, insurance, taxes—were based on prices cur-rent in Baltimore, Maryland, at the time the study was made.

To point up the conclusions this study suggests, let us assume that your car is developing mechanical troubles. The front end is beginning to shimmy. The tread on the tires is gone. The engine needs new parts. It frequently re-fuses to start. And there are squeaks and rattles, as well as numerous chips and scratches. You would be wise to sell the car immediately, right? Wrong—if you are interested in economical transportation. The DOT study shows that the best way to keep transportation costs down is to use an automobile until it has little or no trade-in value.

Many people trade away perfectly good transportation and waste hundreds of dollars because they have little no-tion of how much their cars cost to own and operate. They know that the purchase price is the first step in a long line of costs, but they often do not take into consideration de-preciation, repairs and maintenance, replacement tires, ac-cessories, gas, oil, insurance, garaging, tolls, and taxes.

In addition, many motorists put too much emphasis on the cost of repairing an old car. They rationalize that they need a new car by pointing to the frequent repair bills on their old car. If they continue to trade in their old car, even as often as every year or two, they reason, they will save on repair bills and come out ahead.

Depreciation exceeds repair bills

Their reasoning is faulty because the cost of transportation does not work that way. The DOT study shows that the biggest cost in owning a car, after the initial purchase, is *not* the cost of repairs, as most people believe. It is depreciation, or the loss in resale value of the car. And it is the depreciation that will be highest on a new car—old cars have already depreciated substantially. After depreciation, the study shows that the next biggest cost factor in operating a car over a ten-year span is repairs and maintenance, followed by the third biggest cost item—fuel. The ten-year average cost of repairs is slightly more than two cents per mile—just about one-fourth of the per-mile depreciation cost during the first year of driving, and about half of the per-mile depreciation cost over the full ten-year period. It is easy to see why DOT says: "Depreciation is by far the greatest single cost of owning and operating an automobile, and in the great majority of cases the age of the car is more important than its mileage in determining its resale or trade-in value."

Estimating car's depreciation

There is no set rule by which you can accurately figure how much your car has depreciated. The actual dollar depreciation will depend on market conditions and can be learned only by checking one of the used-car price guidelines to find the cash value of your car on the market today. But the DOT statistics do provide a basis for estimating the depreciation on your car. The DOT study projected a 28 percent ($1,226) depreciation loss on the car during the first year of its operation. Over the ten-year period, the car would continue to depreciate by the following rates and amounts. These figures show that the biggest depreciation losses occur during the first three years of a car's life, and suggest that that might be a good time to trade.

| | Drop in Value | |
Year	Percent	Dollars
1	28%	$1,226
2	21	900
3	15	675
4	11	500
5	9	376
6	6	259
7	4	189
8	3	121
9	2	85
10	1	48

But how do these costs compare with the repair and maintenance expenses? Translating the dollar cost figures per year into cents per mile, the DOT study shows the following comparisons:

| | | Cents per Mile | |
Year	Mileage	Depreciation	Repair & Maintenance
1	14,500	8.46	.56
2	27,500	6.92	.89
3	39,000	5.87	2.11
4	49,000	5.00	2.96
5	58,900	3.80	2.78
6	68,800	2.61	2.95
7	78,300	1.99	4.19
8	86,800	1.42	2.02
9	94,300	1.13	3.26
10	100,000	.84	.51

These figures indicate that, although repair expenses begin to rise in the third year, it is not until the sixth year of a car's life that they begin to equal depreciation cost. In addition, repair and maintenance expenses hit their highest peak when the car is approximately seven years old—or has reached 78,000 miles.

Think about trading after 60,000 miles

Assuming the same yearly mileages that the study does, it would appear that the critical time to start thinking of buying a new car comes when your car is above five years old — or has reached 60,000 miles. The study assumes a series of outlays over the years for such things as tire replacement, starter repair, carburetor overhaul, and replacement of the fuel pump, radiator hoses, muffler, tail pipes, and shock absorbers. But by the time the car has 70,000 miles on it, DOT assumes that major repairs will have to be made—the study specifically provides for a valve job costing more than $100.

From these figures, then, it is clear that expenses for repair and maintenance do begin to climb during the third year, reach their peak during the seventh year, and then drop off to virtually nothing during the tenth year. But at no point in the life of the car cited by the DOT study did the repair and maintenance costs come close to the depreciation expense of buying a new car instead of keeping the old one. You can see this more clearly if you use dollar figures instead of per-mile costs. According to the study, the total dollar cost of operating a three-year-old car—including all expenses and not just depreciation and repairs—is $1,655, compared to $2,325 for a new car. This is a difference of $670, and these figures do not even take into consideration the fact that the new-car owner is probably paying more than $100 in interest on his loan.

Another way to look at depreciation is in terms of cost per driven mile. This is computed by dividing the depreciation cost by the number of miles driven. The more you drive, the lower the cost per mile. Of all drivers, the ones who can best justify frequent trading are those who drive well above 14,500 miles a year. During the first two years, when depreciation is greatest, these drivers will have the lowest-per-mile depreciation cost. Conversely, someone who does very little driving, using his car only, say, on weekends or for getting around town, will have high per-mile depreciation costs and will pay a premium for frequent trading.

If you use your car in your business, incidentally, you should know that you can get the best tax break when its depreciation is highest—since depreciation is tax-deductible. Repair and maintenance expenses also are tax-deductible on such a car. This could make the difference between trading now and waiting.

Long use appears most economical

In general, the DOT study argues for long-term ownership as the most economical choice. As the report put it: "The 'annual trader' always has a new car, but depreciation for a standard-size automobile over a ten-year period costs him about $12,260 (ten times the first-year depreciation)." If the same individual traded in his car every five years, his ten-year depreciation cost would be $7,354—a saving of almost $5,000.

Regardless of whether you are driving a standard-size car, a subcompact, compact, or a limousine, depreciation will follow a typical pattern, and will take a tremendous toll of the value of your car. However, though the pattern is the same, the actual dollar cost of operating a small car is less than that of a large car. The DOT statistics on the next page compare the ten-year average per-mile costs of operating standard, compact, and subcompact cars.

If you are the kind of motorist who finds it too troublesome to drive a car until it finally falls apart but you are interested in keeping your cost-per-mile down, it may be wise for you to switch to a smaller new car, since the

The Cost of Operating a Car

The figures are for suburban Baltimore, Maryland, and would be higher or lower in other areas. The analysis assumes that each car is driven 100,000 miles during 10 years, and shows that the smallest car is the least expensive to operate, but does not compare safety and comfort factors.

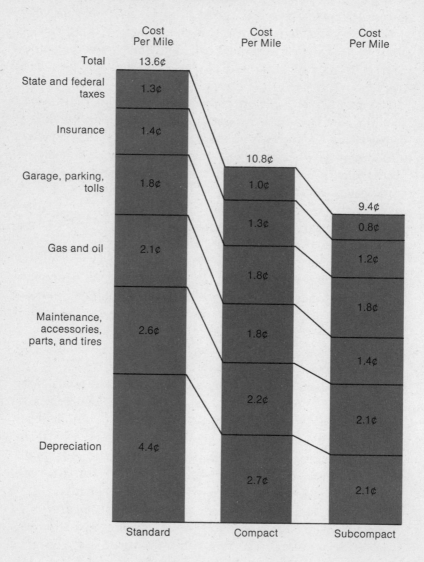

	Cost Per Mile	Cost Per Mile	Cost Per Mile
Total	13.6¢	10.8¢	9.4¢
State and federal taxes	1.3¢	1.0¢	0.8¢
Insurance	1.4¢	1.3¢	1.2¢
Garage, parking, tolls	1.8¢	1.8¢	1.8¢
Gas and oil	2.1¢	1.8¢	1.4¢
Maintenance, accessories, parts, and tires	2.6¢	2.2¢	2.1¢
Depreciation	4.4¢	2.7¢	2.1¢
	Standard	Compact	Subcompact

higher the price of a car, the higher the cost of operation. Because you will pay less for a small car, there will be less depreciation on your investment, and you will have the lower operating costs that come with small-car driving.

When estimating the cost of buying and operating a compact car—one costing $2,700 and having a six-cylinder engine, automatic transmission, and power steering—the DOT study figured operating costs over a ten-year period at $10,808. For a subcompact with standard transmission, the costs came to $9,444—compared to the $13,555 cost to operate a standard-size car for ten years and 100,000 miles.

All down the line, the motorist who owns a compact car saves money, both in the initial price and in operating expenses. While the standard-size car consumes 2.1 cents worth of gas and oil per mile, the cost to run a compact is 1.8 cents, with the subcompact getting by on only 1.4 cents worth of fuel.

As for the crucial total per-mile costs, the standard-size automobile used in the DOT study averages out at 13.6 cents for each mile driven during the ten-year life of the car. The owner of the compact spends 10.8 cents per mile, and the cost-per-mile for subcompact owners is 9.4 cents.

Cost data given

Included in Appendix III are all of the cost data that DOT developed on these three sizes of cars. When using these figures, remember that they are averages, and can provide only guidelines to help you figure your own costs. You have to keep in mind the unmeasurable aspects of operating a car. Thus, for example, it costs less in terms of wear and tear to drive a car long distances on good roads, at reasonable speeds, and with light loads than it does to constantly drive a car in heavy traffic, with much stopping and starting, and with occasionally heavy loads.

What do you do, then, if you do not have an average car? What if your car seems to have more than the average

Mountains of junked cars include some wrecked in accidents and others that have reached the end of the road after providing many years of service.

Scrapped Autos Pile Up

Year	Estimated Number of Cars Scrapped During Year	Scrappage as a Percentage of Total Cars Registered at Beginning of Year	Scrappage as a Percentage of New Car Registrations During Year
1962	4,248,000	6.7%	61.2%
1963	4,610,000	7.0%	61.0%
1964	5,137,000	7.4%	63.7%
1965	6,046,000	8.4%	64.9%
1966	6,136,000	8.2%	68.1%
1967	6,066,000	7.8%	72.6%
1968	6,125,000	7.6%	65.1%
1969	6,364,000	7.6%	66.8%
1970	6,067,000	7.0%	71.5%
1971	7,168,000	8.0%	71.9%

Source: National Automobile Dealers Association Research Department

share of repair troubles? Again, there is no sure way to determine how much additional trouble such a car is going to cause. One thing you could do is to take the car to a diagnostic test center. To avoid being sold repairs, however, make it clear that your purpose in having the diagnosis is to decide whether or not to keep the car.

What you can expect

Here are some other points to bear in mind.

Engine. If you have faithfully changed the oil and filter and had tune-ups performed at the recommended intervals, you should expect to get as many as 100,000 or even 150,000 miles from your engine. Nor should you panic if your engine suddenly begins eating oil. If, for instance, it begins to use a quart of oil every 500 miles, you would only be spending $15 or so more than you normally would spend for every 10,000 miles that you drive. This, therefore, is not any reason to believe that your engine's lifetime is over.

Transmission. There is no set time for how long a transmission will last. This will depend on whether or not it has been abused. But if, every 20,000 miles, the fluid and filter are changed and the bands tightened, all at a cost of about $25, there is no reason that an automatic transmission should not last the lifetime of your car.

Differential. Rebuilding of the gears housed in the middle of the rear axle could cost up to about $100 and make you decide in favor of a new automobile. So if you should hear a noise in the differential, get an estimate before deciding to have it fixed.

Universal joints. Repairs to these small parts that connect the sections of the drive shaft may be necessary at from 40,000 to 100,000 miles. As your car reaches this mileage bracket, ask your mechanic during routine maintenance to check for wear and excessive play in the universal joints. Replacement costs are not high—about $16 per unit for parts and labor. Generally, the front joints wear out in cars with automatic transmissions, the rear ones on cars equipped with standard transmissions.

Shock absorbers. Expect original-equipment shock absorbers to begin showing signs of wear at around 20,000 miles. These are not expensive items.

Exhaust system. If your car is used primarily for short trips, expect your muffler and exhaust pipes to wear out faster than if you use your car primarily for long trips. This is because the parts do not get hot enough on short trips to evaporate the corrosive, acid-bearing water that gets into the system.

Cooling system. Properly maintained, the radiator should last indefinitely; neglected, it is bound to go bad within

30,000 or 40,000 miles, and the cost of repairs could range from $60 to $135. It is important, then, to follow the maintenance instructions in your manual. In general, the water level should be checked each time you get gas, and the system should be drained and flushed every two years or 24,000 miles. Inspect the hoses regularly, and replace them *before* they begin to disintegrate. Also be sure to check the belts for wear and proper tension at regular intervals. Although there is not much you can do to prolong the life of the water pump, you can decrease its life expectancy by keeping the belts too tight. If it does go bad, it will cost you about $25 for a six-cylinder car and about twice that much for a V-8 with air conditioning.

The time when you really will have to trade in your car is not when one or more of the above ailments appear, but when the car has so many miles on it and so much wear that the wiring begins to deteriorate and the brake lines start to rust. Until then, it may pay to keep driving the old car.

BUICK—'63, sta. wag. V6, auto., good cond. Special $175. 671-4042.

BUICK—'71 Elect. 225, 4 dr. Settle estate, Offer. 347-1234.

BUICK—'70, Skylark, 2-dr. hdtp., gold, brn. vinyl roof, V-8, auto., p.s., A/C. Immac. cond. $1895.

CADILLAC—'72 Coupe deVille, Cranberry w/white top, white leather int. Equip. 13,000 mi $5495. 384-1519, aft. 6

CADILLAC—'69 4-dr. sedan, dark green, leather inter., all extras; immac. cond. 1 owner. Garage kept. $2750. 929-1409.

CHEVY—'66 Impala 2-dr. hdtp., '71 engine, excel. cond. Make offer. 781-7694.

CHEVROLET—'66 Malibu, 6-cyl. auto. Special, $265. 671-4042.

CHEVY—'72 conv., low mi., 402 in., loaded with extras, $2200, 554-9768 or 554-3969.

CHEVY—'71 Impala 4-dr. hdtp. Fully equipt. Low mi. $2250. OL 2-5023.

CHRYSLER—'68 Newport, 2 dr. hdtp., auto., r&h, make offer. 927-7060.

CHRYSLER—'67 300, 2-dr. hdtp., AC, like new, 1 owner, 574-9639 or 692-0162.

CHRYSLER—'70 "300" 4 dr. hdtp. air/cond., auto. trans., pwr. ST & Br. am/fm radio, V. Top, w.w. tires, tint glass, other ext

---

auto., r&h, $/95 aft. 11. 636-5471.

FORD — '67 Country Squire Sta. Wag., 10 pass., auto., p.s., p.b., air cond., pwr. winds., pwr. seats, am/fm tape deck, excel. cond., lo. mi. $650. 948-1069.

FORD—'72 Country Squire, 10 pass., AC, AM-FM stereo, lugg. rack, wht. wall tires, elec. winds., P.S., P.B., $3200, call 281-9650.

FORD—'73 Galaxie, Vinyl Roof, Stereo AM/FM, AC, etc. 15,000 mi. Call 528-2584. Ask for Dave.

FORD—'72 Gr. Torino wag., equipd, 13,000 mi. $2950. JA 7-2731.

JAGUAR—'73 XJ6, only 4000 mi., save a $1000 on this all power a/c beauty. Call 768-1747.

JENSEN-HEALEY — '73. Excellent condition. 13,000 miles. 340-1031

PONTIAC—'73, Luxury Lemans, fully equip., AM/FM, tape player, 5000 mi. Elec. windows & sunroof. Gold & white vinyl roof. $3900. 229-4295.

PONTIAC—'69, Grand Prix, 46,000 mi., in excel. cond., priced at $1995, will take a trade, and assist w/financing, 273-4424.

PONTIAC—'72 Granville. Many extras. Make offer over $2750. Va. 560-2336

RAMBLER—'63, 6 cyl., new generator, regulator, battery, starter & good tires. Make offer. 536-7107.

RAMBLER—'67 AMBASSADOR—4-dr. 6-cyl. auto. Good cond. Special $290. 671-4042.

RAMBLER—'68 Spt., air, $495, $15, dep. LA 6-2700.

CHAPTER 10

How to
Sell
Your
Car

When the time comes to replace your car, one of the decisions you will face is whether to trade it in or try to sell it yourself. There are advantages either way.

Trading in your car is certainly the faster, less complicated way of disposing of it, since you do not have to search for a buyer. On the other hand, the dealer is going to have to recondition and resell the car and still make a profit. He will, then, give you only the wholesale value of the car, and the price he quotes you today will almost always be higher than the one he will quote tomorrow. This means that you have to make up your mind quickly as to whether or not to accept his offer. If you wait too long, you could suffer a sizable loss.

Selling your car yourself is a great deal more trouble. You might be able to sell it right away, but you might also have to wait some time before a buyer comes along. If you do not have enough cash to put toward the down payment on a new car, you may have to put off buying it until you have sold the old one. And then you may be without any car at all between the time you sell yours and the time you take delivery on the new car. There are, in addition, legal details, such as transferring the title, that you will have to handle yourself. But you may gain enough extra cash to make this kind of inconvenience worthwhile. Selling it yourself, you will probably get close to the retail value of your car because there is no middleman—and this could mean an additional several hundred dollars that you could apply toward buying your new car. These extra dollars could make the difference between being able to afford the air conditioner or stereo-tape player that you have always wanted in a car and having to do without them again.

Essentially, then, you have to decide whether you want the convenience of doing business with the dealer or the extra cash you will realize by selling your car independently. If you decide on the latter course, here is how the experts advise handling it.

Pricing your car

The first thing you need to do is to determine how much your car is worth. Look in one of the used-car price guide-books to find the *retail* value of your car. You may be able to ask for an amount close to this figure, but you will probably get an amount somewhere between the retail price and the wholesale price. This is because, as an independent seller, you cannot offer the service facilities and warranty coverage of a dealer. Be sure to make the appropriate additions and deductions for any special equipment that you do or do not have on your car. Instructions for doing this are included in the guides.

Next, you might check in the classified section of your newspaper, especially the Sunday edition. You should be able to find some advertisements about cars of the same year, make, and model as yours, and these will tell you how much other people are asking for such a car. The prices listed in these advertisements will probably be somewhat lower than those listed in the guidebooks because, like you, the sellers are independent.

The prices that you have gathered from these two sources will probably vary considerably, but they will guide you in setting a price on your own car. If your car is in excellent condition, you should be able to get an amount close to the higher prices. If your car needs a great deal of mechanical work or if it has a rundown appearance, you may have to settle for a lower price. Avoid setting the price too high—but be fair to yourself and do not set it too low either.

After you have decided on the price you actually hope to get, you might want to set your asking price a little higher. This will put you in a position where the buyer can bargain you down, and you will still get the price you want. If you initially ask for what you want to get, you may have to settle for less than that. Whatever you do, always try to get as much as you genuinely think the car is worth.

Preparing your car for sale

The next thing you might think about is what, if anything, you need to do to the car to make it attractive to a buyer. What you do and how much you do in this regard is strictly up to you, but one good rule to follow is to ask yourself what you would look for in the car if you were the buyer.

One thing you would surely want is a clean car. Most dealers will attest to the fact that a clean, tidy car always sells faster than one that looks as though it had not been cared for. It would be a wise investment of your time to wash the outside of the car. A neat interior is also important, so you might vacuum the rugs and the upholstery, wash the windows, and polish the chrome fittings. You should also remove everything from the glove compartment and the trunk. Be sure, however, to leave the owner's manual in the car for the buyer. If your asking price is particularly high, you might want to do a little more in the cleanup line, like giving the car a good coat of wax.

Anything you spend to make repairs to the car is going to have to come out of your profit—that is, the difference between what the dealer would give you and what you will get by selling the car yourself—so most experts advise that you do very little unless you are selling the car for more than $1,000. You might want to check the fluid levels in the radiator, crankcase, battery, master brake cylinder, and transmission and correct any problems that may exist there, but anything more than this probably would not be cost effective.

It would be to your advantage to be able to show a prospective buyer any receipts for work that you have had done to the car, such as major tune-ups, oil changes, or a brake relining job. This will indicate to him the kind of care you have given the car.

You should tell the prospect honestly about any mechanical defects that you know exist. Failure to do so may constitute misrepresentation, which is a criminal offense in some jurisdictions. But, even if you are scrupulously honest, there could be some serious problem of which you are not aware that might become evident soon after the sale, and you could have difficulty proving that you did not know about it prior to the sale. You would be wise, then, to encourage the prospect to take the car to a diagnostic center or to his mechanic—and to base his decision on their report of the car's condition and not yours. However you handle the matter, always make it clear to the buyer that you are selling the car "as is" and that you will not be responsible for any mechanical problems.

Advertising your car

Now that you know what price to ask for your car and have it ready for inspection, your next step is to find a buyer.

One inexpensive way to reach good prospects is to place a "For Sale" sign in the window of your car with your telephone number on it. You could also place signs on your company and community bulletin boards, and you could pass the word along to your friends that you are trying to sell your car.

These sources do not always produce prospects quickly, so you might also want to place an advertisement in your local newspaper. Before doing this, check the other advertisements to see how they are worded, and use them as a guide in writing your own. Try to give potential buyers as much information as you can without being too wordy. You need to tell the year, make, and model of the car, of course, and you should also give some indication of its condition and the optional equipment it has. Then state the price of the car. And remember that if you word the advertisement to read "asking price," you will indicate to potential buyers that you are willing to bargain. Finally, be sure to include your telephone number, but not your address.

Protecting yourself against pitfalls

Selling your car yourself can be risky, so you should be extremely cautious.

Most experts advise that you never turn your keys over to a prospective buyer so that he can test drive the car by himself. Unless the prospect is a friend, you will be dealing with someone about whom you know absolutely nothing. There have been cases where a seller has turned over his car and its keys to a prospect—and has never seen the car again. To avoid having this happen to you, ride in the car with the prospect if he wants to drive it.

Always insist on payment in cash or by certified check,

since you cannot know whether the buyer has the cash in his bank account to cover a personal check. He could give you a worthless check and then disappear forever—with your car. For the same reason, never agree to time payments. All you may ever see is the down payment, and you may only have that if it is made in cash. Even if you can find the buyer who defaults on payments, you will still have a hard time trying to collect your money. It is hardly worth taking these risks when you can be sure of finding a buyer who will pay cash, even if this means coming down on your price a bit.

Legal Matters Involved in Sale of Car

Make out a duplicate bill of sale.

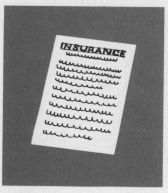

Notify your insurance company.

Transfer your registration card.

Remember the legalities

Then there are the legal details that you must handle.

You are going to transfer the title to the new owner, so be sure that you have it before you begin talking to prospective buyers. If you have lost the title, get another copy from your motor vehicle bureau or the dealer who sold you the car. If you are still making payments on the car, your banker or loan official will have the title, and you will have to get it from him. If your state does not require a title, be sure to have on hand those papers necessary to transfer ownership, such as your bill of sale or registration card.

Follow car inspection requirements.

Remove plates if not transferred.

Transfer the title.

You have to get the lending bank's permission to sell if you are still making payments on the car. And you should arrange to have the buyer take over the payments. This is most important, because it relieves you of any responsibility if he should default.

After the sale has been completed, you will have to transfer the title to the new owner. If instructions for doing this are not on the title itself, or if there is no title, find out what procedure you should follow by calling your motor vehicle bureau. They can also give you the details about transferring your registration card to the new owner and tell you your state's rules about license plates. Plates can be transferred in some states, but not in others, and some states require that they be returned to the motor vehicle bureau. If plates cannot be transferred in your state, remove them from the car before the buyer drives off. This will protect you from responsibility for any misuse he may make of the car.

Many states have inspection requirements. Some require that the buyer have the car inspected and make any necessary repairs before he can register it and obtain title; others require that the seller have it inspected. You can find out the details on this when you call the motor vehicle bureau.

Always make out a duplicate bill of sale. It should include your name, the name of the buyer, the date of the sale, the year, make, model, and serial number of the car, and the price. All of the terms and conditions of the sale should be clearly stated on it, such as the fact that the car is being sold "as is." The bill of sale should be signed by both you and the purchaser, and it should be notarized. Then keep one copy for yourself and give one copy to the buyer. Following this procedure will protect you in the event that questions arise after the sale.

Notify your insurance company immediately when you have sold the car. This will protect you against future claims, and it will ensure that you get a refund for any unused portion of your insurance premium.

Because cars are such a large and expensive item, buying and selling them is complicated. The problems can multiply when you try to handle the sale of your car by yourself. But if you know how to go about it and what pitfalls to watch out for, the experience will probably make you wiser —and possibly richer, too.

The innards of an automobile are as great a mystery to many people today as they were around 1910 when these children explored their family car.

11

How
Your
Car
Works

Although the automobile is the dominant means of transportation in the United States today, few people know how it works. Lacking this knowledge, most motorists find it impossible to understand what is happening when the machine does not work. Let us take a look at what an automobile is and what happens when you get into it, turn the key, shift into gear, step on the gas pedal, and drive off.

The automobile basically consists of a frame, wheels to support the frame and permit it to move freely from one place to another, a body to house the passengers, and a power plant to move the car. In addition, there are a number of support systems to give the passengers a smooth, controlled ride.

Put together, all the parts of the car—except the body— are called the chassis.

The power plant

Taking a close look first at the engine that supplies the power to move the car, we find that it is a *piston-driven internal combustion engine.* This is the engine that has been the basic power plant used in American automobiles for more than sixty years, and although it may face stiff competition from other types of engines in the future, most experts expect it to be in use for many years to come.

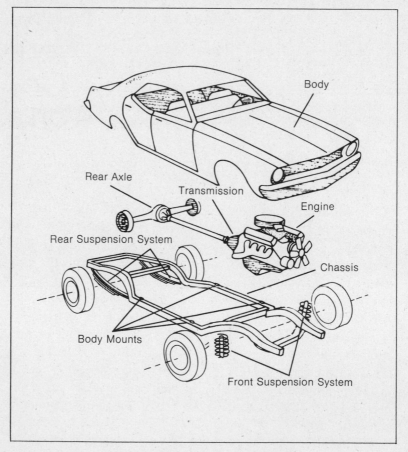

BASIC PARTS OF AN AUTOMOBILE

To say that it is an internal combustion engine means that fuel is burned inside it to produce power. To say that it is piston-driven means that a piece of metal moving up and down inside a container, or cylinder, provides the power to make the wheels go around. This is how it works.

When you want to drive the car, the first thing you do is insert a key into the ignition switch and turn it to the "on" position. When you do this, you activate the main electrical circuits in the car. When you turn the key a little farther —to the "start" position—the battery sends electrical energy to the starter motor. The starter motor then turns a flywheel, which is a heavy, balanced metal disc, or, on some cars, a fluid coupling. The flywheel, or coupling, is attached to the end of a long shaft, called the crankshaft. Actually, the crankshaft is not one long rod, but a series of cranks strung together. As the flywheel, or coupling, starts spinning, so does the crankshaft.

CRANKSHAFT FOR A 6-CYLINDER, IN-LINE ENGINE

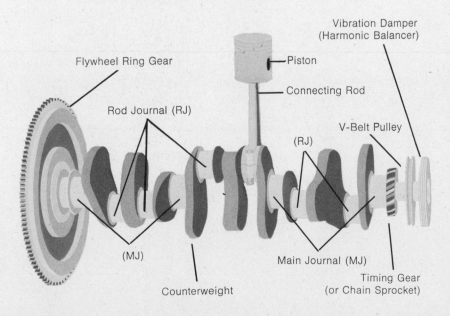

Vibration Damper (Harmonic Balancer)

Flywheel Ring Gear

Piston

Connecting Rod

Rod Journal (RJ)

(RJ)

V-Belt Pulley

(MJ)

Main Journal (MJ)

Timing Gear (or Chain Sprocket)

Counterweight

The crankshaft is the backbone of the engine. It runs the length of the engine, and its spinning motion ultimately turns the wheels of the car. Once started, however, the crankshaft will not continue spinning without renewed energy, and this energy is provided by the pistons.

The pistons fit inside of cylinders and are attached to the crankshaft by connecting rods. As the pistons move up and down, they turn the crankshaft round and round. In this way, an up-and-down motion is transformed into a rotary motion. The engine works on the same principle as a bicycle. When a bicycle rider pushes the pedals up and down, the wheels turn around.

There is only one crankshaft in an engine, but there may be four, six, or eight cylinders. The cylinders may be arranged in a straight line, in two horizontal lines, or in a "V" shape.

CYLINDER BLOCKS

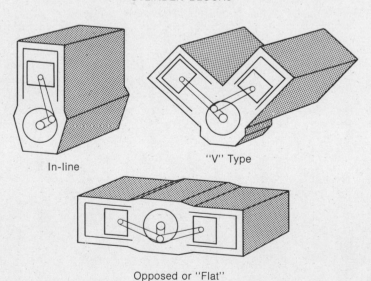

In-line

"V" Type

Opposed or "Flat"

We now know everything about this action except what keeps the pistons moving up and down. The power to do this comes from controlled explosions that are created when a mixture of fuel and air is burned in the spaces at the top of each cylinder.

The standard piston engine has what is known as a four-stroke cycle. This means that the pistons must go up twice and down twice to complete one full cycle. There are two openings in each cylinder which are opened or closed by valves. One is called the intake valve, and when it is open, the fuel-air mixture can flow into the cylinder. The other is called the exhaust valve, and when it is open, the gases that are left after the fuel-air mixture has been burned can be forced out of the cylinder.

INTAKE AND EXHAUST VALVES

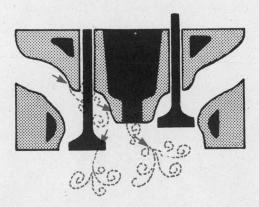

On the first, or intake stroke, of the piston, it is pulled down by the turning crankshaft and the intake valve opens to let the fuel-air mixture into the cylinder.

On the second, or compression stroke, the intake valve closes, the piston is pushed up, and the fuel-air mixture is tightly squeezed into the top of the cylinder. The often-used term "compression ratio" is a measure of how much the mixture is squeezed in the cylinder. To be more specific, it is the ratio of the volume of the whole cylinder to the volume of the small space at the top of the cylinder that contains the compressed mixture. If, for example, the volume of the cylinder is 50 cubic inches when the piston is down as far as it can go and 5 cubic inches when it is up as far as it can go, the compression ratio is 10 to 1—meaning that the mixture has been squeezed into a space 1/10th as large as it originally occupied. If the mixture has been squeezed into a space 1/8th as large, the compression ratio would be 8 to 1. As a general rule, the higher the compression ratio, the greater the horsepower output of the engine.

THE FOUR-STROKE CYCLE

Intake Stroke   Compression Stroke

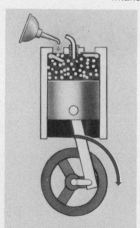  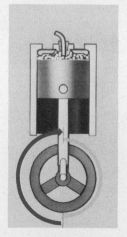

After compression, the mixture is ignited by a spark from a spark plug inserted into the top of the cylinder. This is much the same thing that happens when fuel in a cigarette lighter is ignited by a spark from a flint. When the fuel in a cylinder is ignited, however, it burns and expands with tremendous energy. The more the mixture is compressed, the more energy is produced when it is ignited. The rapid expansion of the burning fuel forces the piston down, and this provides the momentum needed to keep the crankshaft turning at great speed. This is the third, or power stroke.

On the fourth, or exhaust stroke, the piston is pushed up again, the exhaust valve opens, and the waste gases are forced out of the cylinder.

You can see from the diagram that as each piston goes through one full cycle, the crankshaft goes around twice, each valve opens and closes once, and each spark plug fires once. The expanding fuel pushes on the pistons for only a fraction of a second, but this is long enough to keep the

Power Stroke

Exhaust Stroke

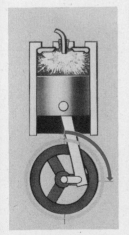

crankshaft turning smoothly. These actions in the engine occur with tremendous speed and precision. For example, to keep a car with an eight-cylinder engine moving at 80 mph, the ignition system would have to supply about 16,000 sparks a minute, or more than 250 sparks every second— and each spark would have to occur at the exact instant that it is needed.

The carburetor

As a driver, you know that your car needs gasoline in order to run. And you know that when you press down on the accelerator pedal, you inject gasoline into the engine. What you may not know is exactly how this happens.

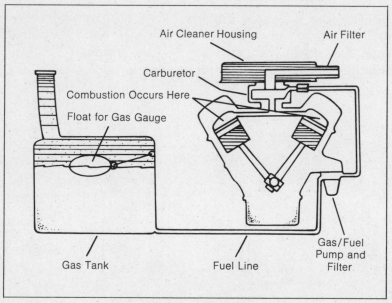

FUELING THE ENGINE

As we have seen, the cylinders do not use pure gasoline; they use a mixture of gasoline and air. The carburetor is the device that has the job of mixing these fuels and supplying the mixture to the cylinders. When you operate the accelerator pedal, you are, to some extent, controlling the activities of the carburetor. Here is how the carburetor works.

First, gasoline is sent to the carburetor fuel bowl from the gasoline tank by a fuel pump. When the piston starts down on its intake stroke, it creates a partial vacuum in the carburetor. As a result, air is pulled in through the top of the carburetor, after it first passes through a cleaner, which filters out any dirt or dust to prevent it from getting into the engine. As the air rushes down through the narrow center of the carburetor, it, too, creates a partial vacuum, which causes gasoline to be sucked in through holes, or jets, in the carburetor. Gasoline then enters the carburetor in the form of a fine spray, or tiny droplets, that will mix easily with the air to make a powerful explosive vapor.

There are one, two, or four "butterfly" valves, or throttle plates, in the carburetor that control the amount of the fuel/air mixture that goes to the cylinders. The carburetor is adjusted so that normally when the engine is idling, the proportion of fuel to air in the mixture will be constant. When the engine is cold, however, it needs more gasoline with the air.

The butterfly valve at the top of the carburetor is called the choke valve. It controls the intake of air. In the past, cars had a choke knob that the driver could operate to control this valve, but in most vehicles on the roads today, this valve operates automatically. When the engine is cold, the valve remains closed and admits only a little air. This makes the mixture rich in gasoline. As the engine warms up and needs less gasoline, the valve gradually opens to admit more air. In this way the heat of the engine controls the valve and determines how much air is admitted into the carburetor.

When you want the car to speed up, you step down on the accelerator pedal, and this operates two things in the carburetor: the lower butterfly valve and the accelerator pump. As your car starts to accelerate, the volume of air drawn into the carburetor momentarily decreases, as does the speed of the air going through the carburetor, which means that less gasoline is pulled in by the vacuum action we have just described. As you depress the pedal, the lower valve opens to draw more air through the carburetor and to permit more of the mixture to flow into the engine. In addition, the accelerator pump injects liquid gasoline directly into the carburetor to give you the richer mixture you need to increase the speed of the car.

The mixture is enriched only as the accelerator pedal moves downward. When you keep a steady pressure on the pedal, the accelerator pump no longer operates, but the butterfly valve remains open. At this point the engine again relies entirely on the fuel drawn into the carburetor by the air passing through it. The mixture, then, becomes thinner, but the engine continues to get the volume of the mixture that it needs to maintain the speed you have reached.

This is what the carburetor and its valves look like:

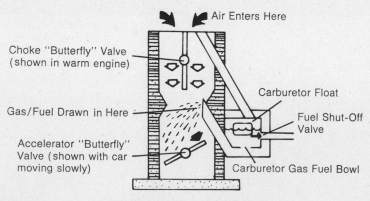

THE CARBURETOR—CUT IN HALF

The valve train

The fuel-air mixture, as we have seen, enters the cylinders through intake valves, and the waste gases are pushed out through exhaust valves. The opening and closing of these valves is a purely mechanical function controlled by the camshaft. This is another metal rod extending the length of the engine that has bumps, or cams, on it—one for each valve in the engine. Through a gear or pulley arrangement, this shaft is turned by the crankshaft, and thus

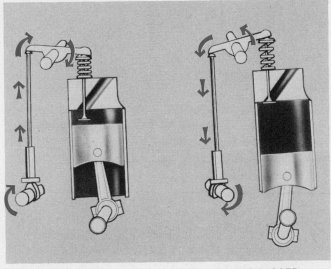

VALVE OPEN   VALVE CLOSED

turns at a precise speed relative to the main shaft. As the camshaft spins around, each of the bumps in turn pushes up on a metal rod, called a push rod. The push rod does what its name implies—it pushes on another metal rod, called the rocker arm. The rocker arm then pushes down on the valve to open it. When the push rod releases the pressure on the rocker arm, the valve closes again.

The electrical system

We have seen how the exploding fuel turns the crankshaft to move the car, but we have not seen the source of the electricity which provides the spark.

Remember that when you turned the ignition key to the start position the battery sent energy to the starter motor. At the same time, electrical energy began to move in another direction—to the spark plugs via an ignition system generally consisting of an ignition coil, breaker points, a condenser, a rotor, a distributor cap, and spark plug wires. (Some cars have an electronic ignition system, with resistors and transistors that do most of the work of the points.)

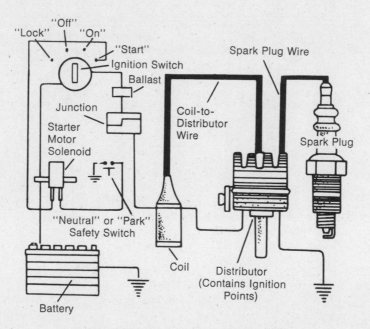

SUPPLYING ELECTRICITY TO SPARK PLUG

Because the average car battery can produce only 12 volts of electricity and because 20,000 or more volts are needed to ensure high voltage at the spark plugs, the voltage coming from the battery must be increased. This is the job of the coil, the points, and the condenser—and the electronic devices in an electronic system. The distributor does what its name implies—it distributes electricity to the right spark plug at the right time. Each spark plug is connected to the distributor cap by a spark plug wire. There is a rotor inside the cap that spins around and sends electricity through the wires to each spark plug in turn. The rotor works something like one hand of a clock. As it "points" to one spark plug wire, it closes the electrical circuit to one spark plug.

At the bottom of each spark plug are two wires, or elec-

PARTS OF SPARK PLUG

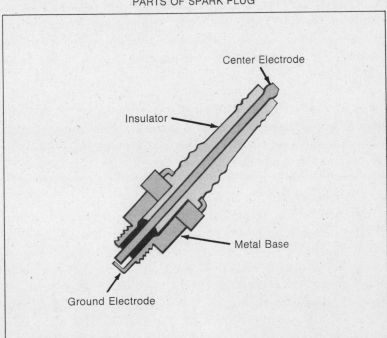

Center Electrode

Insulator

Metal Base

Ground Electrode

trodes. When electricity jumps across the narrow gap from one electrode to the other, a spark results, and this spark ignites the fuel-air mixture in the top of the cylinder, or combustion chamber.

Another part of the car's electrical system is the alternator—or generator on some older American cars and some foreign cars. Their job is to recharge the battery.

The battery has a tremendous amount of work to do. Not only does it have to supply electricity to the starter motor and the ignition circuit, it has to operate all of the other electrical equipment in the car. Each time you turn on the lights or the windshield wipers or the radio, you are using electricity from the battery. Because the battery can supply only twelve volts of electricity, it would soon run down without some provision to recharge it. The alternator or the generator does this job best when the engine is running at high speed. If your car has a generator, the battery will actually be discharging at slow engine speeds or when the car is merely idling. If your car has an alternator, however, the battery will be recharging to some extent even under these conditions.

The alternator or the generator can produce large quantities of electricity, and if all of this were sent to the battery at once, the battery would burn up. The voltage regulator has the job of controlling the amount of electricity that is sent to the battery to recharge it.

The cooling system

Because fuel is being burned in the cylinders, a running engine's heat may reach temperatures as high as 4,000 to 4,500 degrees Fahrenheit, which is almost twice the temperature at which iron will melt. To cool the engine, a small pump constantly circulates water or other coolant from the radiator through hollow spaces called water jackets around the hottest parts of the engine. The water absorbs the heat from the metal and then returns to the radiator. Behind the radiator is a fan, which pulls in air to cool the water again. Air is an efficient coolant, and some cars use it instead of water to cool the engine.

Here is what a water cooling system looks like:

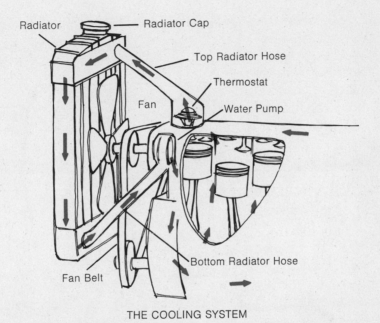

Radiator — Radiator Cap

Top Radiator Hose

Thermostat

Fan — Water Pump

Fan Belt

Bottom Radiator Hose

THE COOLING SYSTEM

The lubrication system

Water alone cannot keep the engine running smoothly; there must also be a lubrication system to keep a thin film of oil between the moving parts. When two pieces of metal rub together, the friction makes the metal hot, and the pieces tend to stick together and not move. If oil is put between the two pieces of metal, the friction and the heat are reduced. Oil has another function, too. It collects any dirt that may be in the engine and carries it away. The dirt is then removed from the oil by the oil filter.

This diagram shows how a pump forces the oil from the oil pan, through tubes and passages drilled in the crankcase and connecting rods, to all the critical points in the engine.

PRESSURE LUBRICATION SYSTEM

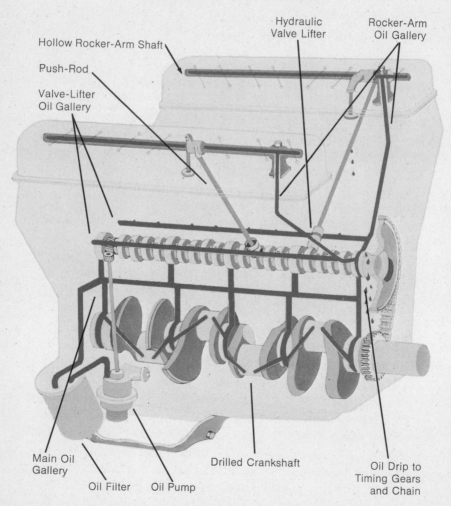

Hydraulic Valve Lifter

Rocker-Arm Oil Gallery

Hollow Rocker-Arm Shaft

Push-Rod

Valve-Lifter Oil Gallery

Main Oil Gallery

Oil Filter   Oil Pump

Drilled Crankshaft

Oil Drip to Timing Gears and Chain

All parts of the engine need oil—except the combustion chamber. If oil should get into the combustion chamber, it would be burned with the fuel-air mixture. This would ruin the spark plugs and drastically decrease the efficiency of the engine. In addition, the car would lose engine oil too rapidly. There are three or four rings that fit into grooves in the pistons and constantly press against the wall of the cylinder to seal off the combustion chamber. These rings are called piston rings. The top two or three rings prevent the fuel-air mixture from leaking out of the combustion chamber; the bottom ring, which is actually a three-piece unit, keeps the cylinder wall clean of oil and prevents oil from leaking into the combustion chamber.

PISTON RINGS

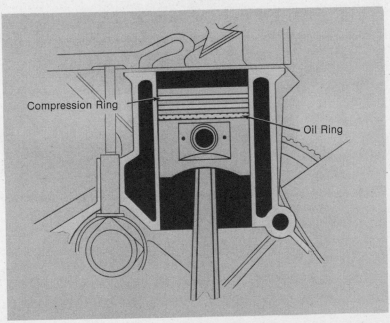

Compression Ring

Oil Ring

The exhaust system

We have seen how the explosions within the engine produce waste gases that are forced out of the cylinders through the exhaust valves. One of these gases is carbon monoxide, which can be dangerous in large amounts without proper ventilation. Thus it cannot be allowed to escape into the car. When the exhaust gases leave the cylinders, they enter the exhaust manifold. From there they go through pipes to the muffler(s) and then out the tail pipe(s). The job of the muffler, of course, is to quiet the exhaust noise. Some cars also have a resonator to further reduce noise.

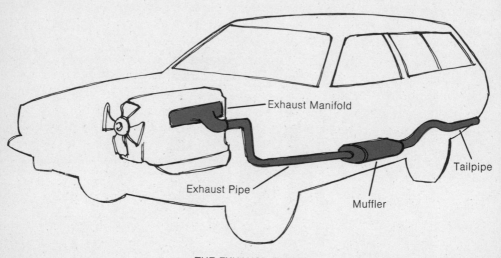

Exhaust Manifold

Tailpipe

Exhaust Pipe

Muffler

THE EXHAUST SYSTEM

The power train

You will recall that the crankshaft is the backbone of the engine. This spinning shaft turns the camshaft and the fan, and it runs the alternator, the fuel pump, the oil pump, and the water pump. Its main purpose, however, is to turn the wheels of the car.

In order to understand how one spinning shaft can do all of these jobs, we need to understand some simple principles about pulleys and gears. These devices enable you to transmit a turning motion from one unit to another and at the same time increase the power and speed of the turning and even change its direction.

A bicycle provides a common example of a pulley. As a rider turns the pedals—or the crank—he at the same time turns the rear wheel. The discs are the pulleys; the chain is the belt.

Although pulleys are not used to turn the wheels of an automobile, the principle is used many times in the engine. For example, by putting a pulley on the end of the crankshaft and one on the end of the fan shaft and connecting them by a belt, the turning of the crankshaft will turn the fan. In this way, you have to keep only one part turning in order to turn a great many other parts.

The same principle applies to gears. Gears are wheels with notches, or teeth, around the outside edge. When the teeth of two or more gears fit together, they push each other along so that if one wheel turns, all the wheels turn. A good example of this is the egg beater. As you turn the handle—or the crank—the large gear attached to it turns the small gear attached to the beater.

Gears are always calculated in terms of ratios. When a small gear has to turn completely around twice in order to turn a larger gear completely around once, the ratio is two to one. You can obtain power by increasing the gear ratio —that is, by using a very large gear with a very small gear —and speed by decreasing the ratio—that is, by making the gears more nearly equal in size. This diagram shows how gears work. When the smaller gear has made one complete revolution, the larger gear has made only half a turn. Note, too, that the gears turn in opposite directions.

HOW GEARS WORK

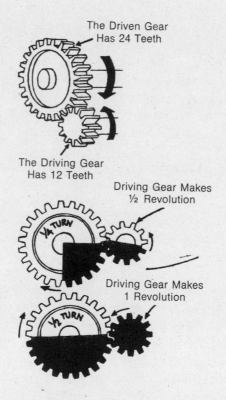

The Driven Gear Has 24 Teeth

The Driving Gear Has 12 Teeth

Driving Gear Makes ½ Revolution

¼ TURN

Driving Gear Makes 1 Revolution

½ TURN

How, then, are gears used to turn the wheels of a car? The turning power of the crankshaft is sent to the wheels through the power train, which generally consists of a clutch, a transmission, a differential, and a drive axle.

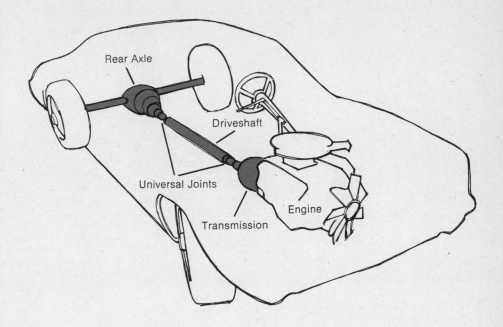

THE TRANSMISSION AND DRIVELINE

You may have wondered how a car can stand perfectly still while the engine is running and generating so much power. This is made possible by the clutch, which is located just behind the engine and in front of the transmission.

When you are sitting in your car with the clutch pedal pushed all the way to the floor, the flywheel, which is attached to the end of the crankshaft, spins freely and the car does not move. As you ease the pressure on the pedal and let it rise, the clutch, which consists of several discs or plates and a very strong spring, is pushed tightly against the flywheel and begins to turn with it. As the clutch discs start spinning, another shaft attached to the clutch and extending back to the transmission also starts spinning. In this way the turning power of the crankshaft is started on its way to the rear wheels. This is what the clutch looks like:

THE CLUTCH

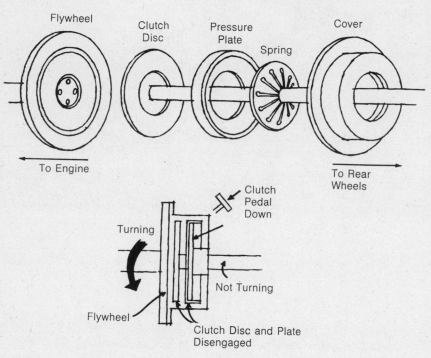

Flywheel   Clutch Disc   Pressure Plate   Spring   Cover

To Engine

To Rear Wheels

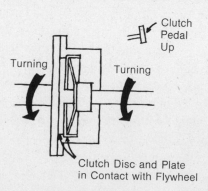

Clutch Pedal Down

Turning

Not Turning

Flywheel

Clutch Disc and Plate Disengaged

Clutch Pedal Up

Turning   Turning

Clutch Disc and Plate in Contact with Flywheel

The spinning power of the crankshaft has now been transferred to the clutch shaft, but it cannot go directly to the rear wheels in this form. It takes a tremendous amount of power to start a car moving from a dead stop, and when the engine is idling or running at very low speeds, it does not produce much power. We need gears to enable us to increase the power of the turning force. We have said that you can increase the power by increasing the gear ratio, and this is how it works:

Going back to the egg beater again, you can see that if there is a large gear attached to the crank handle and a small gear attached to the beater, the beater will whirl around many times for every one turn of the handle. The beater will go very fast, but will not have much power. But if there were a small gear attached to the handle and a large gear attached to the beater, the small gear on the handle would turn several times in order to make the beater go completely around once. The beater would turn slowly, but it would have developed enough power to beat a thicker substance.

This is exactly what happens in the transmission—which is a box full of gears—when you put the gear selector into first gear. The crankshaft will be spinning very fast, but by means of a large gear in the transmission attached to the drive shaft, the drive shaft will turn more slowly and with great power. In this way, by controlling the gear shift lever, you can harness the engine's output to start the car moving or to drive it up a steep hill.

The gear ratio in first gear is usually three to one. This means that the crankshaft will revolve three times in order to turn the drive shaft once. When you put the car in second gear, the gear ratio is reduced—usually to one and a half to one—because now the car is moving easily and you need less power and more speed. When you put the car in third gear, the gear ratio is one to one. In this gear, all you need is speed, and so the drive shaft can revolve once for every full turn of the crankshaft. When you put the car into reverse gear, you need power again. This time the large gear on the drive shaft meshes with a special small reverse gear.

TRANSMISSION GEARS

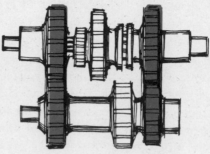

First Speed

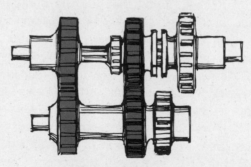

Second Speed

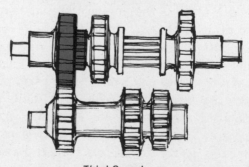

Third Speed

Many cars, of course, have automatic transmissions. These work on the same principles as a manual transmission, except that there is no clutch pedal for the driver to operate. The work of the clutch is done by a special oil and an oil pump in the transmission itself.

By means of gears in the transmission, then, the crankshaft turns the drive shaft, which, as we have seen, extends

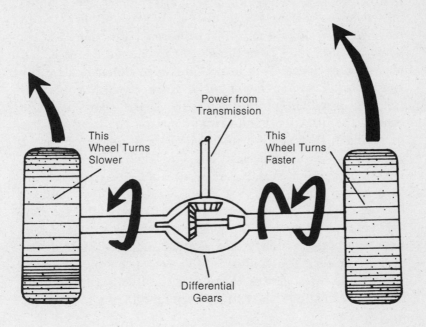

Power from
Transmission

This
Wheel Turns
Slower

This
Wheel Turns
Faster

Differential
Gears

TURNING A CORNER

back to the rear axle. Because the drive shaft is attached to the rear axle, it has to be flexible. The rear axle follows every contour of the road—the bumps and holes as well as the smooth parts. The rest of the car remains rigid. If the drive shaft were rigid also, it could not turn and at the same time bend with the movements of the axle. Two universal joints in the drive shaft give it the flexibility it needs. These joints work something like your wrist—they permit bending and twisting at the same time.

How, then, is the turning power of the drive shaft transmitted to the rear axle? The rear axle, after all, is going to have to turn in a completely different direction. As we noted earlier, gears have the ability to change the direction of a turning force. This principle is also illustrated by the egg beater. There is, then, a set of gears, called the differential, in the middle of the rear axle. These gears not only change the direction of the rotary motion coming from the drive shaft, they also permit the wheels to turn at different speeds. This is an important consideration for turning corners. When a car is going in a straight line, both wheels turn at the same speed, but when a car is going around a corner, the outside rear wheel must turn faster than the inside rear wheel. You will understand why this is so if you have ever seen a line of ice skaters pivoting around one central skater. The skater in the center merely steps in place while the skater at the end of the line has to skate so fast that sometimes she cannot keep up and has to drop out of the line.

Steering and suspension

In most cars, no power is sent from the engine to drive the front wheels. They are merely pushed along by the rear wheels. We saw this in the bicycle, where the turning pedals drive the rear wheel only; the front wheel is for balance and steering. The same thing is true in the automobile, but the steering is a bit more complicated.

When you turn the steering wheel, the turning motion is transmitted to special gears in a steering box and from there to a steering arm, called a pitman arm. The pitman arm then pushes and pulls on metal rods, called tie rods, that extend between the front wheels of the car. The tie rods are attached to the front wheels by steering knuckles, which work something like door hinges and permit the wheels to swing to the right or the left. The steering knuckles turn on special bearings called ball joints.

If your car has power steering, there is a special pump and piston in the steering box that relieves you of about 80 percent of the effort normally required to steer a car.

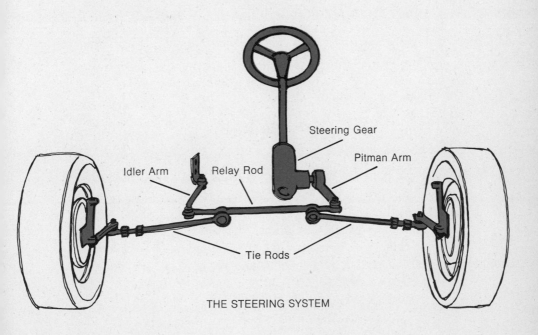

THE STEERING SYSTEM

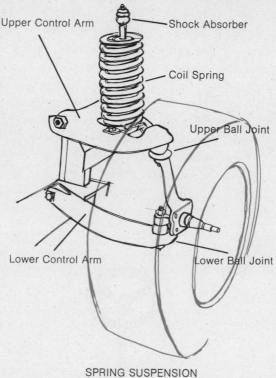

Upper Control Arm — Shock Absorber

Coil Spring

Upper Ball Joint

Lower Control Arm — Lower Ball Joint

SPRING SUSPENSION

All roads are hard and have bumps and holes that would make riding in a car extremely unpleasant if it were absolutely rigid. The passengers would be jostled from side to side and bumped up and down. There are a number of provisions made in modern cars to prevent such discomfort. The tires, first of all, cushion the ride. Gone are the days when tires were made of solid rubber—not to mention the days of wooden wagon wheels.

In past decades the front wheels of cars were suspended on a solid axle extending from wheel to wheel. But this, too, gave a rough ride, and the frame has taken over the job of the front axle in modern cars. Most passengers cars now have independent front suspensions, which use either coil springs or torsion bars, together with shock absorbers, to produce a soft, smooth ride.

The job of the springs is to cushion the car from bumps and holes. But if the car were equipped only with springs, each time it hit a bump, it would bounce up and down until all the energy was used up. This kind of bouncing would not only be unpleasant for the passengers, it would be unsafe, because the wheels would keep losing contact with the road. The job of the shock absorbers, then, is to control the bouncing and keep the car on the road.

Some cars have torsion bars instead of springs. These are metal bars that provide elasticity through a twisting motion.

TORSION BAR SUSPENSION

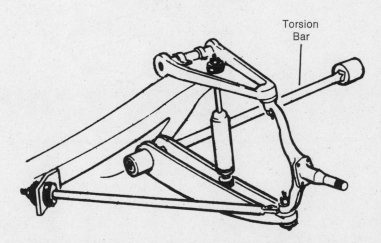

Torsion
Bar

The rear wheels also have to be cushioned from road shock. Typical rear suspensions use coil or semielliptic leaf springs and shock absorbers. This is what they look like:

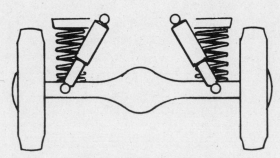

Rear Coil Spring Suspension

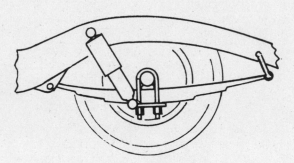

Rear Leaf Spring Suspension

We have all had the experience, at one time or another, of being thrown to the right or left when the vehicle we were riding in turned a corner. To prevent this, some cars have stabilizer bars, which are metal rods that extend between the two wheels, usually at the front of cars.

The braking system

Now suppose you want to stop the car. You step on the brake pedal, and the car comes to a halt. Here is how this happens. Behind the brake pedal is a master hydraulic cylinder containing brake fluid. When you step on the brake pedal, it pushes a piston in the master cylinder which forces out the brake fluid. The fluid goes through tubing, or brake lines, into the hollow brake cylinders located at each wheel.

WHAT THE BRAKE PEDAL OPERATES

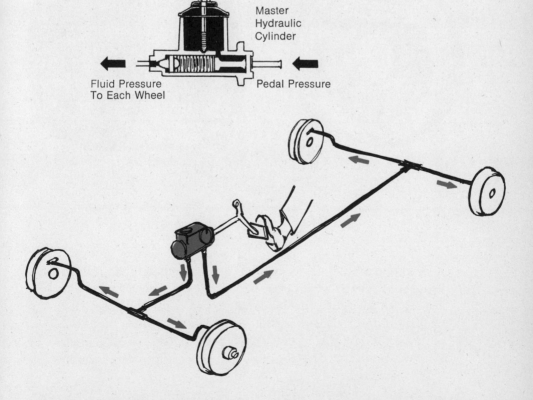

Master
Hydraulic
Cylinder

Fluid Pressure
To Each Wheel

Pedal Pressure

When the brake fluid enters the cylinder, it pushes outward on two pistons that in turn push against brake shoes,
which are covered with a special friction material called
brake linings.

The brake shoes are forced against the inside of the spinning metal brake drum and, because the drum is connected
to the wheel, the car slows down.

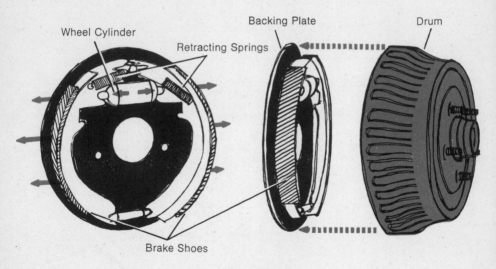

DRUM BRAKE

Some cars have disc brakes. These are usually found on
the front wheels, with drum brakes on the rear wheels, but
sometimes all four wheels are equipped with these brakes.
On disc brakes, a large metal disc called a rotor is mounted
on the inside of the wheel. When the brakes are activated,
calipers lined with friction material squeeze the disc to stop
it from turning.

Disc brakes are generally considered superior to drum brakes, and they are—if all four wheels are equipped with them. But if disc brakes are used together with drum brakes, their performance may be little better than that of drum brakes. This is due to engineering problems created when both types of brakes are operated by the same pedal.

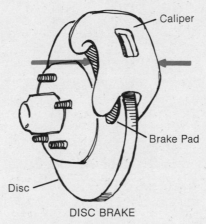

DISC BRAKE

Disc brakes on all four wheels will give excellent braking performance and good durability. Because they are exposed to the air, they run cooler than drum brakes and thus are not as subject to brake fade, or the loss of braking power because of excessive heat buildup. In addition, the spinning action of the discs throws water off the brakes, so they are not as apt to get soaked and thus fail to work properly.

Because disc brakes are usually, but not always, power assisted, they are often more expensive to buy than drum brakes, and they are sometimes more expensive to repair.

This, then, is basically how your car works. The knowledge you have gained does not qualify you to become a mechanic, but it will enable you to understand your mechanic when he starts talking about such things as rotors and ball joints. It will also give you the necessary background information for fully utilizing the advice about preventive maintenance later in this book.

As motor vehicles come under fire for polluting our air, auto makers are attempting to solve the problem by developing "clean" engines.

CHAPTER 12

The Impact of Pollution Controls

We live in an era of grave national concern about what is happening to our natural resources. One concern in particular—about the quality of the air we breathe—is having a profound impact on the automobile and oil industries, and, in turn, on motorists. A desperate race with the clock to perfect devices that will control the harmful pollutants spewed into our air by automobiles is taking place throughout the world. These devices range from units that can be added to the existing piston-driven engine to completely new concepts in engine design.

The basic problem with the internal combustion engine is that when the fuel-air mixture is burned in the closed space of the cylinders, the burning is incomplete. Whenever fuel is burned, chemical reactions take place that change the original substance into other substances. If the fuel in the automobile engine were completely burned, the end products would be water and carbon dioxide, both of which are harmless. But because the fuel in the standard piston-driven engine is not burned completely, three types of gases that can be harmful to health are produced and passed through the car's exhaust into the air.

One such gas is carbon monoxide. Sufficient exposure to this gas can impair judgment, and, because it puts stress on the heart, people with heart disease have low tolerance for it. However, the data are inconclusive as to exactly what levels are unsafe. A class of gases called oxides of nitrogen are also produced in the engine. These gases are considered poisonous and may cause respiratory illness. Hydrocarbons are another by-product of combustion, and although they are not themselves considered harmful in the amounts in which they are produced, they (as well as oxides of nitrogen) react with sunlight to form photochemical oxidants—or the smog that is afflicting so many of our cities. Because it makes breathing difficult, smog can be especially harmful to older persons and those with allergies or other existing respiratory problems. At this time the experts do not agree as to exactly what levels of these automobile emissions are unsafe. Nevertheless, controls are being instituted.

Additives increase pollution

Some of the additives in gasoline also contribute to the pollution problem, either directly by being emitted through the exhaust or indirectly by deactivating some emission-control devices. We need to know something about gasoline in order to understand why this is so.

Gasoline is a highly volatile liquid obtained from petroleum (crude oil). To say that it is volatile means that it changes into vapor rapidly. We have already seen that when it is burned, it produces a number of waste gases. The oxidation process also causes the formation of gum,

What Kind of Gasoline Should You Buy?

Many motorists are perplexed when it comes to buying gasoline. Should they use leaded, low-lead, or unleaded fuel? And what about octane—should they use regular or premium or one of the blended gasolines? They also want to know if brand is important.

Generally speaking, brand makes little difference. Virtually all of the major oil companies put the same additives in gasoline:

- Carburetor detergents and other engine cleaning additives
- Fuel line and carburetor anti-icers
- Additives that help prevent spark plug fouling and preignition
- Antirust, antigum, and antiwear additives

The things that really count are the octane rating of the gasoline and its lead content. Regular gasoline usually has an octane rating of about 94, premium gasoline has a rating of 100 or more, and blends may have ratings somewhere in between. As a starting point, you should follow the recommendations in your owner's manual. However, the octane requirements of the same make and model car can vary by as many as ten numbers when the car is new. And as the car gets older, the octane requirement can increase four to six numbers due to combustion deposits.

What all of this means is that cars are highly individual, and you should experiment to find out what your car's octane requirements are. Any gasoline that does not produce knock will be suitable. According to the American Petroleum Institute, mild knocking will probably not damage an engine, but intense, sustained knocking could damage the pistons. It is always wise, then, to eliminate knock when it occurs by switching to a higher octane gasoline.

High-compression engines have a greater tendency to knock than low-compression engines and usually require a premium gasoline. Other factors that can increase the octane requirement include:

- High air or engine temperatures
- Driving at low altitudes
- Low humidity
- Advanced spark timing
- Lean carburetor settings
- Consistent sudden acceleration or stop-and-start driving

The octane requirement of your car, then, will depend not only on the kind of car you drive, but also on where and how you drive your car.

As we point out, the trend now is to unleaded gasolines in preparation for the introduction of automobiles with the more complicated pollution-control devices that require unleaded fuel. This is why cars manufactured after 1970 have been designed to run on unleaded fuel of lower octane numbers. Most automobiles manufactured through the 1970 model year were designed to run on fully leaded gasoline, although many can use the new low-lead and unleaded fuels. You would be wise to follow the recommendation in your owner's manual regarding the lead content of the gasoline you use.

How to Save Gasoline

Faced with the increasing costs of operating an automobile, as well as the need to conserve natural resources, it is important to get as many miles as possible from each gallon of gasoline. Here is how you can achieve this goal:

• Keep your car tuned up. A misfiring spark plug can waste up to two miles per gallon of gasoline. A faulty carburetor choke can waste up to three miles per gallon, and a clogged air filter can waste up to one mile per gallon.

• Avoid "jackrabbit" starts—they can cost you as many as two miles per gallon of gasoline.

• Drive at as steady a speed as possible—stopping and starting gradually. Needless stopping can waste up to two miles per gallon. Keep a reasonable distance from the car ahead and try to anticipate traffic conditions.

• Reduce speed in highway driving. The faster your car travels, the harder your engine has to work to overcome air resistance. Driving at 70 mph instead of 50 mph can waste about four miles per gallon.

• Keep tires properly inflated. Low pressure in the tires creates more rolling resistance, and the engine has to work harder to overcome it. This can reduce your gasoline mileage by as much as a mile per gallon.

• Do not idle the engine unnecessarily. An idling engine uses gasoline. Particularly, do not idle the engine to warm it on a cold day. This is hard on the engine in addition to wasting gasoline. The car will warm up faster if you drive slowly for the first few miles.

• If your car has a manual transmission, shift into third gear as soon as you can. The gasoline waste can be as much as 45 percent when you race your car in second gear.

• Combine trips to the supermarket, drugstore, bank, and cleaners.

• Try to organize or join a car pool to get you to and from work. Fewer cars on the road mean less gasoline being burned.

• Keep your use of the air conditioner to a minimum. This device puts a heavy load on the engine and can cost you up to two miles per gallon.

which will foul the engine. In the refining process, then, certain substances are added to inhibit gum formation.

By various means, water gets into gasoline in the refinery's transportation pipes and storage tanks, and can cause rusting in a car's fuel system. So the oil companies add corrosion inhibitors to prevent this. They also add substances to prevent ice from forming in the carburetor, which can occur at certain temperatures. Dirt in the air that enters the carburetor can accumulate there and cause rough idling, stalling, and decreased fuel economy. Detergents are added to gasoline to control these deposits. Deposits can also form on the intake valves, causing loss of power and even valve burning, so more chemicals are added to control this problem.

All of these additives perform functions vital to good engine performance, but they are of no known ecological importance. There are, however, two other substances added to gasoline at the refinery that affect both engine efficiency and pollution control.

The more important of these two substances is lead, which is added in the form of tetraethyl- or tetramethyllead. Gasoline obtained directly from petroleum does not burn smoothly. Because of certain reactions taking place within the engine, gasoline can ignite in the combustion chamber at several points other than at the spark plug. The result is that the gasoline is completely burned prematurely and starts pushing on the piston before it reaches the top of its upward stroke. This produces a sharp metallic noise, or "knock," as well as a loss of power. In the early 1920s, researchers discovered that by adding lead, they could produce a gasoline that would not knock and would burn more slowly and evenly, with a corresponding increase in power. A gasoline's resistance to knock is defined in terms of octane. The higher the octane rating of a gasoline, the greater its knock resistance.

The addition of lead to gasoline made high-compression

engines possible. But as compression ratios rose, another problem was created. The high temperatures that develop in these engines can cause carbon deposits on the cylinder walls to glow and ignite the mixture prematurely. This is known as preignition, and results in pinging and rumbling noises in the engine. These glowing deposits can also cause the engine to continue running after the ignition has been turned off, a condition known as dieseling. Phosphorus is added to gasoline to prevent preignition.

Controlling emission of lead

These two substances—lead and phosphorus—create real problems for pollution control. Some experts are convinced that particulates of lead passing into the air through the exhaust are harmful to our health. Lead, of course, is toxic to humans, and there are some data which indicate that the blood levels of lead in our population are increasing. Although the evidence that automobile emissions are responsible is not conclusive, the decision has been made to control the emission of lead through the exhaust and to reduce the lead content in gasoline. Some cars are being equipped, or will soon be equipped, with particulate traps, but the real answer seems to be to eliminate the lead from gasoline— for other important reasons. Again, we need some background in order to understand what is happening here.

Antipollution devices cause problems

People who own late models have already experienced trouble with the operation of their cars—difficult starting, stalling, loss of power, and decreased fuel economy. This kind of poor performance is caused by the existing pollution-control devices, and as these devices become more complex, motorists' problems may worsen.

In the 1960s, the positive crankcase ventilation (PCV) valve was required on all American cars to feed unburned hydrocarbons back into the cylinders to be burned. Later,

1973 and 1974 Emission-Control System

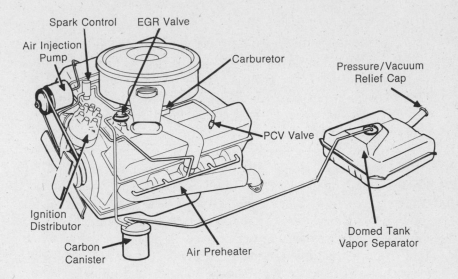

Spark Control

EGR Valve

Air Injection Pump

Carburetor

Pressure/Vacuum Relief Cap

PCV Valve

Ignition Distributor

Carbon Canister

Air Preheater

Domed Tank Vapor Separator

1975 Emission-Control System

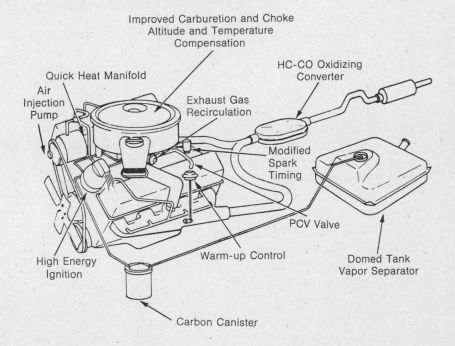

Improved Carburetion and Choke Altitude and Temperature Compensation

Quick Heat Manifold

Air Injection Pump

Exhaust Gas Recirculation

HC-CO Oxidizing Converter

Modified Spark Timing

High Energy Ignition

Warm-up Control

PCV Valve

Carbon Canister

Domed Tank Vapor Separator

pumps were installed to force air into the exhaust, thus helping to oxidize some of the hydrocarbons and carbon monoxide. In 1971, devices to control the evaporation of hydrocarbons from gasoline tanks and carburetors were added. Two years later, exhaust gas recirculation (EGR) systems to control nitrogen oxides were required on all cars. These devices reduce combustion chamber temperatures, and can be blamed for the starting and stalling problems so many motorists have experienced.

Some cars are also equipped with electronic ignition, which provides a surer, stronger spark and minimizes the chance that a spark plug will misfire. If a spark plug does not fire when it is supposed to, the gasoline is not burned properly, with a resulting increase in the pollutants emitted from the exhaust.

All of these devices have substantially reduced pollution from automobiles, but the results fall far short of the standards set up by the Environmental Protection Agency (EPA). What this means, then, is more devices to affect engine performance and economy.

The catalytic converter

The device to which Detroit is committed is the catalytic converter, which fits into the exhaust system and uses catalysts to change carbon monoxide and hydrocarbons into harmless carbon dioxide and water and to strip the oxygen from nitrogen oxides. These converters, which use rare, imported metals—platinum, ruthenium, and palladium—as catalysts, are expensive and fragile. Experts say that these devices will add about $200 to the initial cost of the car, and will cause fuel economy losses of 5 to 30 percent, depending on the size of the car. Although the law requires that the converters last for 50,000 miles, the need for relatively frequent repair or replacement would make them even more expensive.

To compound the problem, engine conditions have to be

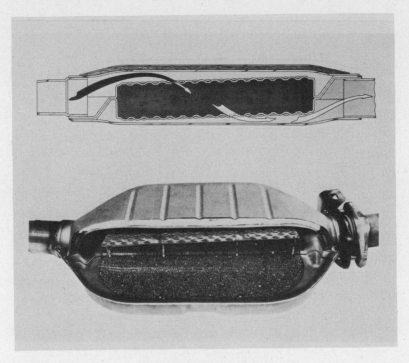

CATALYTIC CONVERTER

optimum for these devices to work. They do not operate well during engine warmup, when gasoline burns less completely than during normal operation. The unburned fuel passing through the exhaust can ignite the catalyst bed and even cause it to melt. The stresses of stop-and-go and downhill driving can also dangerously overheat this device. Also, lead in gasoline can "poison" or deactivate it, and phosphorus can cause it to deteriorate. (Lead salts also corrode the materials used in thermal reactors, another control device, and more expensive materials would be needed if leaded gasoline is used.)

In preparation for the converter, as well as to reduce lead in the air, EPA decreed that by July, 1974, gasoline stations would have to supply at least one grade of unleaded, 91+ octane gasoline. The pumps for these fuels and the gasoline tanks of cars with converters will be specially equipped so that leaded gasoline cannot be pumped into these cars by mistake. Because the converters are so fragile and undependable at their current stage of development, proposals have been made for the creation of state or federal inspection systems to police these devices.

But the story does not end here, because when lead is removed from gasoline, other problems ensue, and this accounts for the low octane requirement of the new gasoline. Remember that high-compression engines are designed to use high-octane gasoline. Unleaded, low-octane gasoline used in these engines can cause knock and possibly valve recession—which means that the seal between the valve and its seat will be destroyed, resulting in a loss of compression and power. Although certain phosphorus additives might prevent valve problems, they would create others. They could cause holes to be burned in the pistons, and, as we have noted, phosphorus can deactivate the catalysts. A number of aromatics can be added to increase gasoline octane, but they are so expensive that the cost of gasoline would be too high. Even getting the octane up to 91 without the use of lead will increase the cost of the gasoline by an average of one cent per gallon over the cost of conventional leaded gasoline, or an average of $10 annually per car.

Return to low-compression engines

The only alternative, then, has been to go back to low-compression engines, which also, because of their lower combustion temperature, produce fewer pollutants. Almost 90 percent of the engines manufactured in this country since 1971 have been low-compression engines designed to be able to use unleaded, low-octane fuel. This, again, is going to cost the motorist more money, because these engines have average fuel economy losses of 5 percent. Add these increased fuel costs to the initial cost of the converter, plus the cost of its maintenance, and you have a sizable increase in the cost of owning and operating a car.

The High Cost of Cleaner Air

	Sticker Price Rise	Yearly Maintenance and Operation	National 10-Year Cost
Engine modified to meet 1973-74 standards	$100	$ 5	$10.8 billion
Catalytic converter to meet 1975 standards	185	10	40.9 billion
Combination of devices to meet 1976 standards	205	42	70.8 billion

Source: Environmental Protection Agency

On the brighter side, however, is the fact that lead fouls spark plugs, clogs oil filters, and hastens the deterioration of mufflers and tail pipes. The saving to the motorist that will result from the longer life of these parts may equal the increased amount he will pay for fuel.

But even with all the added trouble and expense the catalytic converter will cause, American auto manufacturers cannot guarantee that it will be able to meet the standards for oxides of nitrogen, the most difficult of the pollutants to control. Because of time and cost factors, however, Detroit is locked into its decision to use this device—possibly for at least as long as it continues to build huge, piston-driven engines.

How the Wankel works

Elsewhere, car manufacturers seem to be having more success in controlling pollutants with little loss in power and efficiency. One of the most dramatic developments in engine design is the Wankel rotary engine, which since 1967 has been offered as optional equipment in its Mazda cars by Toyo Kogyo Co., Ltd., of Japan. This engine is also

designed on the internal combustion principle, but where
the piston engine delivers power through either four, six,
or eight reciprocating (moving up-and-down) pistons, the
Wankel delivers power through two triangular-shaped rotors. Each rotor is enclosed in a housing shaped like a modified figure eight which engineers call an epitrochoid. The
rotors move in a kind of hula-hoop motion around a power
output shaft, and this shaft and the rotors are the only
moving parts in the engine.

We have already seen how the major action takes place
on top of the pistons in the conventional engine. The actions that give the Wankel engine its power are spaced out

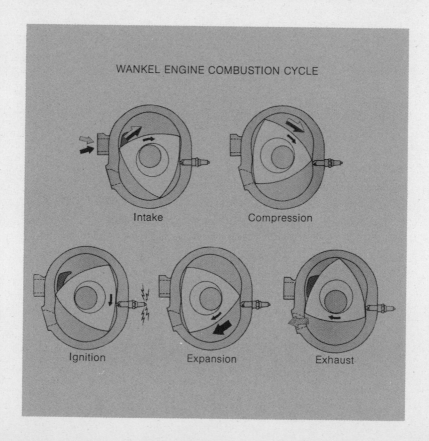

WANKEL ENGINE COMBUSTION CYCLE

Intake   Compression

Ignition   Expansion   Exhaust

along the three working surfaces of the twin rotors. There are four "strokes" to the Wankel's operational cycle, like the cycle of the standard piston engine, but each face of a rotor is engaged in one phase of the cycle at any given moment. As the rotor spins around, each of its sides forms a chamber that draws in fuel, compresses it, and then—after ignition—forces out the exhaust. Each rotor, in effect, does the same amount of work done by three cylinders in the conventional engine.

The diagram opposite shows the Wankel's intake, compression, ignition, expansion, and exhaust stages.

There are three power "strokes" to one full turn of each rotor, and each time a rotor makes a full turn, the output shaft makes three full turns. You can see in the diagram the gear arrangement in the center of each rotor that is used to turn the output shaft.

Because this engine is so small—it is half the size of a comparable piston engine—there is plenty of room under the hood for a big thermal reactor. This device mixes fresh air with the carbon monoxide and hydrocarbons in the exhaust to ignite them and complete the combustion process. Because exhaust temperatures in the Wankel are high, the thermal reactor can work more efficiently than it could on a piston engine. In addition, combustion temperatures are low, which means that fewer oxides of nitrogen are produced.

Because of its Wankel engine, the Mazda met the original 1975 pollution-control standards at an early date. And it was able to do this without great sacrifices in car performance and fuel economy. The Mazda produces plenty of power; in anywhere from eight and a half to ten and a half seconds, it can accelerate smoothly from 0 to 60 mph. In independent tests the car averaged 14.2 miles per gallon (mpg) in city driving and 17.8 mpg in extended driving on interstate highways. In mixed city/highway driving, the car averaged 16 to 17 mpg.

Stratified-charge system

Although Mazda has been able to meet the 1975 standards, it, too, may have trouble meeting the 1976 standards for oxides of nitrogen. Some experts believe, however, that the Wankel engine could easily be adapted to the new stratified-charge system developed by Honda—the only system that, according to its developers, can meet these standards. As an added bonus, the Wankel shows promise of being able to do this without a significant loss in performance and perhaps with even better mileage. Stratified charge works well on small engines. The cost of adapting it to larger engines is exorbitant, and on these engines expensive fuel-injection systems are necessary.

In the stratified-charge system, no extra emission-reducing devices are added to the engine. Emissions are controlled through a modification of the cylinders themselves. The system is based on the principle that very lean mixtures—that is, mixtures with much more than the usual amount of air—produce fewer pollutants. The problem is that if the mixture is lean enough to be effective for pollution control, it cannot be ignited by a spark plug. Honda solved this problem by building a tiny combustion chamber on top of the cylinder. A rich fuel mixture (a stratified charge) is injected into this chamber and ignited by the spark plug, and this burning fuel, in turn, ignites a lean mixture injected into the larger chamber. The Honda system also uses dual carburetors—one carburetor to supply the mixture to each type of chamber.

Clearly, the automobile industry is in a state of turmoil. And the changes to come may prove to be more dramatic than those that have already occurred.

New types of engines explored

All of the solutions to the environmental problems that we have discussed involve some modification of the basic internal combustion engine. But because problems the man-

The Six-Part Cycle of the Honda Stratified-Charge Engine

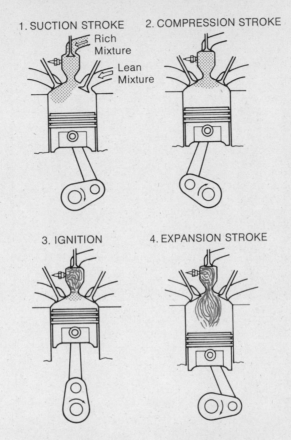

1. SUCTION STROKE
   - Rich Mixture
   - Lean Mixture

2. COMPRESSION STROKE

3. IGNITION

4. EXPANSION STROKE

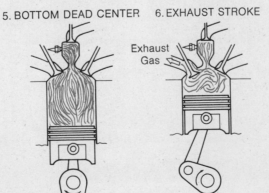

5. BOTTOM DEAD CENTER

6. EXHAUST STROKE
   - Exhaust Gas

The Decline in Auto Pollutants

Percentage reductions as compared to cars without emission controls (1962 and earlier), based on federal requirements for new cars in the model years shown.

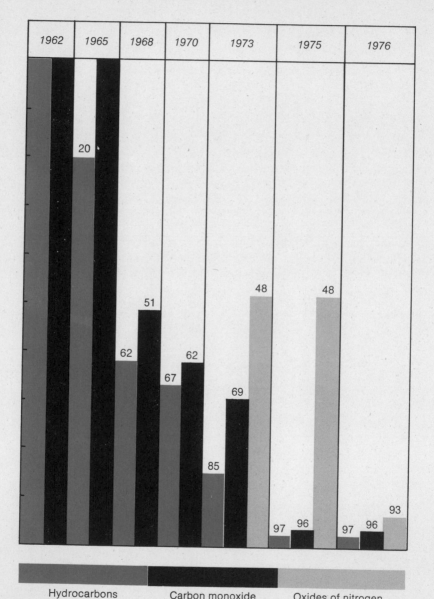

Source: Ford Motor Company

ufacturers have encountered are so great, they are beginning to turn their attention to other possible solutions. The Ford Motor Company, for example, together with the Thermo-Electron Corporation and EPA, is exploring the possibilities of the Rankine cycle engine. Essentially, this engine works on the same principles as the Stanley Steamer, where liquid is heated in a boiler, and the vapor is injected through valves into a reciprocating engine. Instead of using water, however, the Rankine engine would use trifluoroethanol, an organic fluid which will not freeze in winter. As for the Rankine's emissions: nitrogen oxide emissions are well below the 1976 standards and hydrocarbon and carbon monoxide emissions are well below the 1975 standards. General Motors Corporation also is developing a turbine engine that would use an organic fluid, and Chrysler Corporation is working on both turbine and piston steam engines.

Several automobile manufacturers are experimenting with gas turbine engines that might meet 1976 standards —if the problems of cost, durability, and performance are solved. More work is being done with diesel engines, including the development of a rotary diesel; the existing engines cannot meet the 1976 standards for nitrogen oxide emissions. And, of course, the idea of an electrically powered vehicle is being resurrected. These cars would be pollution free, but the problem of producing economical fuel cells that will have a reasonable mileage interval between recharges has not been solved.

Some or all of these developments may well be in the automobile world of the future. For the present, however, we have to deal with the familiar piston-driven internal combustion engine. Now that we know its inner workings and some of its problems, we need to know how and when to get it repaired and how to take care of it so that it will provide the maximum in dependability and performance.

Finding a good mechanic is an important aspect of being a car owner. The recommendations of satisfied customers provide the most reliable method for selecting a mechanic who will do repair work correctly.

13

The Mechanic: How to Deal With Him

The task of getting your car serviced or repaired can be one of life's most frustrating experiences. Arranging for service, taking your car to the shop, waiting for the car to be repaired, and then all too often returning the car to have the job done correctly can bring on a feeling of helpless rage. The cost in terms of your time and energy is high, to say nothing of your money.

Each year in the United States some $25 billion are spent on automobile repairs. There are about 60 million cars in this country that are between two and ten years old, which means that they are prime candidates for repair work. But often the cry is heard that repairs are unsatisfactory and prices too high. Frequently, the customer does not know the value of the job being done. He (or she) feels all alone in a no-man's land, not knowing what parts are needed or what parts are being supplied. The car owner is at the mercy of the mechanic. Even if he had the opportunity to shop around for parts, he would not know what parts to buy. Sometimes, he does not even know if the repair work is really necessary.

Motorists can deal with mechanics better if they know how their cars work, and become more knowledgeable about the business of automobile repairs.

Good mechanics in short supply

There are in the United States some 400,000 automobile repair facilities and about 800,000 auto mechanics. With only one mechanic for every 150 cars on the road, there is a need for an additional 125,000 to 200,000 properly trained mechanics. With more models, more options, and more style changes in the increasing number of cars using the roads, the need for able mechanics has never been greater.

The severe shortage of mechanics, due in part to noncompetitive fringe benefits and the poor image of the trade, has created one of the most serious consumer crises in the nation. Of the thousands of complaints received each month by the President's special assistant for consumer affairs, those about automobile service and repairs make up the largest single category, outnumbering by four to one all other complaints filed with this office. The complaints run the gamut from poor workmanship, the use of inferior parts and accessories, and long delays in completing repair work, to charges that parts paid for are not installed, and that some repairs are totally unnecessary.

The system is not in the consumer's favor. In the United States, beauticians, real estate agents, even barbers, are required by law to have a license. But the automobile repairman, whose incompetent work could cause the death of innocent people, is not required by any state to have a license. Although many auto repair shops require mechanics to serve an apprenticeship, any person can pick up a pair of pliers or a wrench and call himself a mechanic. He is not required to have any special kind of equipment. If he does a poor job and you refuse to pay him, he can, in most states, hold your car under a mechanic's lien until the dispute is settled. Even if he is found guilty of cheating you, few states have any kind of system in which the mechanic can be fined or suspended from carrying on his business.

Flat-rate manuals

Unfortunate, too, for the motorist is the fact that when determining prices, most of the country's automobile repair businesses use flat-rate manuals, which show the length of time a particular repair job is estimated to take—not the actual time it may take a mechanic to do the job.

One set of flat, or fixed, rates is determined by the automobile companies to enable them to set limits on their warranty work. But most automobile shops do not use the manufacturers' manuals for figuring the bulk of their work. They use other, privately published manuals which add more time to the allowances in the manufacturers' manuals and figure a longer time for each job.

When it comes to warranty work, the mechanics use the manufacturers' manuals—as required by the manufacturers. But for cash retail work, repairmen prefer the independent manuals—for the obvious reason that they get more for their services. Most experts say that a reasonably competent mechanic can beat the time in the independent flat-rate manuals by as much as 50 percent.

The original idea behind flat-rate manuals was to protect the motorist from paying an hourly rate to an incompetent mechanic. But today this system works against the customer more often than not. If the mechanic works on a commission basis, which most do, the more jobs he can squeeze into a day, the more money he can make. This means that the customer may get shoddy work because it was done in a hurry by someone seeking increased income.

Furthermore, even a competent mechanic cannot afford to spend the time necessary to make an adequate diagnosis. If he is to earn money, he must do the job as quickly as possible. Instead, then, of trying to find out what is wrong with your car before he replaces any parts, he may replace parts until he hits on the one that corrects the problem. And many times it is less time consuming under this system to install a new part than to repair the old part. These widespread practices—a direct result of the system—can sometimes be extremely costly to the consumer. To compound the problem, the service adviser and the parts manager often work on a commission basis, too, so that the more repairs and parts they sell, the more money they receive.

Finding a good repair shop

Recommendations of friends and acquaintances provide the best guidance when deciding where to take your car for service or repairs. You might visit a few of the recommended repair shops and find out how they determine prices. If you can locate a shop that charges by the hour and pays its mechanics a salary, you might do well to take your business there. In the final analysis though, you should pay more attention to recommendations than to prices. It is better to pay a higher price and have the job done correctly than to pay a lower price for unsatisfactory work that entails one or more return trips to the shop.

To help you in your search, you should know something about the different types of repair shops.

Authorized new-car dealerships. Don't expect to meet the mechanic face to face here. Be prepared to meet a service adviser, who will make a note of your problem and pass the information on to a mechanic. The service adviser will ask you to sign a repair order authorizing work to begin on your car and will call you with details of the work to be

The Rising Cost of Auto Repairs

The table compares the cost of replacing frequently damaged parts of a popular model 1967 car involved in an accident in 1967 and the 1972 model of the same car damaged in 1972. Although labor charges vary widely, the average charge climbed from about $6 an hour in 1967 to about $9 an hour in 1972.

1967

	Parts	Labor	
Bumper	$ 50.20	$28.80	
Grille	25.75	8.40	
Hood	74.00	12.60	
Front Fender	61.95	21.60	
Total	$211.90	$71.40	$283.30

1972

	Parts	Labor	
Bumper	$118.62	$ 59.40	
Grille	64.91	26.10	
Hood	124.53	19.80	
Front Fender	122.07	46.80	
Total	$430.13	$152.10	$582.23

Source: Insurance Information Institute

done as soon as a mechanic has checked the car. The main advantage of a new-car dealership is expertise in a particular line of cars and immediate access to an extensive parts inventory—the average major automobile dealer's stockroom may hold as many as 19,000 different parts for one full line of cars.

General repair garages. These shops are often patterned after the service departments of new-car dealerships. They, too, have service advisers who will write up the repair order. Because he is in direct competition with new-car dealers, the owner or manager may charge a little less for labor and pay his mechanics a little more to attract the best. This type of operation also is usually large enough to have an adequate supply of parts available.

Specialty shops. These shops specialize in selling or repairing a specific part of your car—brakes, mufflers, shock absorbers, front-end repairs, transmissions, or engines— and are usually franchised by a national company. An important factor here is not to be overly influenced by television commercials that sing the praises of these shops, most of which are operated by independent businessmen who have bought a nationally known name and reputation for a franchise fee. The shop is only as good as the man who runs it. Patronize a franchised garage for the same reasons you would any other repair shop—because friends and acquaintances have praised its services.

Department store auto repair centers. These centers specialize in tune-ups, front-end alignments, and the repair or replacement of brakes, mufflers, and shock absorbers. They also sell tires, batteries, and accessories. Often you can get good parts more cheaply here than you can elsewhere, but be careful not to buy more than you really need.

Small one- or two-man garages. These shops, which often have a run-down appearance, are hard to find now, and are among the few places where you actually meet the mechanic, who, incidentally, is likely to tell you quickly what is wrong with your car, how long it will take to fix it, and how much it will cost. These small shops usually offer good service at lower prices and can be excellent places to do business.

Gas stations. This is the most frequented type of repair shop. The skill of the mechanics ranges from the worst to the best. Sometimes first-class mechanics from new-car dealerships moonlight evenings and weekends at these stations, but most gas station mechanics are not likely to know how to do complicated repair work. Even so, these people help many motorists, since they are often available late at night and on weekends when large repair shops are closed.

Collision repair shops. These shops mainly do body and chassis repairs on automobiles damaged in accidents, so the bulk of their work is covered by insurance. This is the type of shop where you will often get used parts and experience undue delay in getting your car repaired. Sometimes an insurance adjuster will specify used parts; other times the shop is forced to install used parts because the insurance company will not pay enough to cover the cost of using new parts. Delays occur when the shop's sources of new parts (the new-car dealership) and of used parts (the junkyard) do not have the needed parts. Knowing that the parts are not immediately available, the shop may nevertheless promise quick repairs in order to get the job.

Other independent shops. These include economy paint shops and shops that repair such things as air conditioners or radios.

Diagnostic centers. These facilities use costly devices to analyze your car's ailments. Although they basically are a good idea, they often are connected to a garage where repair work is done and are just a gimmick to sell repairs.

Complaints analyzed
The Better Business Bureau of Metropolitan New York

recently did a study of the auto repair industry which is helpful in evaluating the performance of these different types of repair facilities. An analysis of the complaints the bureau received showed that:

• Allegations that work was charged for but not done or that the repairs were ineffective were leveled at virtually every type of shop and were the predominant complaint. The bureau found, however, that incompetency rather than dishonesty was the cause behind the complaints.

• Complaints that the shop sold unnecessary repairs were directed mainly toward those specialty shops that sell brakes, mufflers, shock absorbers, and front-end repairs. And of the few complaints involving misleading advertising, four out of six were directed toward these shops, which, incidentally, do the most advertising.

• The bulk of the complaints regarding the installation of used parts and undue delay in completing the work were directed toward collision repair shops, as were complaints regarding theft of the car, parts, or personal property.

• Five out of every six complaints were directed toward the independent shops, which were also the least anxious to respond to complaints. Says the bureau:

> Of the four out of every ten firms that failed to respond to the consumer complaint presented by the bureau, 42 percent were independent shops and 22 percent were authorized dealer shops, suggesting that there is greater indifference to consumer complaints on the part of the independent shops. General repair shops, collision shops, and gasoline stations combined accounted for 80 percent of the "no replies" within the independent group.
>
> While the consumer is not always right, the fact that the company will not acknowledge his complaint when coursed through an impartial third party convinces him that he is. There may be instances where lack of administrative help results in an occasional

failure of a business firm to respond, but the persist-
ent failure of a company to acknowledge complaints
can only lead to the conclusion that it is indifferent
and apathetic, reason indeed for consumer criticism of
the industry in general.

The bureau has found that most complaints about "unauthorized repairs" or "charging more than the estimate"
involve a communications gap between the customer and
the shop. In many of these cases, a mechanic discovers that
additional repairs are needed and makes them without first
calling the customer to get his approval. When the customer later receives a larger bill than he expected, he is
upset and resentful. To avoid having this happen to you,
tell the service adviser or mechanic to call and give you an
estimate if he finds that the car needs additional repairs.

How to protect yourself

Here are some other things you can do to promote a hap-
pier relationship between you and the repair shop:

• Always try to deal with a business in your own
neighborhood. Even if it is a little more expensive than
other places, you could be better off because it needs the
local goodwill to stay in business.

• Inquire of all repair shops how long they have been
in business in order to avoid fly-by-night operations.

• Do not be reluctant to ask anyone who is going to
work on your car about his experience and qualifications. If
you are not satisfied that the mechanic has sufficient experience, do not permit him to touch your car.

• Never accept a repair shop's word about what a job
will cost without making some investigation of your own to
determine if the cost is fair.

To find out how much a particular job should cost, you
have to know how much time the job takes and how much
the shop charges per hour for labor. To get an idea of the

time, check a current edition of either *Chilton's Labor Guide and Parts Manual* or *Motor's Mechanical Time and Parts Guide*. You might be able to find a copy of one of these flat-rate manuals in the reference section of your public library. If it does not have one, your local gas station will, and the manager would probably be willing to let you look at it.

In figuring the cost of a particular job, these manuals assume a certain hourly rate, but they also include conversion tables that enable you to find the total charge for a job at many different rates. If, then, you know the approximate time a job should take and the hourly rate a shop charges, you can easily determine whether a price quoted to you is reasonable or not. If the price quoted seems unreasonable, call other repair shops to obtain their estimates.

• When dealing with repair shops, ask whether you will be billed by the flat-rate manual or by the clock hour. You may find that you are paying a higher hourly rate by the clock method, but if the shop has good mechanics, you will probably pay less in the long run, and you may get a better job done.

• If you are ever charged what you consider to be an outrageous fee, one far in excess of the estimate, find out how the labor charge was figured. If it was based on a flat-rate book, ask for an hourly rate in an effort to have the charge reduced. Should this tactic fail, you could write to your local Better Business Bureau (BBB) or to the Federal Trade Commission in Washington, D.C., giving details of the case. As a last resort, you could take your case to a small claims court. If in the beginning, however, you make it clear to the repairmen that you will hold them to within 10 percent of the estimate, they will be less likely to exceed the estimate by a large amount.

• Before you pay your bill, read it carefully. Each area of work should be itemized with the name, number, and cost of every part, plus the labor charges. Make sure, then, that you have not been charged for something you did not authorize. If you find that you have, ask for an explanation of the charge.

• Choose the day that you take your car in for service. Avoid Mondays—too busy. Thursdays and Fridays are the slowest and thus the days when the service writer will have the most time to give you. Also watch the time of day. Mid-afternoons are less busy than mornings.

• Make a careful and complete list of all the things you want the mechanic to check or repair. Do not rely on your memory, because you are likely to forget something when you are distracted by all the activity at the shop. If your car has a specific problem, try to describe it accurately. If, for example, you say that the left wheel makes a squealing noise, this tells the mechanic one thing. If you describe it as a grinding noise, this tells him something else. In the first case, it may be a noisy grease seal and he may advise you to do nothing. In the second case, rivets on the brake shoes could be scoring the brake drums—a serious condition that should be corrected promptly. If you, on the other hand, merely tell him that there is an unusual noise in the front of the car and ask him to check it, he may have to spend hours looking for the problem. You can save his time and your money by observing carefully—what it sounds like or looks like, what it does, how often it does it, exactly when it does it—and then describing these symptoms in detail to the mechanic or the service adviser.

• After you have made a list of all the things you want checked or repaired, give a copy to the service adviser and ask him to sign it along with a note saying that these are the only items you want done. As an extra precaution, you may want to ask for a copy of the repair order before any work is done on the car to ensure that nothing is added to the order after you have signed it. Before signing the order, make sure that no unauthorized repairs have been added. The wording on the repair order should be specific.

If a mechanic is instructed to check something, ask that a notation be put next to the item requesting him to call you for your approval before any work is done. And never approve work by telephone without getting an estimate. If the estimate seems too high, tell the mechanic not to do the work. Then shop around; you may find that you can do better elsewhere.

• If your car fails a state inspection, bear in mind that you need not have the car repaired by the garage performing the inspection. Again, shop around until you find a place that is satisfactory to you.

• If you are involved in an accident and the police call a tow truck, be aware that you are not under any obligation to have the truck haul your car to its own body shop. The truck must take the car to the shop of your choice. Once in the shop, get a full estimate of all charges (plus any storage fees) before you authorize any work. As you would for any repair job, ask for an itemized bill.

• If a body and fender repairman offers to help you avoid paying the deductible on an insurance claim, take your business elsewhere. In such a shop, the chances are good that you will be cheated in some way—by the installation of inferior parts, for example.

• Ask your insurance company or agent—*not* a claims adjuster—for the names of body and fender shops they have dealt with and know to be honest and fair.

Tricks dishonest mechanics use

Honest mechanics are either competent or incompetent. While the latter can cause you severe headaches, they are at least honest. Your real troubles begin when you deal with the dishonest mechanic. This man knows a great deal about cars, and he also knows how to play on your fear for your safety. He will bilk you—and you will drive out of his shop feeling gratefully confident that he has saved your life.

Knowing certain facts about how your car works and how unscrupulous mechanics operate can save you grief—and money. It helps, too, if you can watch while the mechanic is working. Unfortunately, however, few motorists can afford to spend time standing around until a mechanic can begin work on their car. In addition, many shops have rules against customers going into the work area. But when you can watch, be sure to do so.

Two times when you can and should pay attention to what the mechanic is doing are when you call a tow truck to get your car started and when you pull into a station for gas. Many thousands of dollars would be saved annually if motorists were aware of how they can be cheated in these situations.

What can happen when you call the tow truck? First, the operator touches a responsive chord by enlisting your aid. He asks you to get into the car and try to start it while he works on the engine. When you obligingly get into the car you cannot see that the mechanic has not hooked up the battery cables properly. All looks well from inside the car —but all is far from well. As a result, your car will not start, and the mechanic is allowed to tow it into his shop, where he is free to cheat you for "repairs." Be sure, then, that he hooks up his cables to the metal terminals on your battery and not to the rubber cables. Then let *him* start the car.

Many things can happen when you do not pay attention in a gas station. For example:

• The mechanic can insert the dipstick so that it shows insufficient oil. Then, when you agree to add oil, he takes an empty oil can, inserts the pouring spout, and starts pouring. Frequently, he has to cover the bottom of the can with a grease rag so that you will not notice the other holes in the can. So you pay for oil that you did not need and did not get.

• The mechanic can conceal a razor blade between his

fingers and cut your fan belt so badly that it must be replaced immediately. When he shows it to you, you are aghast, and usually grateful that he discovered it in the nick of time.

• He can also slash or puncture your tires and disconnect wires while you are away from the car. Repairing the damage will make him a tidy profit.

When a mechanic in a gas station opens the hood of your car, remain beside him. And, if at all possible, do not leave your car unattended while you go to the rest room, especially if you are on a trip. If you are traveling alone, lock the hood if you can, and make it clear that you are aware of the condition of your tires before leaving the car unattended.

More unscrupulous practices

Here are additional common types of trickery you can protect yourself against:

Automatic transmission. If a mechanic removes the transmission pan, points to bits of metal in the transmission and says it needs overhauling, tell him to put the pan back on, and get away as quickly as possible. It is entirely normal to find a few metal particles in most transmissions.

According to the BBB, rebuilt or new transmissions are needed in only 5 percent of all transmission repairs. Even if you find your transmission leaking, you should not take this as a sign that it needs an overhaul. It may just need new seals, a job that will cost about $50—instead of the $250 or so that a rebuilt transmission will cost. Most transmissions can be repaired by doing a seal job, making linkage adjustments, or replacing the motor mounts or other components.

One expert believes that in 75 percent of all instances where cars have to be towed in because of transmission problems, all that is needed is a change of fluid and a new filter. To avoid this kind of inconvenience and the risk of being tricked into paying for a major overhaul, change the fluid and the filter at a maximum of every 24,000 miles.

If, however, you are convinced that your car does need a major transmission repair job, be sure that the work is guaranteed—in writing—for at least 90 days or 4,000 miles.

Battery. Many motorists spend money unnecessarily to buy new batteries because they do not know that their old batteries are still usable. The best way to determine whether or not a battery needs replacing is to load test it. This test requires the use of special equipment, which many mechanics have, and a lot of know-how, which many mechanics do not have. In most cases, then, you will have to rely on the hydrometer test. This test can tell you whether the battery needs replacing or whether it merely needs recharging—*if* you know how to interpret the readings properly.

A hydrometer is a glass tube with a rubber syringe bulb on one end to suck fluid into the tube and a rubber pickup tube on the other end. By drawing fluid from each battery cell in turn, you can read on a scale inside the glass tube the specific gravity of the electrolyte in that cell. Because its temperature can affect the specific gravity of a liquid, the readings must be temperature corrected. A good hydrometer will have a built-in thermometer which will give an automatically corrected reading. If the readings are not temperature corrected, they are meaningless.

The following charts indicate how the readings should be corrected for temperature and how to interpret the test results. Fully charged batteries will have corrected readings between 1.260 and 1.280; fully discharged batteries will have corrected readings as low as 1.110 to 1.130. Remember, though, that a battery can be fully discharged and still be good. It would merely need to be properly recharged. Only if there are more than 50 points between the corrected readings of the highest and the lowest cells

Hydrometer Corrections

Hydrometer Test

Temperature of electrolyte (degrees F.)	Add or subtract	Difference between highest and lowest cells	Specific gravity lowest cell (80°F.) corrected	Battery
160	+.032	Less than	More than	Good, and
150	+.028	50 points	1.230	satisfactorily
140	+.024			charged
130	+.020			
120	+.016	Less than	Less than	Good, but
110	+.012	50 points	1.230	needs
100	+.008			charging
90	+.004			
80	.000	More than	— —	Defective;
70	−.004	50 points		should be
60	−.008			replaced
50	−.012			
40	−.016			
30	−.020			
20	−.024			
10	−.028			
0	−.032			

should the battery be discarded and replaced. Otherwise, have the battery recharged.

A slow charge is best, but a fast charge is all right if it is done properly. If the mechanic gives your battery a fast charge, he must be sure that the electrolyte is at the proper level in each cell, that the cell vents are functioning properly, that he is using the correct charging rate for your battery, and, most importantly, that he makes provision for slowing or stopping the charge if the electrolyte reaches 125 degrees. The battery can be damaged if the electrolyte gets too hot.

Never use an additive to rejuvenate your battery. It will

cause the battery to perk up temporarily—but it will also have done irreparable damage, and you will have to replace the battery.

If the case of the battery has been split, cracked, or otherwise physically damaged beyond repair, the battery must be replaced.

Brakes. Be extremely wary about advertised low-priced brake jobs. A good brake relining job on all four wheels could cost $80 or more, but the safety good brakes provide is well worth the money.

Ask friends and acquaintances to recommend a good brake specialist. An incompetent or dishonest repairman could endanger your life by using inferior parts, or putting in brake linings of the wrong size, or failing to reattach the brake springs.

Carburetor. If gasoline is leaking near the carburetor, do not be in a hurry to buy a new or rebuilt one. The leak may be caused by loose fuel line connections or a sticking float valve.

Many worn-out carburetor parts can be replaced with new ones that come in a kit costing considerably less than a new or rebuilt carburetor. Always encourage the mechanic to *repair* the carburetor if he can.

Engine. Beware of advertisements that promise inexpensive repair jobs. These are often nothing more than ruses to get you into the shop. Once he has your car, the unscrupulous mechanic will call and tell you that your engine needs major repairs. Then he charges you—but does not do the work. He gets away with this by steam-cleaning and painting the engine so that it looks as though he overhauled it or installed a rebuilt one. He also makes the minor repairs that were actually needed.

And if you see "labor plus parts" advertised, don't assume that the price listed includes both labor and parts. This tricky wording may mean that the quoted price is for labor only, and the parts cost extra.

Shock absorbers. "There are probably more shock absorbers unnecessarily replaced on cars through the use of scare tactics than any other part on the car," one expert believes. One of the tactics used is to squirt oil on the shock absorbers while a car is on the lift for an oil change or a lubrication job.

Remember the tests that you can make to find out whether or not your shock absorbers are inadequate: Press down firmly on each corner of the car and let go. The car should rise to its normal position and then stop. If it continues to bounce, the shock absorber is probably defective. To test the front shocks, drive the car at about 5 mph and step lightly on the brake pedal several times. If the front end bounces, the shock absorbers probably should be replaced.

There is no way to anticipate exactly when the shock absorbers will need replacement. Much will depend on the kind of driving you do. But you should expect to replace original shock absorbers by a maximum of 24,000 miles.

Incidentally, when buying new shock absorbers, always replace them in pairs on the same end of the car; never buy just one.

Steering and suspension. This is another category in which people are actually grateful when they are cheated —because they saw with their own eyes the "dangerous" condition of their car. The parts and services most often oversold in this department are idler arms, ball joints, and front-end alignments.

The idler arm—part of the steering mechanism under the front end of the car—can actually go bad in as few as 20,000 miles, but it is still a grossly oversold item. The mechanic may try to sell you a new one when you complain of your steering wheel shimmying at high speeds. To correct the shimmy, try balancing the wheels first.

The mechanic might also turn one of the wheels outward and shake it. This will make the whole front end look as

How to Test Shock Absorbers

If the car sways excessively when making a tight turn, the shock absorbers are bad.

If the car continues to bounce for two or more times after you have bounced it three times by hand, the shock absorbers are bad.

If the tires are unevenly worn or have cupped or chopped treads, bad shock absorbers may be the cause.

though it is going to fall apart, and you are about to be
tricked into buying an idler arm or ball joints or anything
else the mechanic feels he can sell you. You should know
that only if the mechanic leaves the wheel pointing
straight ahead when he shakes it is he performing any kind
of a legitimate test for front-end looseness.

It is even more impressive when the mechanic pushes up
on the wheel, causing it to clunk dramatically. This "dangerous free play in the ball joints" he has just shown you
is in most cases inevitable—and completely normal—if he
jacks up the car improperly. Using this trick, he can sell
you new ball joints but *not* install them, and then jack up
the car properly so that you can see for yourself that there
is no longer any free play.

Ball joints are the part in the front end of a car that
need replacement least often; they are usually good for
75,000 to 100,000 miles. The only genuine test for them is
made with a ball-joint gauge. Excessive tire wear is the
usual symptom of worn ball joints. Ball-joint failures causing the wheel to come loose are extremely rare.

Another highly oversold item is a front-end alignment.
The problem here is that usually you do not get what you
pay for. All the mechanic has to do is squirt oil all over the
tie-rod sleeves and then scratch them with a wrench—being
careful not to turn anything. If he does this, no one—not
even a master mechanic—could tell just by looking whether
or not he actually aligned the front end. Your protection
against this trick is to know these facts:

• Most people think their cars need an alignment when
they really need new tires. This is why they are often told
that they need new tires as well as an alignment. It is the
new tires that correct the steering problem that prompted
the customer to seek help—not the alignment job he paid
for and did not get.

• The two things that indicate a need for an alignment
are: excessive wear on *only one side* of one or both of the

front tires; and if a car drifts left or goes straight when you take your hands off the wheel going 30 to 35 mph (the car should drift to the right because of the slope of the road).

• You do not knock the front end out of alignment every time you hit a hole or bump against the curb. These things are hard on tires—not on the alignment. A correct alignment will last from two to seven years.

• The only way you can tell whether an alignment was actually performed is through the use of an alignment gauge.

• A proper alignment will take from one to three hours to do and will cost between $10 and $35.

Water pump. This is another frequently oversold item. The first sign of water pump trouble is an engine that overheats. But overheating can be caused by a loose fan belt, a loose radiator hose clamp, a hole in the radiator hose, a defective radiator cap, or a clogged cooling system. These possibilities should be checked before you okay the installation of a new pump.

Improving auto repair standards

Some efforts are being made to correct the deficiencies of the auto repair industry.

A nationwide move is under way to elevate the status of the mechanic by licensing him, a move it is hoped will boost the quality of repair services. And some mechanics are being tested and certified—on a voluntary basis—by a new organization, the National Institute for Automotive Service Excellence. In 1972, this institute, in cooperation with the Educational Testing Service (ETS) in Princeton, New Jersey, gave the first examinations for mechanics ever given in this country. Of the 11,146 mechanics who took the four, three-hour written tests, some 75 percent passed at least one of the sections, and 12 percent, or 1,369 mechanics, passed all four.

Proof that mechanics are interested in the program—and the right to wear an armpatch attesting to their competence—is the fact that they came from all parts of the United States to take the tests, which required a $40 fee.

The program was established "to promote the highest standards of automotive services for the public good," said the sponsoring institute, which claims the support of every facet of the automotive service industry. The institute notes that consumers complain more about incompetent workmen than about dishonest practices.

It says, "Many, many good mechanics want recognition, stature, and better career opportunities. Certification will mean the mechanics servicing cars and light trucks are qualified and thoroughly know what they are doing. This certification program, with its scope and stature, will show the gap between a knowledgeable 'pro' and a handyman. And the time for 'Certified Mechanics' is now."

Attesting to this is a recent Automobile Club of Missouri study, which showed that of some 6,500 repairs recommended by its Saint Louis diagnostic center and performed by various shops, only 65 percent were done satisfactorily. An alarming 57 percent of the front-end work and 17 percent of the brake work was deemed unsatisfactory.

The serious implications for the motorist of poor repair work are revealed in a University of Indiana study. A review of some 1,000 accidents found mechanical defects to be a factor "in not less than 14 percent" of the cases. Leading the list were brake defects, a factor in 43 percent of these accidents.

Before anyone can take the ETS test, proof of at least two years of work experience must be shown. The examination is divided into four parts and covers: (1) engines and fuel induction, ignition, and exhaust systems; (2) manual and automatic transmissions, clutches, drive lines, and axles; (3) suspension, steering, and brake systems; and (4) starting and charging systems, electrical systems (body and chassis), and basic air-conditioning systems. Here are some typical questions in the test. See if you can answer all of them correctly.

1. A compression test revealed that one cylinder is excessively low. A cylinder leakage test indicated that there is excessive leakage. During the cylinder leakage test, air could be heard escaping through the tail pipe. These findings indicate which of the following?

    (A) broken piston rings
    (B) a faulty head gasket
    (C) a faulty exhaust gasket
    (D) an exhaust valve not seating

2. When interference-grinding valves and seats, if the valve seat is faced at 45°, then an acceptable angle for facing the valve would be:

    (A) 44°
    (B) 45°
    (C) 46°
    (D) none of these

3. All of the following can cause excessive oil consumption. During the first 20,000 miles of engine operation, however, the cause is *least* likely to be:

    (A) bad compression rings
    (B) a plugged PCV system
    (C) plugged cylinder-head return holes
    (D) improper valve guide clearance

If you knew the correct answers (1. D; 2. A; 3. A), you could probably qualify (if you have the practical experience) for certification as a master mechanic. But, as noted earlier, anyone can now practice as a mechanic with no training at all.

Licensing auto repair shops

In only two states, Connecticut and California, are auto repair shops themselves required to have a license. In Connecticut, where twelve full-time investigators look into complaints and inspect dealerships and repair shops to ensure that they employ competent mechanics, more than sixty licenses were suspended or revoked by the commissioner of motor vehicles in 1972.

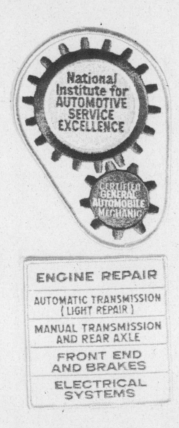

Shoulder patch worn by general automobile mechanics certified under the program developed by the National Institute for Automotive Service Excellence. Bars worn below the patch indicate all the tests in which the mechanic has achieved excellence.

In California, where a board composed of industry, consumer, and government representatives has the authority to suspend licenses or take dishonest garage owners to court, numerous complaints were immediately received from the victims of shoddy repair jobs when the state's Bureau of Automotive Repair began operations in 1972.

Many legislators would like to see all the states have such power. Realizing that the authority to license shops will enable the states to investigate complaints, United States Senator Vance Hartke of Indiana has proposed legislation that would license auto repair shops throughout the country. Some legislators advocate more extensive controls, including the licensing of mechanics and insurance adjusters and the quality-grading of replacement parts.

As for legislation that already has been passed, the most noteworthy is the 1972 Motor Vehicle Information and Cost Savings Act which, among other things, directs the secretary of transportation to undertake a study to determine how various automobile models rate in terms of damage susceptibility, withstanding crashes, and ease of diagnosis and repair. Another provision of the act requires that the secretary help set up five to ten demonstration auto diagnostic centers to provide data for establishing safety standards. It is believed that a nationwide network of such centers operated by people who do not do repair work, and thus have no vested interest in diagnostic test results, would be effective in decreasing the number of auto repair frauds.

Do-it-yourself repair centers

Because they are shocked by the high cost of auto repairs and tired of being swindled at gas stations and repair shops, many motorists are using the numerous do-it-yourself auto repair centers that have sprung up around the country. These shops make available to their customers the expert advice of a mechanic and the use of a large variety of tools that will enable them to do everything from changing spark plugs to installing new engines.

Some motorists are not even leaving their homes to have their cars repaired; repairmen come to them. Making "house calls," mechanics in vans containing all the up-to-date equipment necessary to fix common car ailments are finding an increasing demand for their services. The average minimum charge for driveway-to-driveway service is about $10.

Some mobile mechanics are setting up franchises, and the day may soon come when you will find it more convenient and less time consuming to leave your ailing auto where it is for repair instead of taking it to a garage.

CHAPTER 14

An Ounce of Prevention...

Costly repair bills and the inconvenience of not having the use of your car can be avoided by regularly investing a few dollars in its routine care. In this age of pollution-control devices, regular attention to your car is especially vital to its efficient performance as well as to our clean air.

The first thing you should do is to read your owner's manual from cover to cover and familiarize yourself with the information it contains. This is probably the most important book you will ever read about your particular car. It gives you instructions for operating the car, technical data, and most importantly, the maintenance schedule you should follow. Remember that as long as the car is under warranty, you must follow this schedule exactly or you may void the warranty. Further than this, many experts advise that for the best performance and longest service, you treat your car as though it were under warranty throughout its life.

While your car is under warranty, the warranty work must, of course, be done by an authorized dealer, but the routine maintenance can be handled by any mechanic you choose. If you do not go to a dealer, be sure that your mechanic uses only those lubricants and parts that will meet the manufacturer's specifications. Again, you may void the warranty if you do otherwise. It is a good idea, too, to get a receipt from the shop stating the types of materials used, and keep this information with your warranty in case any questions should arise when you are making a warranty claim.

In any event, you should set up and follow some schedule of regular maintenance with your mechanic. Here are some of the more important maintenance tips to remember:

Emission system

On most cars today, the emission system must be checked and adjusted and some parts replaced each 12,000 miles or twelve months, whichever comes first.

This maintenance service includes checking and possibly replacing the points and the condenser (unless your car has an electronic ignition system), the rotor, distributor cap, coil, spark plug wires, and spark plugs. On some cars, the idle speed and mixture will have been set at the factory; on others, they will have to be adjusted. The valve clearances must also be adjusted on some cars, but not on others. Then the ignition timing must be reset.

Depending on how your car is equipped, these various emission systems and their components must be checked and adjusted or replaced as necessary: the fuel vapor emission control system, the positive crankcase ventilation (PCV) valve and hoses, the evaporative emission canister, and the exhaust gas recirculation system.

Most motorists are familiar with the first part of this

procedure—the old-fashioned tune-up—which involves inspection and adjustment of the ignition system. While it was always important to have this done regularly on older cars, it is critically important to do these checks—as well as the emission system checks—on today's cars. Failure to do them will result not only in poor engine performance, but also ineffective emission control.

Although most manufacturers specify this service at 12,000 miles or twelve months, you may need to have it done earlier if you notice a drop in gasoline mileage, a loss of power, or difficulty in starting your car.

Oil

"How often should I change the oil?" is a question many motorists ask, but unfortunately, there is no simple answer. Some car manufacturers recommend that under normal operating conditions the oil be changed every 6,000 miles or four months, whichever comes first. Others recommend an oil change every 4,000 miles or three months, whichever comes first. Most agree, however, that the oil be changed more often under severe conditions—frequent driving on dusty roads or in sandy areas; mainly short-trip driving; extended periods of idling or low-speed operation, such as police, taxi, or door-to-door delivery service; or towing trailers for long distances. Check your owner's manual for the recommendations for your car. These recommendations represent maximum intervals, and you may void your warranty if you change the oil any later.

Some sources, recognizing that most motorists do not drive under ideal conditions, recommend changing the oil more frequently than most manufacturers do—especially in the cold months when water condensing in the oil pan can dilute the oil. The American Petroleum Institute (API) recommends changing the oil every 3,000 miles or three months, whichever comes first.

Why the need to change oil so often? Although oil itself

VIEW UNDER THE HOOD

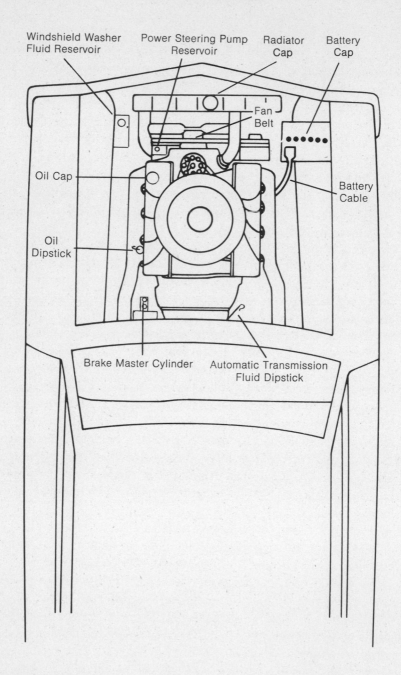

Windshield Washer Fluid Reservoir

Power Steering Pump Reservoir

Radiator Cap

Battery Cap

Fan Belt

Oil Cap

Battery Cable

Oil Dipstick

Brake Master Cylinder

Automatic Transmission Fluid Dipstick

never wears out, the important additives in the oil do. One of the by-products of combustion that can contaminate the oil is water. The combination of water and combustion gases forms acids which can cause corrosive wear and rusting. Metal particles from the engine and dirt coming through the air filter can also collect in the oil. These contaminants can cause serious engine damage. The refiners, then, add chemicals and detergents to the oil to neutralize the effects of the corrosive substances and to prevent the formation of sludge and varnish, which can clog the oil passages. When these additives become depleted, the oil must be drained and replaced with new oil.

All cars are equipped with oil filters to remove the engine-damaging abrasive materials that collect in the oil. When the filter becomes so clogged with contaminants that the oil cannot flow through, a bypass valve opens to permit unfiltered oil to reach the engine parts. For this reason, the oil filter must be replaced regularly. Most car manufacturers recommend a new filter every other oil change, although other experts feel that it is a worthwhile investment to replace the filter each time you change the oil.

Whatever oil maintenance schedule you follow, never exceed the intervals recommended by the car manufacturer. Changing the oil and oil filter frequently and regularly is one of the most important things you can do for your engine. It is certainly much cheaper in the long run than a ring or valve job.

When you change the oil, make sure that the car has first had a good run during which the engine has been operating at normal temperature. Oil flows more easily when it is hot, and so will drain faster. More important, however, is the fact that running the car for a while will assure the carry-off of impurities in the oil when it is drained. If you drain the oil when the engine is cold, these impurities may remain in the crankcase and mix with the new oil.

Pay attention, too, to the type of oil you put in the en-

Guide to SAE Viscosities of Motor Oil

Lowest Atmospheric Temperature Expected	Single-Viscosity Oils	Multiviscosity Oils
32° F.	20, 20W, 30	10W-30, 10W-40
0° F.	10W	10W-30, 10W-40
Below 0° F.	5W*	5W-20, 5W-30

*SAE 5W single-viscosity oils should not be used for sustained high-speed driving (above 60 mph).

Oil Classifications

New API Engine Service Classifications	Previous API Engine Service Classifications	Recommended Use
SA	ML	Straight mineral oil. Not suitable for use in late model automobile engines.
SB	MM	Inhibited oil. Provides minimum protection. Not suitable for use in late model automobile engines.
SC	MS	Meets warranty requirements for 1964 through 1967 passenger car engines.
SD	MS	Meets warranty requirements for 1968 through 1970 passenger car engines and certain 1971 models as specified in the owner's manual.
SE	None	Meets warranty requirements for certain 1971 and all 1972 and later model passenger car engines. Suitable for use in any automobile engine.

gine. For best performance, select an oil of the right service classification and viscosity.

The API has established a classification system that enables you to select engine oils according to their performance characteristics and whether they satisfy the changing warranty maintenance service requirements of the car manufacturers. A classification system of "SA" through "SE" is used for passenger cars. Any oil other than "SE" is not recommended for cars manufactured after 1971, and "SE" oil can be used in all automobile engines regardless of their age. The chart opposite will give you the service classifications that could also be used in older cars.

Oils also come in different weights, or viscosities. Viscosity, of course, denotes the ability of the oil to flow easily at different temperatures. Cold causes oil to thicken; heat causes it to thin out. Because it is vital to always keep a certain amount of oil between all of the moving parts in an engine, the oil must be neither too thick nor too thin.

The Society of Automotive Engineers (SAE) has developed a number system to denote the viscosity of an oil. The numbers they use, singly or in combination, are: 5W, 10W, 20W, 20, 30, 40, and 50. If the number has a "W" (for winter) with it, the oil is suitable for use in colder temperatures. If the number has no "W," the oil is suitable for use when temperatures are higher. Multiviscosity oils, which are assigned combination numbers, have relatively small changes in viscosity over a wide range of temperatures and thus are suitable for year-round use. A multiviscosity 10W-30 or 10W-40 oil satisfies most motorists. See the chart opposite and check your owner's manual for the recommendations for your car.

As for oil additives, most experts advise against using them routinely as preventive maintenance. The chemical balance in your regular motor oil could be upset by these additives, possibly resulting in damage to your car's engine. And you may void the warranty on your engine if you use an oil additive. Some experts say that these additives might be useful if your car already has serious internal engine problems, but even then you may be risking further engine damage. The only acceptable oil additive would be a viscosity additive if you are using a 40- or 50-weight oil. The best thing you can do for your engine to protect it from wear and damage is to use a quality oil made by a reputable company. These oils already contain all the additives your engine needs.

Lubrication

The chassis on most cars should be lubricated regularly. The main points that need lubrication are the upper and lower ball joints, the ends of the steering tie rods, the idler arm, and the front and rear universal joints.

Some of the newest cars are permanently lubricated at the factory and need no attention. Others are semipermanently lubricated, and the manufacturers recommend that the seals be checked every six months for damage and that the car be relubricated every 36,000 miles or thirty-six months, whichever comes first. Some experts recommend that if these cars have removable seals, grease fittings be installed so that the car can be lubricated more often. Do not, however, do this until your car is out of warranty; you will invalidate the warranty if you do.

Cars with regular grease fittings should be lubricated each time you get the oil changed. The cost of lubrication is a very small—and wise—investment in good performance.

Transmission fluid

Many drivers overlook this entirely or wait until it is too late and the transmission has to be replaced. The fluid in an automatic transmission should be checked every three months, or more often if you see any leaks beneath the transmission.

The fluid level should be checked with the engine at normal operating temperature and idling, the parking brake engaged, and the car on level ground. Put the gear selector in each gear momentarily, ending in "park" or "neutral." (Check your owner's manual for the proper gear.) Then remove the transmission dipstick, wipe it clean, and reinsert it. When you remove it again, check the fluid level. It should be at or slightly below the full mark—never above it. Add or drain fluid as necessary to bring it to the proper level.

When you are checking the level, also check the color and odor. If the fluid is very dark and has a strong odor, change the fluid and filter immediately and have the bands tightened. This condition can be caused by severe usage.

For specific instructions on when to change the fluid, even if no trouble signs appear, check your owner's manual. Generally, it is best to change the fluid at a maximum of 24,000 miles or twenty-four months, whichever comes first.

Some motorists assume that if the car does not move when it is in gear and the engine is running, extensive and expensive transmission work is required. This may be the case, but more often than not, all the car needs is a change of transmission fluid and a new filter.

If the transmission works, but slips intermittently, this may be a sign that the fluid level is low. This symptom may be accompanied by the engine racing on a turn or a hill. If the fluid level is all right, have the transmission bands checked, and adjusted if necessary.

Most manufacturers do not recommend the use of additives in the transmission.

The fluid level in a manual transmission should be checked each time the car is lubricated.

Filters

It is important to clean the carburetor air filter occasionally—at least every twelve months or 12,000 miles. This is how your car breathes, and if the filter is clogged with dirt

the fuel-air ratio is upset. This filter—as well as the fuel filter—will need to be replaced every year or two, depending
on the manufacturer's specifications.

Brakes

You should have the brake shoes, or linings, inspected
and the brakes adjusted, if necessary, every 12,000 miles or
once a year, whichever comes first. You can probably expect to replace the linings at about 24,000 miles.

When brake linings are replaced, you should treat them
gently for 400 to 600 miles so that they will seat properly.
Avoid panic stops and apply the brake pedal by pumping
instead of maintaining a constant pressure. Always allow
extra distance for stopping, because new brake shoes are
not as efficient as shoes that have been broken in.

Generally, there should be between one and a half to two
and a half inches of brake pedal travel. If there is more
than this, have the brakes inspected and adjusted.

If your brakes appear sluggish, it may be that sludge
formed by heat and moisture has collected in the brake
fluid. Since hydraulic brakes are a closed system, each time
the brakes are used the same fluid will be forced into the
wheel cylinders to stop the car. So brake fluid should be
checked each time you have the brakes inspected, and it
should be replaced if necessary. Check your owner's manual, however, for the precise intervals for your car.

Although leaks in the brake system are not common, they
do occur. The first sign of a leak will be a sinking brake
pedal. If this happens, look for oil stains on the inside of
each wheel, on the master brake cylinder, or around the
hoses and tubes leading to the wheels.

Also remember that the self-adjusting brake mechanism
will not be actuated if you rarely back up—which may be
the case if, for instance, you have a circular driveway. The
car has to be operated in reverse occasionally to adjust
the brakes. So, regardless of the type of driving you do,

make a point of backing up once in a while—in order to stop faster when you are driving forward.

Front wheel bearings

These should be cleaned, inspected, and repacked periodically. Check your owner's manual for the exact mileages, but generally this should be done at 12,000-mile intervals, or whenever you have the brakes inspected. These small parts are very important and do an enormous job in relation to their size—each bearing supports the entire weight of one-quarter of the car. It is most important that they be in good condition and properly lubricated. The rear bearings, incidentally, do not have to be serviced in this way. They are different types of bearings and are lubricated by grease in the differential.

Drive belts

You should occasionally try to determine if the drive belts are too loose—at least once a year or every 12,000 miles. In most cars there will be one to five belts which drive such accessories as the water pump, the power steering pump, the generator/alternator, and the air-conditioning compressor. To check the tension in the belts, press down firmly at the center of the longest span. In general, a belt should not deflect more than one-half inch, but this can vary on different cars, so check the specifications for your car. If any belts are too loose, have them tightened by your mechanic.

From time to time—when checking the oil or the battery, for instance—look closely at the belts. Make sure, first of all, that they are not cracked or frayed. Then examine their *inner surfaces* to see if any pieces have fallen away. Also check to see if the sides of the belts are extremely shiny or if any thread ends are showing. If any of these wear symptoms show on a belt, have it replaced immediately.

When a belt is replaced, it usually has to be readjusted

within 100 to 200 miles. Ask your mechanic if this needs to be done.

If you hear a squealing sound from under the hood, it may be caused by a loose or faulty belt.

Cooling System

Check your owner's manual for the proper water level setting, and check the level each time you get gasoline. If you need to add water, do not overfill the system, because the coolant will be lost through the overflow tube when the engine heat expands it.

Always keep at least 50-percent antifreeze solution in the system at all times. In the winter, this will protect down to −34 degrees F. Add more antifreeze according to the chart opposite if you need protection down to a lower freeze point.

Despite its name, antifreeze is just as important in hot weather as it is when the temperature plunges. It raises the boiling point of the coolant to about 265 degrees F.—53 degrees above the boiling point of water. This is particularly important with today's engines, which run so much hotter than the engines of ten years ago. Antifreeze also contains corrosion- and rust-inhibiting chemicals.

Be sure to have your mechanic check the degree of your antifreeze protection at least twice a year—at the beginning of the winter and summer seasons.

If your radiator leaks, an antileak compound could be quite effective. There is no trick to the familiar television commercial showing a man punching holes in a can of antileak antifreeze. The liquid does not flow out because little plastic particles plug the round holes, and they will do this in your radiator—if there are any little round holes in it. But the more common leaks are the "moving" kind, found along the seams, which open and close when the radiator expands and contracts as it heats and cools. Antileak antifreeze does not work well for seam leaks.

Protection Against Freezing

This table shows in degrees below 0°F. the protection you can expect from a given amount of antifreeze/coolant.

Cooling System Capacity, In quarts	Quarts of Antifreeze/Coolant					
	5	6	7	8	9	10
10	— 34	— 62				
11	— 23	— 47				
12	— 15	— 34	— 57			
13	— 9	— 25	— 45	— 66		
14	— 5	— 17	— 34	— 54		
15	0	— 12	— 26	— 43	— 62	
16		— 7	— 19	— 34	— 52	
17		— 4	— 14	— 27	— 42	— 58
18		0	— 10	— 21	— 34	— 50
19			— 7	— 16	— 28	— 42
20			— 3	— 12	— 22	— 34

If the label says an antifreeze is permanent, this does not mean it will last forever. It means that the product is for year-round use. In general, the cooling system should be drained, flushed, and refilled every twenty-four months. But sometimes the coolant will need changing more often than this, so it should be checked periodically. If it is ever discolored, faded, or filled with sediment, or if you see scales forming around the hoses, the system needs flushing.

Remember that draining and flushing are two different

matters. When the cooling system is drained, it is merely emptied of coolant. When it is flushed, the coolant is first drained and replaced with a cooling system cleaner and water. This solution is circulated through the cooling system by running the engine, and then is drained. This process is repeated until the liquid draining out of the engine is nearly colorless.

Cooling system hoses deteriorate. They should be inspected by your mechanic at least once a year and replaced if necessary.

If, in spite of the antifreeze, your engine overheats, do not touch the radiator cap until the engine temperature is normal. Then loosen the cap, but do not remove it—and take care to wear a glove or wrap the cap in a cloth as you slowly turn it to the left. Loosening the cap will allow the steam and pressure to escape so that you can later remove it safely.

Do not add cold water while the cooling system is overheated. When you do add water, keep the engine running at idle speed so that the cold and warm water will mix gradually. This will prevent a sudden temperature change, which could damage the engine.

If the radiator has boiled over for no apparent reason, consult your mechanic. The radiator cap may be rusted or it may not be rated at the correct pressure for your car, or the spring and gasket may be rusted or worn. By maintaining pressure in the cooling system, the cap prevents coolant from boiling at temperatures as high as 260 degrees. The cap should also be checked routinely at least once a year.

When the car is standing in bumper-to-bumper traffic and is in danger of overheating, do everything possible to take the load off the engine. Keep the gear selector in neutral to prevent overheating of the transmission. And not only should you turn off the air conditioner, you should, believe it or not, turn on the heater. This will dissipate the heat from the engine and lower the temperature of the coolant. Although you will feel very uncomfortable, your car will keep going when others will not.

As a final tip about the cooling system, be advised never to put cardboard in front of the radiator to hasten the warm-up time or to get more heat from the heater. This could cause the coolant to boil and dangerously overheat the engine. You should also remove any bugs and leaves that may be blocking the radiator or the air-conditioning condenser.

Battery

Each time you get gasoline, or once a week in the summer, check the fluid level in the battery. This is particularly important today when engines run so hot. Be sure that the amount of liquid in *each* of the cells is checked because they rarely consume the same amount of electrolyte, which is a solution of sulphuric acid and water. The liquid should be high enough to cover the battery plates at all times.

If you have to add water, distilled water is best, but tap water that does not have an extremely high mineral content will not harm the battery. If you want to be absolutely certain that the battery contains distilled water and not tap water, it is best to add the liquid yourself, because most service stations use tap water. If you add water yourself, be sure never to expose the battery to an open flame or electric spark, and do not allow battery fluid to touch your skin or eyes, or any fabrics or painted surfaces.

If you find that you have to add water frequently—more than once a month or even every hundred or so miles— there may be a malfunction in the charging system. If the battery is overcharging, the liquid will boil away. Have your mechanic check the voltage regulator, and if it is putting an excessive amount of voltage into the battery, have him adjust it, if possible, or replace it. (Electronic voltage regulators are not adjustable.)

Second only to changing the oil frequently, keeping the

battery clean is an excellent way to prevent car trouble.
Each time you get an emission tune-up, ask your mechanic
to clean all the dirt and corrosion off the posts, cable terminals, cables, carrier, and hold-down apparatus. Any heavy
buildup of corrosion can cause the battery to leak current
and slowly discharge, with the result that one day you
might not be able to start the car. After he has cleaned the
battery, the mechanic should check it for cracks and leaks,
tighten the cable terminal bolts, and make certain that the
battery is secure on its mount. He might want to check the
battery's charge, too, and recharge it if necessary. All of
this should be a routine tune-up procedure, but it is advisable to specify it to be sure that it is done.

Rustproofing

Frequent washings and waxings will help prevent rusting, but you may want to consider a professional rustproofing job. If you have your car rustproofed, you may save
hundreds of dollars in car wear—and perhaps even your
life. According to the *American Journal of Public Health,*
some 600 people die every year in the United States due to
poisonous carbon monoxide gas seeping into cars that the
occupants parked with the engine running. Declared the report: "Rust was a major factor in most cases, having
caused a combination of exhaust system defects plus holes
in the body. Even two-year-old cars had significant rust
damage."

Contrary to popular opinion, tarlike undercoating may
not be the best way to protect your car against rust. Because some types can actually trap moisture and plug
drainage and ventilation holes, undercoating could cause a
car to rust faster.

The cost of professional rustproofing may range as high
as $100. Since much of the worst kind of rust works from
the inside out, the rustproofer will drill small holes in all of
the car's boxed-in areas, such as doors, rocker panels, and

quarter panels, and then spray the interior surface with the antirust compound. Many rustproofing guarantees cover five years or 50,000 miles.

In searching for a good professional rustproofer, seek out those who rustproof fleets of commercial cars and trucks. Check with the manager of beverage delivery fleets where you live or with the maintenance manager of your area's utilities trucks.

Tires

The air in the tires should be checked periodically—preferably once a week. The sticker in your car will give you the proper pressures. Because gas station air towers are notoriously inaccurate and because tire pressures should be checked when the tires are cold—that is, when the car has been stationary for at least three hours—it is wise to invest in an inexpensive tire gauge. Then you can check the pressure before you go to get gas and either jot down on a sheet of paper or mark with your finger in the dust on the hubcap the number of pounds of air that need to be added to or released from each tire. If, for example, a tire is supposed to be inflated to 26 pounds, but has only 24 pounds in it, mark the tire "+2." Then when you get to the gas station, you can tell the attendant to increase the pressure in that tire by two pounds. Taking the trouble to keep your tires properly inflated will mean better, safer handling of your car and longer tire wear.

As you drive your car, the tires will heat up, which will cause the inflation pressures to increase. This is why you must check the pressures when the tires are cold. Do not think, however, that you should "bleed" the tires—let air out of them—after you have driven the car. Tires are designed to adjust to the increased pressures caused by driving, and the pressures will drop back to normal when the tires cool off.

Always maintain the proper differential in pressure in

Tires in Various Stages of Inflation
(Exaggerated Views)

UNDERINFLATION
Tire flexes and builds up excessive heat.
Tread life reduced and risk of sudden tire failure increased.

OVERINFLATION
Tire runs hard.
Tread life reduced and possibility of impact damage increased.

CORRECT INFLATION
Tire makes proper contact with the road.
Tread life and safety improved.

the front and rear tires to compensate for differences in weight distribution in the car. The only times when the pressures should be increased over those recommended by the manufacturer are when you will be carrying a heavy load, when you will be doing extensive turnpike driving, and when using snow tires. For turnpike driving, increase the pressure four pounds per square inch (psi) in each tire; for snow tires, increase the pressure four psi in these tires only.

Most manufacturers recommend that you rotate tires every 6,000 to 8,000 miles in the way shown on the next page.

Be sure to heed these words of caution, however:

• If you have different types of tires on the front and rear axles, rotate these tires on the same axle. Exception: If you have only two radial tires, do not rotate them.

• Never change radial tires from one side of the car to the other. You will have drastic handling problems if you do. These should be moved only from front to rear on the same side of the car if all four tires are radial tires.

• Do not rotate studded tires. When you take them off for the summer, mark the direction in which they have been rolling. Then remount them on the same wheels so that they roll in the same direction. The studs may work loose if they roll in the opposite direction.

• Although sudden tire failure is not as common as it once was, it is still a good idea to keep the best tires on the rear of the car if all of your tires do not have equal wear. A blowout in the rear could cause you to lose control of the car. Putting the best tires in the rear will give you better traction and handling, too.

Finally, have the balance of each tire checked before you remount it, and recheck the inflation pressures after the tires are back on the car. When you are rotating the tires is also a good time to check for unusual wear patterns and to look for and remove any stones, glass, or other foreign

How to Rotate Tires

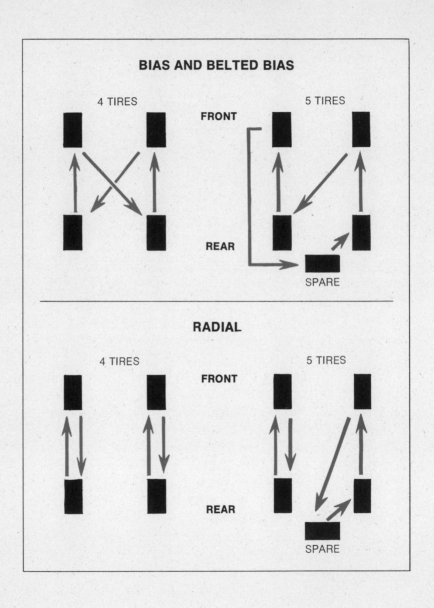

BIAS AND BELTED BIAS

4 TIRES   FRONT   5 TIRES

REAR   SPARE

RADIAL

4 TIRES   FRONT   5 TIRES

REAR   SPARE

material that may have become embedded in the tire treads.

Here are additional tips on tire care:

• Avoid constant high speeds. High speed generates heat, which accelerates tire wear and increases the risk of tire failure.

• Avoid hard, fast driving on bad roads, which can cause cuts, blowouts, and bruises.

• Avoid constant, abrupt braking. Decelerate before you reach a corner, not when you reach it.

• Avoid fast, "jackrabbit" starts. These drastically shorten the life of treads.

• Avoid hitting your tires against curbs when turning corners or parking. This can damage the sidewalls.

• Never use a tube in a tubeless tire as a substitute for a permanent repair. Only in an emergency should temporary repairs be made from the outside of the tire, such as externally applied plugs and aerosol sealants. Most industry-approved methods involve repairs made from the inside of the tire.

What not to do

Most of the maintenance advice so far falls under a "what to do" heading. Here are some important "don'ts":

• *Don't* race your engine after starting it. This is a waste of gasoline. It will pour gas through the carburetor and could cause excessive wear because the engine will be racing before the oil has had a chance to circulate through it.

• *Don't* race the engine just before turning off the ignition switch. This will not make the car easier to start the next time. It will prime the cylinders with raw gasoline that will wash off the protective oil film and hasten wear of the engine.

• *Don't* start your car with the radio, headlight, heater, or air conditioner on. This may strain the battery and shorten its life.

Causes of Rapid Tire Wear

UNDERINFLATION—*causes rapid wear on shoulders.*

EXTREME CORNERING—*causes tread shoulders to be worn smooth.*

INCORRECT CAMBER—*causes more wear on one side of tire.*

OVERINFLATION—*causes rapid wear on center of tread.*

FAULTY BRAKES OR INCORRECT WHEEL BALANCE—*causes irregular wear on tire.*

MISALIGNMENT—*causes feathered edge on tread.*

Causes of Invisible Injury to Tires

Hitting a curb or chuck hole can cause nonrepairable injury although there is no visible sign of damage.

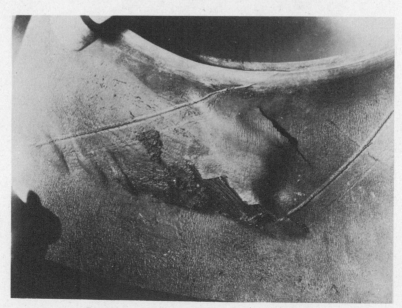

Driving on an extremely underinflated or flat tire causes interior damage which cannot be repaired.

• *Don't* repeatedly press the accelerator if the carburetor should flood. This will only worsen the flooding. Simply depress the accelerator pedal fully and hold it to the floor while you turn the ignition. This will permit more air to enter the engine and dissipate the gasoline.

• *Don't* apply your brakes while driving on bumps or while going across railroad crossings. The shock could go through the entire braking system and put undue strain on the various components.

• *Don't* shift into "park" position while the car is moving. This could snap off the lock pin in the transmission that prevents the rear wheels from moving and could mean an expensive transmission repair job.

• *Don't* apply the parking brakes during cold, wet weather—except on steep hills. If you put the gear selector in "park," this usually will be enough to prevent the car from rolling. If you apply the parking brakes and there is a sudden drop in temperature, the brake cable could freeze, making it impossible to move the car. If this should happen, run the engine for a while. This may generate enough heat in the muffler to thaw the brakes. If this does not work, get help. *Never* force the car.

• *Don't* overload the car's trunk. This could cause the vehicle to steer erratically and the front end to rise, thus aiming the headlights too high and cutting down on the visibility of the road.

• *Don't* continue to drive if you hear a rhythmic thumping noise from your tires. Such a noise on a normal stretch of road could indicate that there is a bulge in your tire and it may blow out. Stop the car as soon as you can do it safely, and check *both* sides of the tires for bulges or other signs of damage. If you see any damage, change to the spare.

• *Don't* continue to drive if the steering wheel turns more than two inches in either direction before the front wheels move. This could indicate dangerously worn steering parts. The condition should be checked immediately with a qualified mechanic.

• *Don't* continue to drive if the temperature light on the dashboard goes on. To prevent an overheated engine from causing expensive internal damage, stop the car as soon as possible and let the engine cool off.

• *Don't* overfill the crankcase with oil. When churned by the engine parts, the excessive oil will become foamy and could cause the hydraulic valve lifters to collapse. The best oil level is at the "full" mark on the dipstick. The oil should never be above or below the "full" mark.

Symptoms, possible causes and cures

Despite all the excellent care you give your car, unexpected troubles will develop occasionally. What we offer here and in Appendix VI are possible causes and cures—not definite diagnoses. But this information may be useful to you in describing your car's condition to your mechanic. It might save his time—and your money.

"Dieseling." This condition, in which the engine continues to run after you turn off the ignition, may be caused by a hot spot or glowing particle of carbon in the combustion chamber which provides enough heat to ignite the idle mixture from the carburetor. The problem can be worse in hot weather, and is aggravated by emission-control devices.

The condition may result from using gasoline of the wrong octane. Try using a higher octane gasoline. If this does not cure the problem, have your mechanic check the engine's idle speed and ignition timing as well as the carburetor throttle linkage. Also be sure the cooling system is not running too hot.

Difficult starting. Have your mechanic check the points, plugs, ignition coil, and the possibility of a short somewhere in the electrical system. Also have him check the PCV valve.

Engine runs unusually rough or stalls. This can be a problem on today's cars with complicated emission systems. Have your mechanic check the ignition system and timing, the fuel system, the exhaust gas recirculation system, the crankcase ventilation system, and the compression pressures in the cylinders.

In cold weather, when gas has trouble vaporizing, it is vital that you keep your car's battery, starter, and ignition system in top condition to avoid stalling. The automatic choke must also be in perfect working order.

Car stalls and will not start. If this happens in hot weather when you step on the gas pedal, it could be due to "vapor lock," caused by the expansion and boiling of gasoline from too much heat. Let the car cool before trying to start it again. This could take as long as one hour. To prevent this problem, make sure you are using the grade of fuel recommended for your car. Also ask your mechanic to make certain that the exhaust manifold heat riser valve is not stuck.

Stall-like sounds at high speeds. A poorly set carburetor could cause this condition. So could a dirty air filter, which could prevent the engine from getting the air it needs at high speeds.

Backfiring. Have the ignition system checked, including the wires, spark plugs, and points, and have the timing reset. If this does not cure it, get a compression check, which may reveal a sticking valve. Continued backfiring could cause engine damage, so it is important to correct the condition quickly.

Pinging noises on acceleration. This could be caused by gasoline of insufficient octane. Switch to a higher octane gasoline, and if that does not cure the problem, have the ignition timing checked.

Rapid hammering sound. If you hear this from the engine, you should suspect a loose crankshaft connecting rod or bearing, or insufficient oil or water. To avoid further damaging your engine, stop the car immediately and get the vehicle to a mechanic.

Increase in oil consumption. If oil mileage drops suddenly, look first for a leak—the engine may not be burning oil at all. A gradual increase in oil consumption could be caused by sustained high-speed driving, heavy start-and-stop operation, or overfilling the crankcase. If you cannot find the answer in any of these simple areas, have the engine checked for internal problems.

Exhaust smoke. If you see blue or black smoke from the exhaust, have your mechanic check the fuel and ignition systems and the engine cylinder compression pressures. White smoke could mean a bad modulator valve in the transmission or more serious internal engine problems. (Do not confuse this with steam caused by condensation of water in the exhaust gases.)

Rumbling sound under the rear. This probably is a sign that the muffler or tail pipe is rusting through. If the noise suddenly increases, look for holes in the exhaust system components or a break in its connections. Any defective parts should be replaced immediately; there is always the danger of poisonous carbon monoxide fumes seeping into the car.

Generator light on the dashboard. If this light comes on, it probably means trouble in the battery. Have the battery and its cables and connections checked immediately. A slipping drive belt also could be the cause of the difficulty, as could sticking alternator or generator brushes. Do not operate the car until you determine the source of the problem and correct it.

Leaks or seepages. If you notice spots of fluid beneath your car, get the vehicle up on a hoist and have the entire underside checked, including the fuel route, the oil pan, and the oil filter. Leaks also can be caused by faulty or loose hose connections, radiator corrosion, or deteriorated valve cover gaskets.

Gasoline odor. This could be caused by flooding the engine, but the odor should go away as soon as the excess gas is cleared out of the engine. If the odor persists, check the fuel system vent and the fuel tank cap. If these are not causing the problem, check the entire fuel system for leaks.

Steering wheel shimmies. Usually this is caused by wheels that are out of balance, out-of-round tires, or a bent wheel rim.

Car shakes at high speeds. The source of this trouble will most likely be in the wheels or the axles. However, shaking also may be caused by worn universal joints at each end of the drive shaft.

No air from air conditioner. Ask your mechanic or service station attendant to check the fuse and the blower switch. If both are all right, have the unit checked by an air-conditioning expert.

Pulling to one side when braking. This could be caused by improper air pressure in the tires. If the pressure is correct, have your mechanic check for fluid on the brake linings and also whether adjustment to the brake shoes is needed. If, however, these symptoms occur on a new car or on an old car with new brake linings, it may be that the linings have not seated properly. If the problem is not in the brake system, have the front-end alignment checked.

Brake pedal goes to the floor. This is known as brake fade, and is usually due to excessive heat buildup or loss of fluid. Do not drive the car; tell your mechanic to check the entire brake system.

Excessive brake pedal travel. Excessive travel—more than one and a half to two and a half inches—could indicate a leak in the system and could result in brake failure.

Spongy brake pedal. This is usually caused by air in the

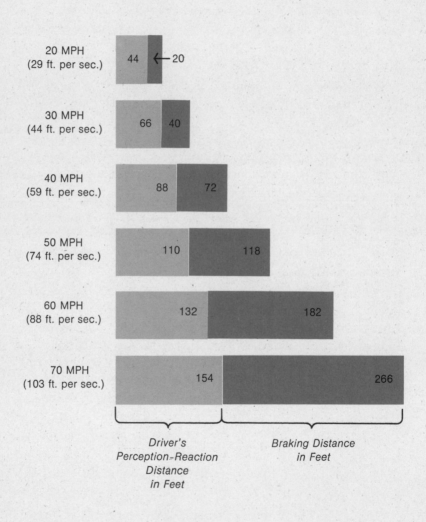

Stopping Distances on Dry Pavement for Cars With Good Brakes

20 MPH (29 ft. per sec.) — 44, ← 20

30 MPH (44 ft. per sec.) — 66, 40

40 MPH (59 ft. per sec.) — 88, 72

50 MPH (74 ft. per sec.) — 110, 118

60 MPH (88 ft. per sec.) — 132, 182

70 MPH (103 ft. per sec.) — 154, 266

Driver's Perception-Reaction Distance in Feet

Braking Distance in Feet

brake system, but it could be the result of something more serious. Have the air bled out of the hydraulic system and then have the entire braking system checked.

Brake pedal pulsation. This could come from an out-of-round drum, thickness variations in a disc brake rotor, or a loose support plate. As with other braking problems, this could lead to sudden, total brake failure. If at any time your brakes do not stop the car surely and in a straight line, if the pedal travels more than the acceptable distance or feels other than firm, or if steady pressure on the pedal causes it to fall all or most of the way to the floor, do not drive the car and have the braking system checked immediately.

Ignoring any of these warning signs can only lead to more serious problems, including higher repair bills later, increasingly poor performance, or even an accident. Follow the example of the experts and practice preventive maintenance. Your life could depend on it.

Appendix

State Motor Vehicle Registrations

	Autos	All Motor Vehicles	Percent Change in Motor Vehicle Registrations, 1971-1972
Alabama	1,746,518	2,227,293	6.4
Alaska	101,080	148,756	—1.3
Arizona	971,681	1,301,870	9.9
Arkansas	732,378	1,070,295	1.4
California	10,560,142	12,852,228	3.9
Colorado	1,271,366	1,679,702	8.5
Connecticut	1,695,458	1,860,385	3.9
Delaware	269,676	322,971	2.0
Florida	4,132,336	4,835,986	6.7
Georgia	2,371,746	2,959,454	7.5
Hawaii	392,458	447,409	5.0
Idaho	381,854	549,834	8.0
Illinois	4,903,960	5,643,853	4.2
Indiana	2,306,789	2,908,543	1.4
Iowa	1,449,638	1,917,075	4.1
Kansas	1,220,430	1,691,501	5.8
Kentucky	1,515,550	1,967,620	5.8
Louisiana	1,518,246	1,942,263	6.0
Maine	450,861	564,782	5.2
Maryland	1,831,917	2,130,458	6.4
Massachusetts	2,543,081	2,821,596	4.5
Michigan	4,265,042	5,010,537	5.7
Minnesota	1,871,521	2,368,127	3.3
Mississippi	919,967	1,249,152	6.2
Missouri	2,026,903	2,618,164	4.8
Montana	374,690	584,116	14.4
Nebraska	777,619	1,080,885	4.7
Nevada	297,824	399,046	7.1

	Autos	All Motor Vehicles	Percent Change in Motor Vehicle Registrations, 1971-1972
New Hampshire	367,856	436,158	7.2
New Jersey	3,463,443	3,858,631	3.2
New Mexico	499,693	710,765	7.5
New York	6,359,081	7,118,566	3.3
North Carolina	2,530,456	3,219,776	7.3
North Dakota	289,648	463,622	4.4
Ohio	5,486,751	6,224,278	3.0
Oklahoma	1,326,180	1,887,210	5.5
Oregon	1,227,057	1,496,115	4.5
Pennsylvania	5,460,277	6,311,330	4.8
Rhode Island	475,251	536,284	5.4
South Carolina	1,202,961	1,497,389	8.3
South Dakota	311,876	462,613	4.7
Tennessee	1,819,121	2,293,635	7.4
Texas	5,553,182	7,315,711	4.7
Utah	538,479	740,507	4.1
Vermont	214,993	261,296	10.2
Virginia	2,167,217	2,602,773	8.0
Washington	1,702,412	2,242,060	3.6
West Virginia	668,740	873,606	5.7
Wisconsin	1,970,777	2,378,836	6.7
Wyoming	173,572	273,608	6.3
District of Columbia	239,059	259,492	—0.2
Total	96,948,813	118,618,162	5.0

Source: Federal Highway Administration, 1972 estimates

Taxes Paid by Highway Users

(Millions of Dollars)

State	Total	Federal Taxes			State Taxes	
		Motor Fuel, Oil, and Vehicle Use	Autos, Trucks, Buses, and Trailers	Parts, Accessories, Tires, Tubes, and Tread Rubber	Motor Fuel	Registration Fees and Other
Alabama	$ 286	$ 71	$ 39	$ 12	$ 123	$ 41
Alaska	22	4	3	1	8	6
Arizona	180	43	25	7	73	32
Arkansas	188	43	24	7	80	34
California	1,946	398	244	69	685	550
Colorado	202	49	32	8	79	34
Connecticut	260	52	33	9	117	49
Delaware	55	12	8	2	20	13
Dist. of Columbia	52	10	7	2	18	15
Florida	682	142	102	24	270	144
Georgia	413	107	61	18	185	42
Hawaii	46	10	9	2	13	12
Idaho	73	17	10	3	28	15
Illinois	980	194	144	33	342	267
Indiana	497	111	66	19	219	82
Iowa	303	60	34	10	108	91
Kansas	216	52	29	9	88	38
Kentucky	294	65	33	11	112	73
Louisiana	271	66	42	11	127	25
Maine	94	21	12	4	43	14
Maryland	368	69	51	12	122	114
Massachusetts	380	92	61	16	154	57
Michigan	790	175	146	31	287	151
Minnesota	341	77	47	13	131	73
Mississippi	196	47	23	8	92	26
Missouri	382	103	58	18	125	78

State	Total	Federal Taxes			State Taxes	
		Motor Fuel, Oil, and Vehicle Use	Autos, Trucks, Buses, and Trailers	Parts, Accessories, Tires, Tubes, and Tread Rubber	Motor Fuel	Registration Fees and Other
Montana	78	18	10	3	32	15
Nebraska	158	34	20	6	70	28
Nevada	57	14	8	2	22	11
New Hampshire	73	14	12	3	29	15
New Jersey	591	126	86	22	219	138
New Mexico	113	27	14	5	45	22
New York	1,142	236	190	40	407	269
North Carolina	507	108	57	18	240	84
North Dakota	63	13	8	2	22	18
Ohio	892	201	130	34	346	181
Oklahoma	280	62	37	10	98	73
Oregon	212	48	30	8	74	52
Pennsylvania	910	194	130	33	381	172
Rhode Island	71	15	9	2	30	15
South Carolina	210	54	28	9	99	20
South Dakota	67	15	8	2	25	17
Tennessee	378	82	48	14	166	68
Texas	1,144	269	151	45	336	343
Utah	91	23	13	4	39	12
Vermont	54	9	7	2	19	17
Virginia	431	94	57	16	164	100
Washington	369	66	34	11	145	113
West Virginia	166	31	22	5	66	42
Wisconsin	362	81	49	14	141	77
Wyoming	50	11	6	2	20	11
TOTAL	$17,986	$3,935	$2,507	$671	$6,884	$3,989

Source: Federal Highway Administration, 1971 estimates

Estimated Cost of Operating
A Standard-Size 1972 Model Automobile [1]

(Total costs in dollars; costs per mile in cents)

Item	First Year (14,500 miles)		Second Year (13,000 miles)	
	Total Cost	Cost per Mile	Total Cost	Cost per Mile
Costs excluding taxes:				
Depreciation	1,226.00	8.46	900.00	6.92
Repairs and maintenance	81.84	.56	115.37	.89
Replacement tires	17.90	.12	16.05	.12
Accessories	3.21	.02	3.08	.02
Gasoline	286.75	1.98	257.16	1.98
Oil	11.25	.08	11.25	.09
Insurance [2]	164.00	1.13	156.00	1.20
Garaging, parking, tolls, etc.	208.36	1.44	199.22	1.53
Total	1,999.31	13.79	1,658.13	12.75
Taxes and fees:				
State:				
Gasoline	74.62	.51	66.92	.52
Registration	30.00	.21	30.00	.23
Titling	177.15	1.22	—	—
Subtotal	281.77	1.94	96.92	.75
Federal:				
Gasoline	42.64	.30	38.24	.30
Oil [3]	.22	—	.22	—
Tires	1.38	.01	1.24	.01
Subtotal	44.24	.31	39.70	.31
Total taxes	326.01	2.25	136.62	1.06
Total of all costs	2,325.32	16.04	1,794.75	13.81

Item	Third Year (11,500 miles)		Fourth Year 10,000 miles)		Fifth Year (9,900 miles)	
	Total Cost	Cost per Mile	Total Cost	Cost per Mile	Total Cost	Cost per Mile
Costs excluding taxes:						
Depreciation	675.00	5.87	500.00	5.00	376.00	3.80
Repairs and maintenance	242.65	2.11	296.09	2.96	275.54	2.78
Replacement tires	23.72	.21	44.40	.44	43.95	.44
Accessories	2.96	.02	2.83	.03	2.82	.03
Gasoline	227.58	1.98	197.72	1.98	195.83	1.98
Oil	12.00	.10	12.00	.12	12.75	.13
Insurance [2]	156.00	1.36	147.00	1.47	147.00	1.49
Garaging, parking, tolls, etc.	190.08	1.65	180.94	1.81	180.33	1.82
Total	1,529.99	13.30	1,380.98	13.81	1,234.22	12.47
Taxes and fees:						
State:						
Gasoline	59.22	.52	51.45	.51	50.96	.52
Registration	30.00	.26	30.00	.30	30.00	.30
Titling	—	—	—	—	—	—
Subtotal	89.22	.78	81.45	.81	80.96	.82
Federal:						
Gasoline	33.84	.29	29.40	.30	29.12	.30
Oil [3]	.24	—	.24	—	.26	—
Tires	1.82	.02	3.42	.03	3.39	.03
Subtotal	35.90	.31	33.06	.33	32.77	.33
Total taxes	125.12	1.09	114.51	1.14	113.73	1.15
Total of all costs	1,655.11	14.39	1,495.49	14.95	1,347.95	13.62

[1] This estimate covers the total costs of a fully equipped, medium-priced, standard-size, 4-door sedan, purchased for $4,379, operated 100,000 miles over a 10-year period, then scrapped. Baltimore area prices, considered to be in the middle range, were used.

[2] Insurance rates are for the Baltimore suburbs.

[3] Where costs per mile were computed to be less than 1/20 cent, a dash (—) appears in the column.

Estimated Cost of Operating
A Standard-Size 1972 Model Automobile [1]

(Total costs in dollars; costs per mile in cents)

Item	Sixth Year (9,900 miles)		Seventh Year (9,500 miles)		Eighth Year (8,500 miles)	
	Total Cost	Cost per Mile	Total Cost	Cost per Mile	Total Cost	Cost per Mile
Costs excluding taxes:						
Depreciation	259.00	2.61	189.00	1.99	121.00	1.42
Repairs and maintenance	292.54	2.95	397.56	4.19	171.82	2.02
Replacement tires	45.44	.46	50.69	.53	62.79	.74
Accessories	8.57	.09	8.30	.09	7.65	.09
Gasoline	195.83	1.98	188.03	1.98	168.13	1.98
Oil	13.50	.14	13.50	.14	13.50	.16
Insurance [2]	116.00	1.17	116.00	1.22	116.00	1.37
Garaging, parking, tolls, etc.	180.33	1.82	177.89	1.87	171.80	2.02
Total	1,111.21	11.22	1,140.97	12.01	832.69	9.80
Taxes and fees:						
State:						
Gasoline	50.96	.52	48.93	.51	43.75	.52
Registration	30.00	.30	30.00	.32	30.00	.35
Titling	—	—	—	—	—	—
Subtotal	80.96	.82	78.93	.83	73.75	.87
Federal:						
Gasoline	29.12	.29	27.96	.30	25.00	.29
Oil [3]	.27	—	.27	—	.27	—
Tires	3.50	.04	3.90	.04	4.84	.06
Subtotal	32.89	.33	32.13	.34	30.11	.35
Total taxes	113.85	1.15	111.06	1.17	103.86	1.22
Total of all costs	1,225.06	12.37	1,252.03	13.18	936.55	11.02

Item	Ninth Year (7,500 miles)		Tenth Year (5,700 miles)		Totals and Averages for 10 Years (100,000 miles)	
	Total Cost	Cost per Mile	Total Cost	Cost per Mile	Total Cost	Cost per Mile
Costs excluding taxes:						
Depreciation	85.00	1.13	48.00	.84	4,379.00	4.38
Repairs and maintenance	244.33	3.26	29.17	.51	2,146.91	2.14
Replacement tires	52.80	.70	42.11	.74	399.85	.40
Accessories	6.97	.09	5.79	.10	52.18	.05
Gasoline	148.22	1.98	112.71	1.98	1,977.96	1.98
Oil	12.00	.16	6.75	.12	118.50	.12
Insurance [2]	116.00	1.55	116.00	2.04	1,350.00	1.35
Garaging, parking, tolls, etc.	165.71	2.21	154.74	2.71	1,809.40	1.81
Total	831.03	11.08	515.27	9.04	12,233.80	12.23
Taxes and fees:						
State:						
Gasoline	38.57	.52	29.33	.51	514.71	.51
Registration	30.00	.40	30.00	.53	300.00	.30
Titling	—	—	—	—	177.15	.18
Subtotal	68.57	.92	59.33	1.04	991.86	.99
Federal:						
Gasoline	22.04	.29	16.76	.29	294.12	.30
Oil [3]	.24	—	.14	—	2.37	—
Tires	4.07	.06	3.24	.06	30.80	.03
Subtotal	26.35	.35	20.14	.35	327.29	.33
Total taxes	94.92	1.27	79.47	1.39	1,319.15	1.32
Total of all costs	925.95	12.35	594.74	10.43	13,552.95	13.55

[1] This estimate covers the total costs of a fully equipped, medium-priced, standard-size, 4-door sedan, purchased for $4,379, operated 100,000 miles over a 10-year period, then scrapped. Baltimore area prices, considered to be in the middle range, were used.

[2] Insurance rates are for the Baltimore suburbs.

[3] Where costs per mile were computed to be less than 1/20 cent, a dash (—) appears in the column.

Estimated Cost of Operating
A Compact-Size 1972 Model Automobile [1]

(Total costs in dollars; costs per mile in cents)

Item	First Year (14,500 miles)		Second Year (13,000 miles)	
	Total Cost	Cost per Mile	Total Cost	Cost per Mile
Costs excluding taxes:				
Depreciation	674.00	4.65	519.00	3.99
Repairs and maintenance	79.41	.55	107.14	.83
Replacement tires	15.30	.11	13.71	.11
Accessories	3.21	.02	3.08	.02
Gasoline	244.25	1.68	218.97	1.69
Oil	10.50	.07	10.50	.08
Insurance	155.00	1.07	147.00	1.13
Garaging, parking, tolls, etc.	208.36	1.44	199.22	1.53
Total	1,390.03	9.59	1,218.62	9.38
Taxes and fees:				
State:				
Gasoline	63.56	.44	56.98	.44
Registration	20.00	.14	20.00	.15
Titling	109.86	.75	—	—
Subtotal	193.42	1.33	76.98	.59
Federal:				
Gasoline	36.32	.25	32.56	.25
Oil [2]	.21	—	.21	—
Tires	1.17	.01	1.05	.01
Subtotal	37.70	.26	33.82	.26
Total taxes	231.12	1.59	110.80	.85
Total of all costs	1,621.15	11.18	1,329.42	10.23

Item	Third Year (11,500 miles)		Fourth Year (10,000 miles)		Fifth Year (9,900 miles)	
	Total Cost	Cost per Mile	Total Cost	Cost per Mile	Total Cost	Cost per Mile
Costs excluding taxes:						
Depreciation	394.00	3.42	305.00	3.05	243.00	2.46
Repairs and maintenance	170.61	1.48	218.90	2.19	240.27	2.43
Replacement tires	12.13	.11	34.27	.34	33.93	.34
Accessories	2.96	.03	2.83	.03	2.82	.03
Gasoline	193.68	1.69	168.39	1.68	166.78	1.68
Oil	11.25	.10	11.25	.11	12.75	.13
Insurance	147.00	1.28	140.00	1.40	140.00	1.41
Garaging, parking, tolls, etc.	190.08	1.65	180.94	1.81	180.33	1.82
Total	1,121.71	9.76	1,061.58	10.61	1,019.88	10.30
Taxes and fees:						
State:						
Gasoline	50.40	.44	43.82	.44	43.40	.44
Registration	20.00	.17	20.00	.20	20.00	.20
Titling	—	—	—	—	—	—
Subtotal	70.40	.61	63.82	.64	63.40	.64
Federal:						
Gasoline	28.80	.25	25.04	.25	24.80	.25
Oil [2]	.22	—	.22	—	.26	—
Tires	.92	.01	2.61	.03	2.59	.03
Subtotal	29.94	.26	27.87	.28	27.65	.28
Total taxes	100.34	.87	91.69	.92	91.05	.92
Total of all costs	1,222.05	10.63	1,153.27	11.53	1,110.93	11.22

[1] This estimate covers the total costs of a medium-priced, compact-size, 2-door sedan, purchased for $2,696, operated 100,000 miles over a 10-year period, then scrapped. Baltimore area prices, considered to be in the middle range, were used.

[2] Where costs per mile were computed to be less than 1/20 cent, a dash (—) appears in the column.

Estimated Cost of Operating
A Compact-Size 1972 Model Automobile [1]

(Total costs in dollars; costs per mile in cents)

Item	Sixth Year (9,900 miles)		Seventh Year (9,500 miles)		Eighth Year (8,500 miles)	
	Total Cost	Cost per Mile	Total Cost	Cost per Mile	Total Cost	Cost per Mile
Costs excluding taxes:						
Depreciation	194.00	1.96	152.00	1.60	103.00	1.21
Repairs and maintenance	268.81	2.72	412.04	4.34	177.27	2.09
Replacement tires	38.45	.39	36.89	.39	61.53	.72
Accessories	8.57	.09	8.30	.09	7.65	.09
Gasoline	166.78	1.68	160.06	1.69	143.11	1.69
Oil	12.75	.13	12.75	.13	12.75	.15
Insurance	114.00	1.15	114.00	1.20	114.00	1.34
Garaging, parking, tolls, etc.	180.33	1.82	177.89	1.87	171.80	2.02
Total	983.69	9.94	1,073.93	11.31	791.11	9.31
Taxes and fees:						
State:						
Gasoline	43.40	.44	41.65	.44	37.24	.44
Registration	20.00	.20	20.00	.21	20.00	.23
Titling	—	—	—	—	—	—
Subtotal	63.40	.64	61.65	.65	57.24	.67
Federal:						
Gasoline	24.80	.25	23.80	.25	21.28	.25
Oil [2]	.26	—	.26	—	.26	—
Tires	2.93	.03	2.81	.03	4.69	.06
Subtotal	27.99	.28	26.87	.28	26.23	.31
Total taxes	91.39	.92	88.52	.93	83.47	.98
Total of all costs	1,075.08	10.86	1,162.45	12.24	874.58	10.29

Item	Ninth Year (7,500 miles)		Tenth Year (5,700 miles)		Totals and Averages for 10 Years (100,000 miles)	
	Total Cost	Cost per Mile	Total Cost	Cost Per Mile	Total Cost	Cost per Mile
Cost excluding taxes:						
Depreciation	73.00	.97	39.00	.68	2,696.00	2.70
Repairs and maintenance	78.95	1.05	31.10	.55	1,784.50	1.79
Replacement tires	54.29	.73	41.27	.72	341.77	.34
Accessories	6.97	.09	5.79	.10	52.18	.05
Gasoline	126.43	1.69	96.03	1.68	1,684.48	1.68
Oil	12.00	.16	6.75	.12	113.25	.11
Insurance	114.00	1.52	114.00	2.00	1,299.00	1.30
Garaging, parking, tolls, etc.	165.71	2.21	154.74	2.72	1,809.40	1.81
Total	631.35	8.42	488.68	8.57	9,780.58	9.78
Taxes and fees:						
State:						
Gasoline	32.90	.44	24.99	.44	438.34	.44
Registration	20.00	.26	20.00	.35	200.00	.20
Titling	—	—	—	—	109.86	.11
Subtotal	52.90	.70	44.99	.79	748.20	.75
Federal:						
Gasoline	18.80	.25	14.28	.25	250.48	.25
Oil [2]	.24	—	.13	—	2.27	—
Tires	4.15	.06	3.15	.06	26.07	.03
Subtotal	23.19	.31	17.56	.31	278.82	.28
Total taxes	76.09	1.01	62.55	1.10	1,027.02	1.03
Total of all costs	707.44	9.43	551.23	9.67	10,807.60	10.81

[1] This estimate covers the total costs of a medium-priced, compact-size, 2-door sedan, purchased for $2,696, operated 100,000 miles over a 10-year period, then scrapped. Baltimore area prices, considered to be in the middle range, were used.
[2] Where costs per mile were computed to be less than 1/20 cent, a dash (—) appears in the column.

Estimated Cost of Operating
A Subcompact-Size 1972 Model Automobile [1]

(Total costs in dollars; costs per mile in cents)

Item	First Year (14,500 miles)		Second Year (13,000 miles)		Totals and Averages for 10 Years (100,000 miles)	
	Total Cost	Cost Per Mile	Total Cost	Cost Per Mile	Total Cost	Cost Per Mile
Costs excluding taxes:						
Depreciation	310.00	2.14	285.00	2.19	2,064.00	2.07
Repairs and maintenance	76.15	.53	114.59	.88	1,775.71	1.78
Replacement tires	13.98	.10	12.53	.10	312.29	.31
Accessories	3.21	.02	3.08	.02	52.18	.05
Gasoline	181.84	1.25	163.02	1.25	1,255.15	1.25
Oil	10.50	.07	9.75	.08	103.50	.10
Insurance	145.00	1.00	140.00	1.08	1,251.00	1.25
Garaging, parking, tolls, etc.	208.36	1.44	199.22	1.53	1,809.40	1.81
Total	949.04	6.55	927.19	7.13	8,623.23	8.62
Taxes and fees:						
State:						
Gasoline	47.32	.33	42.42	.33	326.62	.33
Registration	20.00	.14	20.00	.15	200.00	.20
Titling	84.57	.58	—	—	84.57	.08
Subtotal	151.89	1.05	62.42	.48	611.19	.61
Federal:						
Gasoline	27.04	.18	24.24	.19	186.64	.19
Oil [2]	.21	—	.19	—	2.07	—
Tires	.94	.01	.84	.01	20.90	.02
Subtotal	28.19	.19	25.27	.20	209.61	.21
Total taxes	180.08	1.24	87.69	.68	820.80	.82
Total of all costs	1,129.12	7.79	1,014.88	7.81	9,444.03	9.44

[1] This estimate covers the total costs of a low-priced, subcompact-size, 2-door sedan, purchased for $2,064, operated 100,000 miles over a 10-year period, then scrapped. Baltimore area prices, considered to be in the middle range, were used. Since cost data for American-made subcompacts does not exist past the second year, only the first, second, and estimated 10-year totals are shown.

[2] Where costs per mile were computed to be less than 1/20 cent, a dash (—) appears in the column.

Source: U.S. Department of Transportation

Tire Manufacturer Code Letters

Some manufacturers market their tires under a number of different names. This list provides the Department of Transportation code letters for all the major tire manufacturers. The code appears after "DOT" on the sidewall of a tire. When using this list, keep in mind that some tires are made to the specifications of the retailer and not to those of the manufacturer.

Armstrong
CE, CF, CH, CV

Continental
CM, CN, CP, CT, CU

Cooper
UP, UT

Dayton
HX, HY, XV, XW, XY,
YA, YB, YC, YD, YE, YF,
YH, YJ, YK

Denman
DY

Dunlop
DA, DB, DC, DD, DE,
DF, DH, DJ, DK, DL,
DM, DN, DP, DT, DU

Firestone
VA, VB, VC, VD, VE, VF,
VH, VJ, VK, VL, VM,
VN, VP, VT, VV, VX,
VY, WA, WB, WC, WD,
WF, WH

Gates
BW, BX, BY

General
AA, AB, AC, AD, AE,
AF, AH

B. F. Goodrich
BA, BB, BC, BD, BE,
BF, BH, BJ, BK, BL,
BM, BN, BP

Goodyear
MA, MB, MC, MD, ME,
MF, MH, MJ, MK, ML,
MM, MN, MP, MT, MU,
MV, MW, MX, MY, NA,
NB, NC, ND, NE, NF,
NH, NJ, NK, NL, NM,
NN, NP, NT, NU, NV,
NW, NX, NY, PA, PB,
PC, PD, PE, PF

Kelly-Springfield
PH, PJ, PK, PL, PM,
PN, PP, PT, PU, PV,
PW, PX, PY, TA, TB,
TC, TD, TE, TF, TH,
TJ, TK, TL, TM, TN,
TP, TT, TU, TV, TW,
TX, TY, UA, UB, UC,
UD, UE, UF, UH, UJ,
UK, UL, UM, UN

Lee
JA, JB, JC, JD, JE, JF,
JH, JJ, JK, JL, JM, JN,
JP, JT, JU, JV, JW, JX,
JY, KA, KB, KC, KD,
KE, KF, KH, KJ, KK,
KL, KM, KN, KP, KT,
KU, KV, KW, KX, KY, LA,
LB, LC, LD, LE, LF

Mansfield
WL

McCreary
CY

Michelin
FF, FH, FJ, FK, FL, FM,
FN, FP, FT, FU, FV,
FW, FX, FY, HA, HB,
HC, HD, HE, HF, HH,
HJ, HK, HL, HM, HN, HP

Mohawk
CA, CB, CC

Pennsylvania
WK

Pirelli
XA, XB, XC, XD, XE, XF,
XH, XJ, XK, XL, XM,
XN, XP, XT

Seiberling
AV, YM, YN, YP, YT, YU,
YV, YW, YX, YY

Semperit
BT, BU

Uniroyal
AJ, AK, AL, AM, AN,
AP, AU, LH, LJ, LK, LL,
LM, LN, LP, LT, LU

State "No-Fault" Laws

State	No-Fault Benefits
Minnesota	Purchase is optional. Medical: $2,000. Wage loss: $60 week for 52 weeks, starting 14 days after accicent. Death payment: $10,000.
Massachusetts	$2,000 in benefits for medical, funeral, wage loss, and substitute service expenses. Wage loss and substitute service benefits are limited to 75% of actual loss.
Delaware	$10,000 per person and $20,000 per accident. Covers medical costs, loss of income, loss of services, and funeral expenses (limited to $2,000).
Florida	$5,000 per person for medical costs, wage loss, replacement services, and funeral expense (limited to $1,000).
Oregon	$5,000 medical benefits. 70% of wage loss up to $750 month, $18 a day substitute services. Wage loss and substitute services paid from first day if disability lasts 14 days; limited to 52 weeks.
South Dakota	Purchase is optional. $2,000 in medical expense. $60 week for wage loss, starting 14 days after injury, for up to 52 weeks. $10,000 death benefit.
Virginia	Purchase is optional. $2,000 for medical and funeral costs. $100 week for wage loss with limit of 52 weeks.
Connecticut	$5,000 benefits for medical, hospital, funeral (limit $2,000), lost wages, survivors' loss, and substitute service expenses. Wage loss, substitute service, and survivors' benefits limited to 85% of actual loss.

Limitation on General Damages	Vehicle Damage	Effective Date
None.	Stays under tort system.	Jan. 1, 1970.
Can recover only if medical costs exceed $500, or in case of death, loss of all or part of body member, permanent and serious disfigurement, loss of sight or hearing, or a fracture.	Tort liability abolished.	Jan. 1, 1971.
None. But amount of no-fault benefits received cannot be used as evidence in suits for general damages.	Stays under tort system.	Jan. 1, 1972.
Cannot recover unless medical costs exceed $1,000 or there is permanent disfigurement, permanent injury, fracture of a weight-bearing bone, loss of a body function, or death.	Tort liability abolished if damage is under $550, but retained if damage is above that. Florida Supreme Court ruled this unconstitutional July 11, 1973.	Jan. 1, 1972.
None.	Stays under tort system.	Jan. 1, 1972. Jan. 1, 1974, for benefits at left.
None.	Stays under tort system.	Jan. 1, 1972.
None.	Stays under tort system.	July 1, 1972.
Cannot recover unless economic loss exceeds $400, or there is permanent injury, bone fracture, disfigurement, dismemberment, or death.	Stays under tort system.	Jan. 1, 1973.

State "No-Fault" Laws

State	No-Fault Benefits
Maryland	$2,500 in benefits for medical, hospital, funeral, wage loss, and substitute service expenses.
New Jersey	Unlimited benefits for medical and hospital costs. Wage loss up to $100 a week for one year. Substitute services up to $12 a day up to $4,380 per person. Funeral expenses to $1,000. Survivors' benefits equal to amount victim would have received if he had not died.
Michigan	Unlimited medical and hospital benefits. Funeral benefits up to $1,000. Lost wages up to $1,000 per month and substitute services of $20 a day payable to victim or survivor.
New York	Aggregate limit of $50,000 for medical, wage loss, and substitute service benefits. Wage loss limited to 80% of actual loss up to $1,000 per month for three years. Substitute service benefits limited to $25 a day for one year.
Arkansas	Purchase is optional. $2,000 per person for medical and hospital expenses. Wage loss: 70% of lost wages up to $140 a week, beginning 8 days after accident, for up to 52 weeks. Essential services: up to $70 a week for up to 52 weeks, subject to 8-day waiting period. Death benefit: $5,000.
Utah	$2,000 per person for medical and hospital expenses. 85% of gross income loss, up to $150 a week, for up to 52 weeks. $12 a day for loss of services for up to 365 days. Both wage loss and service loss coverages subject to 3-day waiting periods that disappear if disability lasts longer than two weeks. $1,000 funeral benefit. $2,000 survivor's benefit.
Kansas	$2,000 per person for medical expenses. Wage loss: up to $650 a month for one year. $2,000 for rehabilitation costs. Substitute service benefits of $12 a day for 365 days. Survivor's benefits: up to $650 a month for lost income, $12 a day for substitution benefits, for not over one year after death, minus any disability benefits victim received before death. Funeral benefit: $1,000.

Limitation on General Damages	Vehicle Damage	Effective Date
None.	Stays under tort system.	Jan. 1, 1973.
Cannot recover if injuries are confined to soft tissue and medical expenses excluding hospital costs are less than $200.	Stays under tort system.	Jan. 1, 1973.
Cannot recover unless injuries result in death, serious impairment of body function, or permanent serious disfigurement.	Tort liability abolished.	Oct. 1, 1973.
Cannot recover unless medical expenses exceed $500, or injury results in death, dismemberment, significant disfigurement, a compound or comminuted fracture, or permanent loss of use of a body organ, member, function, or system.	Stays under tort system.	Feb. 1, 1974.
None.	Stays under tort system.	July 1, 1974.
Cannot recover unless medical expenses exceed $500, or injury results in dismemberment or fracture, permanent disfigurement, permanent disability, or death.	Stays under tort system.	Jan. 1, 1974.
Cannot recover unless medical costs exceed $500, or injury results in permanent disfigurement, fracture to a weight-bearing bone, a compound, comminuted, displaced or compressed fracture, loss of a body member, permanent injury, permanent loss of a body function, or death.	Stays under tort system.	Jan. 1, 1974.

State "No-Fault" Laws

State	No-Fault Benefits
Texas	$2,500 per person overall limit. Covers medical and funeral expenses, lost income, and loss of services. Purchase optional.
Nevada	Aggregate limit of $10,000. Pays for medical and rehabilitation expenses; up to $175 a week for loss of income; up to $18 a day for 104 weeks of replacement services; survivor's benefits of not less than $5,000 and not more than victim would have received in disability benefits for 1 year; and $1,000 for death.
Colorado	$25,000 for medical expenses. $25,000 for rehabilitation. Lost income: up to $125 a week for up to 52 weeks. Services: up to $15 a day for up to 52 weeks. Death benefit: $1,000.
Hawaii	Aggregate limit of $15,000. Pays for medical and hospital services; rehabilitation; occupational, psychiatric, and physical therapy; up to $800 a month for wage loss, substitute services, and survivors' loss; and up to $1,500 for funeral expenses.

Source: State Farm Insurance Companies

Limitation on General Damages	Vehicle Damage	Effective Date
None.	Stays under tort system.	90 days after adjournment of 1973 regular session.
Cannot recover unless medical benefits exceed $750 or injury causes chronic or permanent injury, permanent partial or permanent total disability, disfigurement, more than 180 days of inability to work at occupation, fracture of a major bone, dismemberment, permanent loss of a body function, or death.	Stays under tort system.	Feb. 1, 1974.
Cannot recover unless medical and rehabilitation services have reasonable value of more than $500, or injury causes permanent disfigurement, permanent disability, dismemberment, loss of earnings for more than 52 weeks, or death.	Stays under tort system.	April 1, 1974.
Cannot recover unless injury results in death; permanent or serious disfigurement that causes mental or emotional suffering; significant, permanent loss of use of a part or function; or unless medical and rehabilitation costs exceed a floating threshold established annually by insurance commissioner. However, this tort limitation does not apply to any motorist who causes property damage.	Stays under tort system.	July 1, 1974.

Symptoms and Possible Causes of Car Trouble

By consulting this chart when your auto malfunctions, you will be better able to communicate with your mechanic concerning the probable cause and the necessary cure.

The Engine

Symptoms \ Causes	Burned or worn valves	Worn piston rings	Worn valve guides	Oil leaks	Valves need adjustment	Faulty valve lifters	Valve sticking	Valve spring broken	Broken timing gear or chain	Broken distributor drive	Broken engine mounts	Damaged main bearing	Damaged connecting rod bearing	Worn piston pins
Engine lacks power	•	•												
Poor fuel mileage	•	•												
Excessive oil use		•	•	•										
Fumes from engine		•												
Light clicking noise					•	•	•	•						
Rough operation						•	•	•						
Engine won't run									•	•				
Engine shakes											•			
Heavy thudding												•		
Sharp metallic knock													•	•

The Cooling System

Symptoms \ Causes	Low coolant level	Cooling system clogged	Loose or broken fan belt	Thermostat stuck closed	Thermostat stuck open	Debris on radiator	Faulty water pump	Collapsed water hose	Leaking cyl. head gasket	Late ignition timing	Heater core clogged	Faulty temperature control	Low refrigerant charge	Loose or broken drive belt	Faulty compressor clutch	Debris on condenser
Engine overheats	•	•	•	•		•	•	•	•	•						
Engine warms up slowly					•											
Insufficient heat					•						•	•				
Insufficient air conditioning												•	•	•		•
No air conditioning													•	•	•	

The Emission Control System

Symptoms	Causes	Clogged or sticking PCV valve	Clogged PCV hoses	Leaking PCV hoses	Faulty air injection pump	Air pump belt slipping	Faulty transmission spark control
Rough idle		•	•	•			
Oil fumes from engine		•	•	•			
Oil on outside of engine		•	•	•			
Squeal or knock					•	•	
Stalling		•	•	•			
Engine overheats							•
Engine lacks power		•	•	•			•
Poor gasoline mileage		•	•	•			•

The Exhaust System

Symptoms	Causes	Hole in muffler	Tailpipe bent or clogged	Exhaust pipe or muffler clogged	Leaking tailpipe	Loose pipe or muffler	Pipe touching frame or body	Loose tubes inside muffler
Loud exhaust		•						
Hissing exhaust			•					
Fumes under car		•		•				
Rattles						•		•
Vibration							•	
Engine lacks power			•	•				
Engine overheats			•	•				

The Electrical System

Symptoms \ Causes	Battery discharged	Loose or broken cables	Faulty starter or solenoid	Faulty ignition switch	Faulty distributor points	Faulty neutral switch	Spark plugs fouled	Improper spark plug gap	Faulty coil	Faulty condenser	Damaged dist. cap or rotor	Damaged ignition cables	Incorrect spark timing	Alternator belt slipping	Faulty voltage regulator	Low regulator setting	Faulty alternator	Battery worn out
Starter won't operate	●	●	●	●		●												
Starter turns, engine won't start				●	●		●	●	●	●	●	●	●					
Engine stalls					●				●	●			●					
Engine misfires					●		●	●	●	●	●	●						
Engine cuts out at high speed					●		●	●	●	●	●							
Engine knocks, or "pings"													●					
Engine lacks power					●		●	●	●	●	●	●	●					
Engine idles roughly					●				●	●			●					
Battery frequently discharged														●	●	●	●	●
Alternator does not charge														●	●		●	

Lighting and Safety Devices

Symptoms \ Causes	Battery discharged	Bulb burned out	Faulty wiring	Fuse blown	Faulty flasher unit	Faulty wiper motor	Faulty wiper linkage	Faulty wiper park switch	Fluid low in reservoir	Tubing disconnected	Clogged nozzle	Faulty washer pump	Faulty stop light switch	Short circuit in wiring
Lights very dim	●													
One light doesn't work		●	●	●										
Turn signals flash on only one side		●	●											
Turn signals do not flash			●	●	●									
Windshield wipers don't work			●	●		●	●							
Windshield wipers don't park								●						
Windshield washers don't work									●	●	●	●		
Stop lights don't work		●	●	●									●	
Stop lights stay on													●	
Headlights flash on and off														●

The Fuel System

Symptoms / Causes

Symptoms	Faulty automatic choke	Low fuel pump pressure	Faulty carburetor adjustment	Fuel line hot—vapor lock	Dirt or water in fuel	Clogged fuel filter	Dirty carburetor	Clogged air cleaner	Faulty accelerating pump	Binding accelerator linkage	High fuel pump pressure	Sticking needle valve
Hard starting when cold	•											
Hard starting when hot	•			•								
Engine stalls	•		•		•		•					
Smoky exhaust	•		•				•	•			•	•
Poor gasoline mileage	•		•				•	•			•	•
Engine "starves" at high speed		•	•		•	•	•					
Rough idle	•		•								•	•
Engine stumbles on acceleration					•		•		•	•		
Flooded carburetor	•		•				•	•			•	•
Engine backfires		•	•		•	•						

The Transmission and Drive Line System

Symptoms / Causes

Symptoms	Clutch needs adjustment	Clutch disc worn	Transmission low on lubricant	Incorrect grade of lubricant	Shift linkage out of adjustment	Low fluid level	Bands need adjustment	Control valve sticking	Throttle linkage needs adjustment	Leaking seals or gaskets	Worn universal joints	Unbalanced driveshaft	Unbalanced tires	Worn rear axle gears	Worn rear axle bearings	Tire noise
Clutch slips	•	•														
Hard shifting	•		•	•	•											
Gears clash	•		•	•	•											
Automatic transmission slips						•	•	•								
Automatic doesn't shift properly						•	•	•	•							
Transmission low on fluid										•						
Rough engagement of Drive or Reverse								•								
Heavy "clunk" at low speed											•					
Vibration at high speed												•	•			
Whine from rear end														•	•	•

The Steering and Suspension System

Symptoms (Causes →)	Low or uneven tire pressure	Steering linkage dry	Front end out of alignment	Suspension arms damaged	Ball joints binding	Sagging springs	Power steering belt slipping	Power steering fluid low	Loose front wheel bearings	Worn ball joints	Loose steering linkage	Steering gear needs adjustment	Worn shock absorbers	Wheels and tires out of balance
Hard steering	•	•	•	•	•	•	•	•				•		
Car pulls to one side	•		•	•					•	•	•	•		
Car wanders from side to side	•		•			•			•	•	•		•	
Uneven tire wear	•		•	•					•	•	•		•	•
Front wheel shimmy									•	•	•			
High-speed vibration													•	•
Car not level				•		•								
Heavy thumps on rough roads				•		•				•			•	
Play or looseness in steering									•	•	•	•		
Rattle in steering gear											•			
Thump from front end				•						•				

The Braking System

Symptoms (Causes →)	Low fluid level	Air in hydraulic system	Brakes need adjustment	Brake fade due to overheating	Grease or fluid on linings	Linings glazed	Wet brakes	Faulty vacuum booster	Linkage binding	Weak flexible hoses	Loose or worn wheel bearings	Loose or worn front-end parts	Front wheels out of alignment	Loose disc brake caliper	Warped brake disc	Eccentric brake drum	Faulty wheel cylinder	Faulty master cylinder	Weak or broken retracting springs	Scored brake drums	Dirt in brake mechanism	Clogged or kinked brake lines
Play in pedal	•	•	•						•								•	•				
Hard pedal				•	•	•	•	•									•	•				•
Spongy pedal	•	•							•													
Pedal sinks to floor	•																					
Pedal vibrates		•							•	•				•	•							
Brakes grab				•															•			
Brakes drag			•				•										•	•				•
Brakes pull			•		•						•	•	•	•		•			•			•
Erratic braking			•		•						•	•		•	•	•			•			
Squeal or chatter			•			•									•	•					•	

Source: Automotive Information Council

Index

acceleration ability, 43, 205
accelerator pedal, 167, 261
accelerator pump, 168
accidents
  bumpers and collisions, 42
  collision insurance and, 80
  collision repair shops, 217
  damage patterns, 91
  dealing with mechanics, 222
  inspecting used car, 55
  in U.S., 21
  liability insurance, 76–79
  mixing tire types and, 111
  safety and size, 31
  tail lights and, 42
  uninsured motorists and, 84
additives
  battery additives, 226
  gasoline additives, 194, 202

additives (*continued*)
  transmission fluid, 245
air conditioners, 250, 265
air cooling system, 172
air filter, 167, 263
air pollution. *See*
  emission-control devices
alignment, need for, 230
American Automobile
  Association, 73
American Mutual Insurance
  Alliance, 88
American Petroleum Institute
  (API), 239
antifreeze, 248, 249
antifreeze windshield washer
  solvent, 133
"aspect ratio" (tires), 113
automatic transmission, 37

automatic transmission
  (*continued*)
  how car works, 183
  life expectancy, 146
automobile body
  care of, 125-134
  checking new car, 49
Automobile Club of Missouri, 232
Automobile Club of Southern
  California, 62
automobile clubs, 84
automobile dealers
  buying new car, 43-49
  financing your car, 67
  safety information, 42
automobile manufacturers
  action on complaints, 17
  pollution controls and, 203
  tire recommendations, 110
  warranty, 63
automobile operation,
    performance, etc.
  cost data on, 28, 143, 274-282
  costs per mile, 141
  how car works, 159-191
  need to know principles, 21
  oil changes and, 239
  suspension system and, 38
  trade-in and, 136
  transmission and, 37
  used-car inspection, 54
automobile registration, 156
automobile sales
  buying new car, 48
  contingent on repairs, 63
  dealing with dealer, 43-49
  how to buy new car, 25-49
  how to sell your car, 149-157
  in U.S., 13
  quotas, 46
  used cars and, 20
  where to buy used car, 53

B

backfiring, 263
ball joints, 185, 230

banks and banking
  buying new car, 26, 48
  financing car, 70
battery, 223, 264
  how car works, 172
  maintenance schedule, 251
belted bias tires, 105, 108
belts, drive belts, 247
Best's Insurance Reports, 84
Better Business Bureau, 44, 54,
  220, 224
Better Business Bureau of
  Metropolitan New York, 217
bias ply tires, 104, 108, 113
bill of sale, 156
blowouts, 255, 261
brake fluid, 246
brake lines, 147
brakes, 261, 265
  how car works, 189
  inspecting used car, 57
  linings, 246, 265
  maintenance schedule, 246
bumpers, 42, 88
business automobiles, 141
"butterfly" valves, 167

C

camshaft, 169
cancellation of insurance, 85
carbon monoxide, 176, 194, 200,
  252, 264
carburetors, 206, 245, 263
  how car works, 166
carpeting, 57, 134
car washes (commercial), 130
catalytic converter, 200, 203
charging batteries, 225
*Chilton's Labor Guide and
  Parts Manual*, 220
choke valve, 167
chrome trim, 128
claim service, insurance, 85
cleaning
  car care and, 128
  selling car, 151

climate
car care and salt, 127
snow tires and, 118
clutch, 179
coil springs, 188
collision insurance, 80
compact automobiles, 30
operating costs, chart, 141
prices, 45
comprehensive insurance, 83
compression ratio, 164
consumer complaints, 14, 217
contracts
financing car, 73
leasing car, 99
convenience, new-car options, 35
convertibles, 35
cooling system
how your car works, 172
life expectancy, 147
maintenance schedule, 248
cords (tire cords), 105-107
corrosion inhibitors, 197
crankshaft, 161, 177-183
credit
consumer credit, 14
financing car, 65-74
new car budget, 26
credit unions, financing car, 67
cylinders, 36, 162, 175

D

dealers. *See* automobile dealers
deductible, insurance, 80-83, 222
defective parts, warranties and, 44
defects, selling your car, 152
defroster, 132
demonstration auto diagnostic centers, 235
department store auto repair centers, 216
depreciation
buying new car, 46
costs per mile, table, 139
exceeds repair bills, 138

depreciation (*continued*)
leasing car, 100
tax deductible, 141
used vs. new car, 51
detergents, 197
diagnostic test centers, 145, 217, 235
diesel engines, 209
dieseling, 198, 262
differential
definition, 184
life expectancy, 146
disc brakes, 190
distributor, 171
do-it-yourself repair centers, 235
doors, ease of access, 32
down payment
buying new car, 26
leasing car and, 98
selling car, 154
drive belts, maintenance schedule, 247
drive shaft, 181
driving conditions
snow tires, 118
tire quiz, 107
drum brakes, 191
dual carburetors, 206

E

Educational Testing Service, 231
electrical system, 224
driving "don'ts," 257
how car works, 161, 170
electrically powered vehicles, 209
electronic ignition system, 170, 200
emergency road service, 222
insurance, 17
emission-control devices, 262
effects of, 18
emotion
buying used car, 54
how to buy new car, 25

engine
    gearshift and, 38
    how car works, 160
    how Wankel works, 203
    inspecting used car, 59
    life expectancy, 146
equity, leasing car, 100
exhaust gas recirculation, 200
exhaust manifold, 176, 263
exhaust system
    exhaust smoke, 62, 264
    how car works, 176
    life expectancy, 146
exhaust valve, 165
exterior of car, inspecting
    used car, 55

F

family needs
    choosing new car, 32
    power windows and, 40
    size of car, 28
fan belt, 177, 224
filters
    fuel filter, 246
    maintenance schedule, 245
    oil filters, 241
finance companies, car loans, 67
financing car, 48, 65-74
flat-rate manual, 213, 220
flood-damaged cars, 57
floor mats, cleaning, 134
flywheel, 161, 179
Ford Motor Company, 209
"For Sale" sign, 153
four-stroke cycle, 163
fraud
    protection against, 20
    tricks dishonest mechanics
        use, 222-231
    unnecessary repairs, 23
front-end alignment, 56, 230
fuel-air mixture, 168
fuel consumption
    emission control and, 18

fuel consumption (continued)
    low-compression engines, 202
    maintenance and, 239
    Mazda, 203
    size of car and, 28
    used cars, 52
fuel-injection systems, 206
fuel pump, 167
full-maintenance auto leasing,
    101
full-size cars, 30, 45

G

gas stations, 217, 223
gas turbine engine, 209
gaskets (windows,
    doors, etc.), 131
gasoline
    how car works, 167
    octane rating, 263
    pollution controls and,
        193-209
gearshift. See transmission
General Motors Corp., 209
General Policyholders
    Rating, 84
generators, 172
glass, cleaning, 132
guarantees, used cars, 53, 63
gum formation, gasoline
    additives, 197

H

hardtops, 32, 131
hard wax, 130
hatchbacks, 32
headlights, 128
headrests, 42
heaters, 251
heavy-duty suspensions, 38
hit-and-run drivers, 83
Honda, 206
horsepower, 36, 164
hoses, cooling system, 250
hubcaps, 40
hydraulic cylinder, 189

hydrocarbons, 194, 200
hydrometer test, 225-226

I

ice, removal from windows, 132
idler arm, 228
idling, 18
ignition system, 170, 238, 263
independent insurance agents, 84
injury to person, liability insurance, 76
inspection (personal)
    buying new car, 49
    buying used car, 54-63
    tire replacement, 118
inspection (state), 64, 156, 222
insurance
    consumer complaints, 14, 17
    credit life insurance, 73
    fraudulent claims, 222
    how much needed, 75-95
    leasing car and, 98, 103
    selling car, 156
intake valve, 163
interior of car
    cleaning, 133
    inspecting used car, 57
intermediate-size automobiles, 30, 45
internal combustion engine, 161

K

"knock," 195, 197

L

"labor plus parts" phrase, 227
law
    insurance claims, 94
    repair overcharges, 220
    selling car, 152, 155
lead, 197, 201, 202
lease-purchase plans, 100
leasing, 97-103
leather upholstery, cleaning, 133

liability insurance, 76
license plates, 98, 156
licensing
    auto repair shops, 234
    mechanic certification, 212, 231
life expectancy of automobile, 136-139
liquid wax, 130
load test (battery), 225
loads. *See* weight
loans. *See* credit
location of dealer, 44
lubrication system
    how car works, 173
    maintenance schedule, 244

M

maintenance
    an ounce of prevention, 237
    auto body care, 125-134
    costs per mile, table, 139
    dealing with mechanic 211-236
    emission control and, 18
    leasing car and, 98, 101
    repair vs. depreciation, 138
    safety and, 23
    selling car, 152
    tax deductible, 141
    when to trade in, 137
manual transmission, 37
master hydraulic cylinder, 189
Mazda cars, 203
mechanics
    dealing with, 211-236
    dishonest, 20
    inspecting used car, 54, 62
mileage
    buying used car, 64
    costs per driven mile, 140
    insurance discounts, 85
    leasing car, 103
    life expectancy of cars, 146
    tires and, 105

mixing tire types, 110-111
model year changes, 46
modulator valve, 264
Motor Vehicle Information and
    Cost Savings Act
    of 1972, 235
"Motor Vehicle Safety Defect
    Recall Campaigns," 64
*Motor's Mechanical Time and
    Parts Guide*, 220
mud
    car care and, 126
    inspecting used car, 56
muffler, 176, 264

N

National Institute for Automo-
    tive Service Excellence, 231
negligence, no-fault and, 95
new cars
    dealers, 54
    how to buy, 25-49
    sales in U.S., 14
    vs. used cars, 51
newspapers, 52, 153
"no-fault" insurance, 17, 94
"no-fault," state laws, 284-289
noise
    convertibles and station
        wagons, 32
    inspecting used car, 59
nylon tires, 105

O

octane rating, 197
odometer, 56
oil
    classifications, 242
    costs, 146
    inspecting used car, 59
    leaks, 56
    viscosities, 242
options
    add to comfort, 38
    buying new car, 35
    checking new car, 49

options (*continued*)
    comparing prices, 43
    maintenance and, 18
    new-car bargaining, 45
overheating, inspecting used
    car, 63
owner's manual, 152, 237
oxides of nitrogen, 194, 205

P

paint
    inspecting used car, 55
    touch-up jobs, 129
parts, replacement parts, 214,
    217
passengers, medical benefits
    insurance, 80
passing ability, 43
phosphorus, 201
photochemical oxidants, 194
pistons, 161, 164, 165, 175
pitman arm, 185
pollution, impact of controls,
    193-209
polyester tires, 105
positive crankcase ventilation
    (PCV), 198
power steering, 185
power train, 177
preignition, 198
premiums, auto insurance, 87
previous owner (used car), 53
prices
    auto insurance, 85
    car costs and insurance rates,
        91
    collision insurance, 80
    cost of no-fault insurance,
        95
    cost of repairs, 211, 224
    depreciation, maintenance,
        139, 274-282
    financing car, 70
    flat-rate repair manuals, 213
    getting prices in writing, 48
    leasing car, table, 102

prices (*continued*)
liability insurance, 79
medical benefit insurance, 80
new cars, 26, 43
options for new cars, 35
planning budget, 26
pricing car for resale, 150
repair overcharges, 219, 220
selling car, 152, 154
trade-in on new car, 48
trade-in vs. selling car, 150
used car, 53
when to trade in, 137
professional people, leasing cars
99
property damage, liability
insurance, 76
push rod, 169

Q

quality standards for tires, 123

R

radial tires, 110, 113, 255
radiator, 248
Rankine engine, 209
rayon tires, 105, 107
rear axle, 184
rearview mirror, 42
rebuilt carburetors, 227
recalls, buying used car, 64
recreational vehicle, 35
registration, 156, 270
reliability, when to trade in, 136
rental cars, 99
repairs
costs per mile, tables, 139
dealing with mechanic, 211-236
diagnostic test centers and, 145
dishonest repairmen, 20
selling car, 152
tax deductible, 141
vs. depreciation, 138
replacement tires, 116

repossessed cars
buying used cars, 64
financing car, 74
reputation of dealer, 44
resale value
collision insurance and, 83
depreciation vs. repairs, 138
leasing car and, 98, 101
options and, 36, 38
when to trade in car, 135-139
resonator, 176
retail value of car, 150
reverse gear, 182, 247
road test
checking new car, 49
checking used car, 62
rotary engine. *See* Wankel
rotary engine
rotation of tires, 255
rotor (disc brakes), 190
rotor (distributor), 171
rotor (Wankel engine), 204
rust and rustproofing, 126, 197, 252
car care and, 126
inspecting used car, 56, 59

S

SA (oil classification), 243
SAE. *See* Society of
Automotive Engineers
SE (oil classification), 243
safety
convertible and, 35
need to know about cars, 21
new-car options, 36
power windows, 40
rating auto models, 235
size of cars and, 30
studded snow tires, 120
2- and 4-door cars, 32
sales contract, signatures, 48
salt, body damage and, 127
seat belts, cleaning, 134
security
car theft, 94

security (*continued*)
  convertibles and, 35
  new-car options, 36
selling dealer, 44
semiautomatic transmission, 37
service stations. *See* gas
  stations
shimmying, 228, 265
shock absorbers, 38, 187
  inspecting used car, 56
  life expectancy, 146
size
  buying new car, 28
  station wagons, 32
  stratified-charge system, 206
  tire size, 111, 113
  used cars, 52
  Wankel engine and, 205
small cars vs. big cars, 30
smog. *See* photochemical
  oxidants
smoke, exhaust smoke, 62, 264
snow tires, 118, 255
Society of Automotive
  Engineers (SAE), 243
"space maker" spare tire, 110
spark plugs, 171, 175, 200
specialty cars, 35, 54
speeds (gearshift). *See*
  transmission
speeds, tires and, 107, 123
sports cars. *See* specialty cars
springs, 38, 188
stabilizer bar, 38, 188
stalling, 263
standard automobile, operating
  costs, chart, 141
starting, difficult, 262
station wagon, 32
steel belted tires, 105
steering wheel, 62
"sticker" price, 45
stopping, 42, 246
stratified-charge system, 206
studded snow tires, 118-120,
  255

subcompact automobile, 28
  operating costs, chart, 141
  prices, 45
suspension system
  how car works, 186
  inspecting used car, 56
symptoms of car trouble,
  262-267, 290-294

T

tags. *See* license plates
tail lights, 42
tail pipe, 264
taxes, 272
taxis, used car, 57
temperature
  cooling system maintenance,
    248
  hydrometer test and, 225
  oil changes and, 241
tests
  auto mechanics, 231
  inspecting used car, 63
  test driving, 153
theft
  comprehensive insurance, 83
  insurance and, 87, 91
thermal reactors, 201, 205
tie rods, 185, 230
tire code, 111
tires, 224, 265
  blowouts, 261
  checking new car, 49
  how car works, 186
  inspecting used car, 55
  maintenance schedule, 253
  manufacturers, 283
  optional equipment, 40
  reserve loads, 43
  tire inflation, 116
torsion bars, 187
trade-ins
  buying new car, 47
  selling car yourself, 149
trailers, tire size and, 113

training, auto repair
   industry, 231
transmission
   definition, 181
   how gears work, 177
   inspecting used car, 59
   life expectancy, 146
   types of, 37
transmission fluid, 244
tread (tires), 116
trifluoroethanol, 209
trunk, 57, 261
tubeless tires, 257
tune-up, 239

U

"umbrella" policy (liability
   insurance), 79
underbody, 56
undercoating, 252
uninsured motorists, 83
U.S. Department of Transportation, 28, 91, 116, 123,
      136, 138-141, 143, 235
U.S. Environmental Protection
   Agency, 200
U.S. Federal Trade Commission,
   220
U.S. National Bureau of
   Standards, 107
U.S. National Highway Traffic
   Safety Administration, 110
universal joints, 146, 184, 265
unleaded gasoline, 201
upholstery, cleaning, 133
used cars
   automobile leasing and, 100
   dealers, 54
   how to buy, 51-64
   need to know system, 20
   price guidebooks, 48
   sales in U.S., 14

V

valve repairs, 140
valve stems, 123
valve systems, valve
   recession, 202
valve train, 163, 169
vandalism. *See* security
vans, choosing, 35
"vapor lock," 263
vinyl hardtops, 131
vinyl upholstery, cleaning, 133
viscosity, oil, 243
visibility, car safety, 42
voltage regulator, 172, 251

W

Wankel rotary engine, 203, 206
warranty, 44, 150, 213, 237, 244
washing car, 125, 130
water cooling system, 173
water leaks, 56, 59
water pump, 47, 231
waxing car, 130
weight
   horsepower ratio, 36
   tire loads, 113
wheel balance, 40, 123, 228,
   255, 265
wheels, suspension system and,
   40
whitewall tires, 131
wholesale value of car, 150
windows, 132
   power windows, 40
   tinted glass, 42
windshield, 132
wiring, 147
"Women on Wheels"
   (program), 21

Y

youth, insurance discounts, 87